MW00635873

THE

DISCIPLINED CONTRARIAN

ESSAYS ON INVESTING, MARKETS, AND PLANNING

The Disciplined Contrarian
Copyright © 2017 by Atwater Malick, LLC, Lancaster, PA

Published by: Atwater Malick, LLC, Lancaster, PA

PRINTED IN THE UNITED STATES OF AMERICA
Interior Design: Infantree, Lancaster, PA
Cover Design: Infantree, Lancaster, PA

ISBN: 978-0-692-95508-6

LIMIT OF LIABILITY AND DISCLAIMER

TO OUR CLIENTS, THANK YOU FOR YOUR
TRUST, LOYALTY, AND SUPPORT.

CONTENTS
AT A GLANCE

TABLE
OF CONTENTS

9

11

PREFACE

e received our license to operate as an independent registered investment advisor on September 19, 2008. At that very moment, the financial markets were collapsing.

Over the last nine years, we've witnessed a remarkable financial crisis, a dramatic bear market, a lackluster economic recovery, a powerful bull market and, recently, one of the most contentious elections anyone can remember.

The essays in this book cover the time period from the fall of 2008 to the summer of 2017. These essays, though, are anything but old news.

Rather, they are more enjoyable with the benefit of hindsight. For one, you can see how right or wrong we were. Most importantly, the lessons in these commentaries should be meaningful in ten, twenty or even thirty years. The fundamentals of investing are enduring.

This book is divided into six parts—The Great Recession and the Financial Crisis; Principals of Contrarian Investing; The Investment Industry; The Investment Environment; The Fundamentals of Investing; and Financial and Retirement Planning. Many of the sections have overlap, but we classified the essays based on what we believe is the primary theme.

You can read the book in its entirety or skim for topics, titles, or dates that are of particular interest.

The "Great Recession and the Financial Crisis" is an adventurous sampling of the wild and unprecedented events of the crisis. It has elements of a living history.

Very near the bottom of the bear market, when we thought the panic had reached a level of lunacy, we wrote the essay "Could It Be?," which turned out to be an amazingly accurate analysis of the conditions in March of 2009; which in hindsight was the bear market bottom.

Additionally, our note entitled "The Rearview Mirror" offers a rebuttal to the consensus opinion of the time that the 2010s would be a lost decade for American investors. It has been, thus far, just the opposite. And lastly, "A Snowball Headed for Hell?" tells why it's often very effective to do the opposite of consensus opinions, especially in the midst of a market setback or crisis.

The section entitled Principles of Contrarian Investing outlines many examples of our belief that following the crowd is the wrong investment strategy. The commentary called "The Disciplined Contrarian" is an excellent overall survey of our thoughts on the subject.

We spend a lot of time in the The Investment Industry section because we find considerable fault with much of the opaqueness and hyperbole inherent in our profession. Readers should be aware that some of the financial services industry is hazardous to their health.

You do not need to work in investments or be familiar with the industry to gain valuable knowledge from this section. For example, we talk about the pitfalls of mutual funds in "Mutual Fundosaurus"; we survey the damage fees, taxes, turnover and market timing do to investors in "The Four Horseman of Portfolio Returns"; we reveal the outrageous and inaccurate claims that salesman make regarding variable annuities in "Variable Annuities: A False Panacea"; and we explore the abuse of alternative investments with retail investors in "Faux-Sophistication."

In The Investment Environment grouping, you will find a number of essays about volatility. Big moves in markets are an essential part of the investing ecosystem. Pay particular attention to our essays from early 2016 when most had already written off the year after a miserable start. You guessed it, they were wrong. In an essay called "Disconnect," we talk about an emerging pattern that we felt was indicative of a near-term bottom. A later piece in this section is "Expensive²," which is a hint of us turning less constructive on forward, long-term market returns beginning in 2017.

We end our discussion of investments with a group of essays we call The Fundamentals of Investing. In these pieces, we explore the importance of individual securities, a long-term mindset and—vitally—doing little things right while avoiding big mistakes. "Investing is Boring" is a crucial reminder of what to do and not do when investing.

The book's final section, Financial and Retirement Planning, is a highly practical guide to retirement savings, investing and spending. The pieces "The Future Started Yesterday"...and Investing in Retirement offer a practical guide to the retirement planning and investing processes. Throughout this section you will also learn more mechanical knowledge on subjects like 401(k) and 529 plans, Social Security and Medicare, health savings accounts, etc.

Following this preface is our Investment Philosophy. This is the overarching statement on how we invest money. We wrote this in mid-2008 and, likely, it will never change—as we said, investment principles are enduring. It will offer you perspective and context as you explore this book.

Lastly, another heartfelt thank you to our clients, whose questions and comments over the years inspired many of these writings.

We hope you enjoy the book.

Ben Atwater and Matt Malick
Fall, 2017
Lancaster, PA

PHILOSOPHY STATEMENT

A s investors, it is easy to get caught up in fads, headlines, paralyzing fear and unreasonable optimism. However, those investors who buy solid businesses at reasonable prices can profit handsomely over the long-term. Benjamin Graham, the father of "value investing" and a mentor to Warren Buffett, once posed the following question: "Ask yourself: If there was no market for these shares, would I be willing to have an investment in this company on these terms?" If we genuinely believe in the long-term business prospects of a company that we own at a fair price, the day-to-day fluctuations of the company's stock price should factor little in our investment decisions. The essence of investing is to know what you own and why you own it.

We consider the contrarian point of view in each investment decision that we make. When the stock market is gripped by fear and pessimism, we remain confident that stock prices will eventually reflect the long-term viability of the underlying companies. When the stock market experiences unjustified and excessive enthusiasm, we become cautious of overvalued stock prices.

We believe the most significant risk-reward decision in investing is the allocation to stocks versus bonds and that this simple determination overwhelmingly dictates portfolio volatility. We do not invest our clients in stocks unless we conclude that an allocation to stocks is appropriate, given each client's risk tolerance and time horizon. Our discussions of risk tolerance include both (1) financial ability to absorb short-term investment losses and (2) psychological ability to handle market fluctuations. For client assets that are not suitable for the stock market, we invest in individual fixed income securities for safety of principal and a steady source of income.

Finally, we pride ourselves on our commitment to active and substantive communication during both bull and bear markets.

THE GREAT RECESSION
AND THE FINANCIAL CRISIS

01

ONE WILD WEEK

L ast week was arguably one of the single most historic weeks in the history of U.S. financial markets and Wall Street. As a matter of fact, Wall Street nearly disappeared.

On Monday, Lehman Brothers filed for bankruptcy, while Merrill Lynch sold itself to Bank of America as oil sunk below $100 a barrel. On Tuesday, the nation's first money market fund, the Reserve Primary Fund, fell below $1.00 of net asset value, an extremely alarming event. By Tuesday's end, the federal government took an 80% stake in AIG worth $85 billion. Wednesday brought not only a stock market plunge, but the beginning of a textbook "full-on" financial panic with investors pulling $89 billion from money market funds. On Thursday, the panic intensified with Putnam and Street State announcing money market failures. Late Thursday afternoon, however, the cable network CNBC released a story that Treasury Secretary Paulson and Federal Reserve Chairman Bernanke are proposing an "RTC-style"[1] mortgage bailout and the equity markets take flight. On Friday investors came to believe that a "run on the banks" financial crisis would be averted as preliminary details of the federal government's giant rescue plan emerged, including a ban on short selling in 799 financial stocks. The weekend brought Congress to the table to debate the details of the plan and obstructionists from both sides of the aisle (i.e. Chris Dodd (D) and Richard Shelby (R)) are slowing progress of the emergency bailout. As a result, the market reacted on Monday in another panic, driving the Dow down 373 points, while oil soared to over $120 per barrel. Today, as the market drops precipitously again, Congress is hearing testimony from Paulson, Bernanke, SEC Chairman Christopher Cox, and Federal Housing Finance Agency Director James Lockhart. In our opinion, lawmakers must act quickly in the spirit of the "Paulson Plan" to avoid more severe destruction of our financial system...

What a time to launch a new investment management firm!

As a matter of fact, we love the timing. As an independent firm, we can truly do what is best for our clients. We choose not to outsource the management of your account to an over-diversified hodge-podge of mutual fund managers with divergent theories and no overarching strategy. Rather, we focus on substance and transparency. By substance and transparency, we mean our clients own a diversified portfolio of individual stocks and bonds, a portfolio where you can see and we can articulate exactly what is happening with your investments. Our portfolios are tax and fee-efficient because we buy individual equities through dollar-cost averaging over the long-term. Individual equity investing avoids the capital gains distributions and the second layer of investment management and administrative fees inherent in mutual funds.

To give you an idea of the types of individual long-term holdings we look for as part of our twenty to thirty stock portfolio (which is diversified extensively by industry group), we are providing brief thoughts on two stocks on our focus list:

ACCENTURE LTD (ACN): Accenture is a Bermuda-based technology and management consulting company focused on providing services and solutions to clients around the world. In fact, only 43% of fiscal year 2007 revenue was U.S.-based while the remaining 57% was derived overseas. As corporations work to restructure to adjust to the slowing world economy, the phone at Accenture is ringing with new clients. From a valuation standpoint, the company's forward price-to-earnings ratio is less than 13 times according to Thomson Financial, while the firm's expected price to earnings divided by growth rate (PEG) over the next five years is 1.19, a favorable ratio. The firm's balance sheet appears immaculate with $3.3 billion in cash and only $2.57 million in long-term debt as of August 31, 2008. It is also reassuring to know that management continues to buy back and retire equity in mass;

> "LAST WEEK WAS ARGUABLY ONE OF THE SINGLE MOST HISTORIC WEEKS IN THE HISTORY OF U.S. FINANCIAL MARKETS AND WALL STREET. AS A MATTER OF FACT, WALL STREET NEARLY DISAPPEARED."

the firm had 989 million shares outstanding at the end of fiscal year 2002 and only 758 million shares outstanding at the end of fiscal year 2007. We expect this decrease to continue.

AIRGAS INC (ARG): Airgas is a Radnor, PA independent distributor of specialty, industrial and medical gases, principally in North America. Distribution comprises roughly 90% of sales and is facilitated through more than 1,100 locations leading to a 25% U.S. market share. In the last 25 years, ARG has been amazingly acquisitive, buying over 350 different companies in an effort to consolidate a fragmented space where 50% of the U.S. market is still in the hands of independent distributors. And herein lies the opportunity for Airgas: continued slow and steady acquisitions in the U.S. and more importantly abroad. Recently Airgas acquired a European distributor with business in the Middle East and Asia. Risks of course are inherent in this equity investment as is any other, particularly with regard to the firm's large amount of debt, 51.4% long term debt to capitalization (as of March 31st) and renewed increases in commodity and transportation costs would cut into earnings. Optimistically, officers and directors own 11.6% of common stock according to the July 2008 proxy.

1: The Resolution Trust Corporation (RTC) was a U.S. government-owned asset management company charged with liquidating real estate assets that were declared insolvent as a consequence of the savings and loan crisis of the 1980s.

02

BETTING ON BAILOUT, BUFFETT IS BUYING

> "WE SIMPLY ATTEMPT TO BE FEARFUL WHEN OTHERS ARE GREEDY AND TO BE GREEDY ONLY WHEN OTHERS ARE FEARFUL."
>
> WARREN BUFFETT

On Wednesday, Warren Buffett's Berkshire Hathaway announced they are buying $3 billion of preferred General Electric (GE) shares that carry a 10% dividend. Berkshire also has the option to buy another $3 billion of GE common stock at $22.25 per share—slightly above today's closing price of $22.15. GE is also raising an additional $12 billion by selling newly-issued common stock in the secondary market.

Just last week, on September 23rd, Buffett rode to the rescue of Goldman Sachs (GS) by investing $5 billion in GS preferred stock with a hefty 10% dividend yield. Buffett also received warrants to buy up to $5 billion of GS common shares. The warrants, which are immediately exercisable, have a strike price of $115 a share. Goldman also said it would raise another $2.5 billion by selling more common stock to the public.

In explaining his rationale for these investments, Buffet has indicated that he is counting on Congress to pass the controversial "bailout bill" that was rejected by the U.S. House of Representatives on Monday of this week. In our recent essay entitled "One Wild Week," we expressed our concern that a lack of government intervention would result in more severe destruction of our financial system. Last night, the U.S. Senate passed the current version of the bill that has been expanded to include newly-added measures such as an increase in FDIC limits, changes to accounting rules, and $150.5 billion in unrelated tax relief. While passage of the bill by the House is far from certain, we think it is critical to avoid an even more precipitous drop in the stock market and destruction of the credit markets.

In the same essay entitled "One Wild Week," we also touched on our approach of making long-term investments in a core portfolio of 20-30 stocks, widely diversified among industry groups. Interestingly, last week we added General Electric to our "focus list" and we're looking for good entry points to begin dollar-cost averaging into the stock. Today's significant decline in the stock price, sparked by general market weakness and GE's $12 billion common stock issue, only makes this company look more appealing for our client portfolios. Before initiating a position, we will look for the stock price to stabilize, at which point we'll begin the process of building a position in GE.

In a CNBC interview yesterday, Buffett said *"Frankly, these markets are offering opportunities that weren't available six months or a year ago, so we're putting money to work."* While Buffet's actions may be a sign that many stocks look attractive to long-term investors, it's important to note that the typical investor also isn't afforded the same opportunities as Buffett. A reputation as the world's greatest investor and $60 billion of cash in the company coffers lead to special opportunities, such as preferred stock with a 10% dividend. We "average Joes" are stuck with the common stock. Nevertheless,

Buffet is one of the smartest investors out there, and his insights are often invaluable. We hope you enjoy these highlights from Buffett's PBS interview with Charlie Rose yesterday.

ON THE CAUSE OF THE CREDIT CRISIS:

"...I would say the biggest single cause was...an incredible residential real estate bubble. I mean, you can go back to tulip bulbs in Holland 400 years ago...human beings...through combinations of fear and greed and all of that sort of thing, their behavior can lead to bubbles. [You had the]...Internet bubble at one time, you've had a...farmland bubble in the Midwest which resulted in all kinds of tragedy in the early '80s. But 300 million Americans, their lending institutions, their government, their media, all believed that house prices were going to go up consistently. And that got billed into a $20 trillion residential home market. Lending was done based on it, and everybody did a lot of foolish things. And [some] people...behaved in a fraudulent way...we'll go back and find the culprits later on. But that really isn't the problem we have. I mean, that's where it came from, though. We leveraged up and if you have a 20% fall in value of a $20 trillion asset, that's $4 trillion. And when $4 trillion lands, losses land in the wrong part of this economy, it can gum up the whole place...[Wall Street got] the mortgage of some guy in Omaha... securitized it a couple of times...All these types from Wall Street...they had advanced degrees, and they look very alert...they came with these things that said gamma and alpha and sigma and all that. And all I can say is beware of geeks bearing formulas."

ON THE "BAILOUT" THAT THE SENATE PASSED WEDNESDAY NIGHT AND THE HOUSE IS SCHEDULED TO VOTE ON FRIDAY:

"Well, I don't think it's perfect, but I don't know that I could draw one that's perfect. But I'd rather be approximately right than precisely wrong, and it would be precisely wrong to turn it down...We have a ter- rific economy—it's like a great athlete that's had a cardiac arrest. It's flat on the floor, and the paramedics have arrived. And they shouldn't argue about whether they put the resuscitation equipment a quarter of an inch this way or a quarter of an inch that way, or they shouldn't start criticizing the patient, because he didn't have a blood pressure test or something like that. They should do what's needed right now. And I think they will. I think the Congress will do the right thing. I think that...something this important, they'll do the right thing. So this really is an economic Pearl Harbor. That sounds melodramatic, but I've never used that phrase before. And this really is one...I mean, if Pearl Harbor came along, you could have said the planning was wrong by the military ahead of time, or maybe the battleships shouldn't have all been in the harbor and all that kind of thing...[As to] the [$]700 billion [price tag], if [the Treasury] buys mortgage-related securities or mortgages themselves at current market prices, they're going to make money over time because the United States government has staying power and it has a low cost of borrowing. And if I could take one percent of that 700 billion pot and take the gain or loss from it and be their partner, and they would buy the stuff at market, I'd make a lot of money... These assets will be worth more money over time...When Berkshire Hathaway laid out three billion dollars for GE today, we didn't spend it, we invested it. When the Federal Government buys the mortgages, they're not spending it, they're investing it. Now, they're investing it in distressed-type assets but they're buying them at distressed prices if they buy them at market. It's the kind of stuff I love to do. I just don't have 700 billion [dollars]. [Directed to Charlie Rose] Maybe we could go in it together. You know, with your money and my brains, I mean, there's no telling how far we'd go."

ON HOW TO SPEND THE $700 BILLION WHEN PURCHASING THE DISTRESSED DEBT:

"And one way to [buy the distressed assets] is if some institution wants to sell you a billion dollars' worth of mortgages, they might have to sell 100 million in the market, and then [the government] buy[s] the other 900 million on the same terms. Now, the very fact that [the 'bailout' plan] has been authorized or will be authorized, I hope, will firm up the market to some degree. And that's fine. But you don't want to have artificial prices being paid."

ON OUR GOVERNMENTAL ECONOMIC CRISIS TEAM:

"I don't think you can have a better Secretary of the Treasury than Hank Paulson...He is in there at the wrong time, [and] probably shouldn't have taken the job. He's a friend of mine. But he knows markets, he knows [how] corporations work, he knows money, and he's got the interests of the country at heart. And so, you've got the right [person at the Treasury]...You've [also] got a wonderful person with Sheila Bair [Chairperson of the Federal Deposit Insurance Corporation]...Sheila Bair, in the last two weeks, has taken 8% of the deposits in the United States and seamlessly moved those over to sound institutions, which, in turn, have gotten more capital...it's been a magnificent job. Eight percent of the deposits in the United States, 10's of millions of depositors, and nobody's ever heard of her. She'll never get a golden parachute or any severance pay or anything. She's done a great job. We've got some great public servants. We have, I think, the right people in there to get the job done, and then they need more tools."

ON THE CURRENT STATE OF CREDIT MARKETS:

"When [$]40 billion of treasury bills are sold like they were last week, seven day treasury bills, at a yield of 1/20th of one percent, that means...a lot of the country is at the point of putting the money under the mattress, 1/20th of one percent away from where it's better to put it under the mattress. You don't want 300 million Americans putting their money under the mattress. This economy doesn't work well without the lubrication of credit and trust."

ON THE AMERICAN CONSUMER:

"If you look at the American public, they've got...[$]20 trillion...worth of residential homes. They've got [$]20 trillion worth of stocks, very roughly. Those are the two big assets of American families. They are both down dramatically for different families. But 95% of the people at least are worse off in terms of their residential wealth plus stock wealth from a year ago or two years ago."

ON UNEMPLOYMENT:

"[The current]6.1[% unemployment rate] is going to go higher. But whether it goes and quits at 7[%] or whether it quits at 10[%] or 11[%] or 12[%] depends on, among other things, the wisdom of Congress, and then [the execution of] the plan that Congress authorizes."

ON THE FUTURE:

"Now the recession is going to get worse. I mean, I don't want to hold out false hopes that...by some magic moment, that things will turn around in a couple months because they [won't]...It's a big mistake to try and mislead people. [The economy] will turn around. I don't know whether it will be six months or whether it'll be two years. This country is going [to] be living better ten years from now than it is now. It will be living better in 20 years from now than ten years from now...Now, we had the great depression, we had two world wars, we had the flu epidemic...we had [an] oil shock...we had all these terrible things happen. But something about the American system unleashed more...potential...Over [the last] hundred years...we had a seven for one improvement [in our standard of living]. So we've got a great system. And we've got more productive capacity now than we ever had. The American worker is more productive than he's ever been. We've got more people to do it. We've got all the ingredients for a sensational future. It's just that right now the athlete's on the floor. But, this is a super athlete."

03

SEPTEMBER STATEMENTS

> "MOST OF THE TIME, COMMON STOCKS ARE
> SUBJECT TO IRRATIONAL AND EXCESSIVE PRICE
> FLUCTUATIONS IN BOTH DIRECTIONS AS THE
> CONSEQUENCE OF THE INGRAINED TENDENCY OF
> MOST PEOPLE TO SPECULATE OR GAMBLE...TO
> GIVE WAY TO HOPE, FEAR AND GREED."
>
> BENJAMIN GRAHAM

In the coming days, you will receive your September quarter-end statements for your personal investment accounts. This will undoubtedly be unpleasant to read, as investors have made a mass exodus from global equity markets—an exodus that has exponentially intensified in October. Despite the extreme pessimism that currently abounds, and more importantly because of it, we are beginning to see some solid investment opportunities. We need to be clear that we have no idea where and when this market will bottom, but we do know that many appealing companies are priced lower than they were ten years ago and we doubt this will be the case in another ten years.

We are facing unprecedented market conditions. On Wednesday, the S&P 500 slid further to 984, extending its 2008 tumble to nearly 35% in the market's worst yearly slump since 1937. The Dow Jones Industrial Average today dropped to 9,258, an over 33% retreat in 2008 that is also the worst yearly slide in 71 years. This selloff is part of a world-wide fire sale in equity markets that has pushed many international and emerging market indexes to even greater percentage losses than here in the U.S. In our view, hedge funds and leverage are exacerbating market turmoil beyond any historical context. Furthermore, it is unparalleled to have six consecutive powerful daily declines without the relief of an intermittent rally or "dead cat bounce."

While we continue to think the recently passed $700 billion Troubled Asset Relief Program (TARP) will help to facilitate the flow of credit, it will not happen overnight, and additional measures are necessary. Today, Secretary Paulson announced it will be at least another two weeks until the Treasury buys any assets through the TARP. This is mind-boggling given the Treasury's outrage at the delays in the legislative process. At this pace, Paulson's team makes Congress look efficient. It is easier to extinguish a house fire five minutes after it starts rather than after it has consumed the whole first floor.

The Fed and the Treasury, although taking the necessary steps to prevent economic collapse, have consistently been a day late and a dollar short. Today's action by worldwide central banks to coordinate a one-half percent international rate cut was another push in the right direction. Even as these actions take effect and governments take additional substantive steps toward liberal monetary and fiscal policy, our economy will face serious recessionary headwinds for the foreseeable future. The present goal should be to stabilize financial markets because their drastic decline is a self-fulfilling prophecy for degradation of the real economy, including large rises in unemployment, credit defaults and foreclosures.

Many investors tend to succumb to a herd mentality resulting in extreme moves, many examples of which we have seen in recent years. For instance, in early 2000, the technology sector represented over 40% of the S&P 500 and now stands at about 16%. Financials are another example of these extremes, representing over 25% of the S&P 500 a little more than year ago. Currently they have fallen to less than 14% of the index. Last spring, the Euro galloped toward €1.60 to the dollar, thus bolstering foreign equity returns, and capital poured into international and emerging market funds. Then came summer when oil rolled to $147 per barrel and investors dumped money into commodity funds hand-over-fist under the guise of "diversification." Currently, we are seeing cash chasing the safety of short-term Treasury securities and real assets such as gold and silver. It appears we are in a consensus environment of extreme negativity.

> "ACKNOWLEDGING WE ARE IN A TEXTBOOK FINANCIAL PANIC OF SEVERE PROPORTIONS, WE MUST ALSO NOTE THAT IN PAST BEAR MARKETS, EQUITIES REBOUNDED BEFORE THE ECONOMY RECOVERED."

Acknowledging we are in a textbook financial panic of severe proportions, we must also note that in past bear markets, equities rebounded before the economy recovered. But, calling a "bottom" to a bear market is difficult, if not impossible. Our goal for clients is to take advantage of depressed stock prices, while protecting against current economic uncertainty. In the equity portion of client portfolios we are using available cash positions to dollar-cost average into select stocks from our "focus list" that display favorable price stability and entry points. But, we need not be rushed. Warren Buffet has stated: "The stock market is a no-called-strike game. You don't have to swing at everything—you can wait for your pitch."

We want to leave you with a few positive thoughts amidst the gloom of the market and the economy. First, there is an old adage "Don't fight the

Fed." This means that traditional monetary stimulus is often effective and if the Federal Reserve is actively working to stimulate the market, the market should respond to treatment. This is also coupled with the extraordinary moves that the Treasury is presently taking. Together, this prototypical Keynesian approach is powerful. Also, investor sentiment is so low that with each passing day one should assume the marginal sellers are exiting the market. This is how bottoms are made. Finally, as we discussed at the top of this email, many quality companies are selling at share prices below what they were ten years ago when people were tripping over each other to buy stocks. We think in ten years you will look pretty smart for beginning to dollar-cost average into some of these companies over the next few months.

04

BEAR MARKET BLUES

As you know, we have been writing fervently over the past four weeks for increased government intervention to stem the textbook panic in the financial sector. After finally ascertaining the seriousness of systemic failure over the weekend, worldwide governments provided the serious intervention that is necessary. Led by British Prime Minister Gordon Brown and French President Nicolas Sarkozy, much of the industrialized world, including the United States, began taking major steps to quiet the financial tsunami. Their general methods include direct capital contributions through equity stakes in financial institutions, guarantees of certain bank debt and inter-bank lending, implicit acknowledgment that another major bank failure like Lehman Brothers will be avoided at all costs, and a wide variety of other lesser but necessary tools.

Most agree that the immediate panic is avoided. However, most also believe that we are in a recession that is intensifying. As we see it, much of the real economy (Main Street) froze recently due to the seizure of commercial paper markets and general consumer apathy. Everything from GDP to 4th quarter corporate earnings will reflect this stoppage.

On a positive note, we saw the kind of market action typical of a market bottom, in the form of a climactic sell-off followed by an immense rally. Last week ended with the largest point swing since the 1896 creation of the Dow Jones Industrial Average: down 697 points, to a 322 point gain, and closing down 128 points. This was quite an end to the worst weekly percentage loss (down 18% on the Dow), also since its establishment in 1896. Then, as a result of world government intervention, the Dow surged 11% on Monday, the largest one-day percentage gain since 1933 and its largest daily point gain ever.

But, as we mentioned in our September Statements email last week, market bottoms are impossible to predict. So, we decided to dig into the history books for guidance and to think about ways to make money in bear markets.

What does history say about the potential downside from here? At Friday's close, the Dow was at 8,451; a 40% decline from its October 2007 peak. This compares to the peak-to-trough drop of 45% in 1973-74. The Dow only plummeted over 50% on one occasion—The Great Depression—between 1929 and 1932. Using the 1973-74 crash as a barometer, the Dow would not fall below 7,700, a 45% drop from the peak of 14,000. However, history is no guarantee of future events.

It is also important to remember that stocks are generally not as cheap as one might believe. According to Birinyi and Associates and WSJ Market Data, as of last Friday the S&P 500 was trading at 17.1 trailing earnings, higher than the long-term historical average. To be gloomier yet, Yale Professor Robert Shiller, predictor of the 2000 market crash and the 2008 housing crash, tracks what he calls the Graham Price-to-Earnings (P/E) ratio. This measure, which was named after Warren Buffett mentor and Columbia University Professor Benjamin Graham, divides the price of bellwether U.S. stocks by inflation-adjusted average earnings over the preceding ten years. At the end of last week, this measure stood at 15 times earnings, below the long-term average of 16.3 dating to 1881, according to Mr. Shiller's data. But bear markets tend to go to extremes. From 1977 through 1984, the Graham P/E averaged 10, even reaching a low of 6.6 in

33

1982. Getting the Graham P/E to 10 now would require a drop in the Dow to 6,000.

While there is clearly risk of further market losses, it's important to look at the current bear market in a larger context. There are two basic categories of bear markets: secular and cyclical. A secular bear market represents a multi-year period of below-average market returns, whereas a cyclical bear market is typically shorter in duration and driven by basic economic cycles. To put it another way, cyclical bear markets are bumps along the road that occur periodically, regardless of the secular trend. While we are undoubtedly in a cyclical bear market, we are also arguably in the midst of the fourth secular bear market since 1900. Here is a chart of those markets:

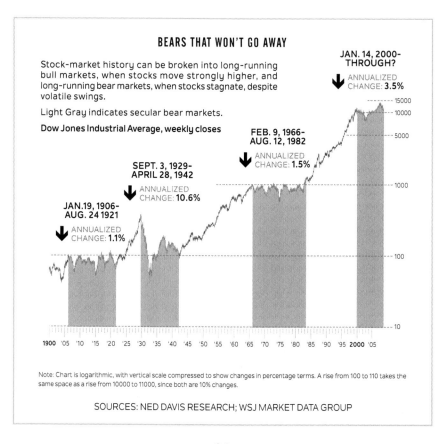

BEARS THAT WON'T GO AWAY

Stock-market history can be broken into long-running bull markets, when stocks move strongly higher, and long-running bear markets, when stocks stagnate, despite volatile swings.

Light Gray indicates secular bear markets.

Dow Jones Industrial Average, weekly closes

JAN. 14, 2000-THROUGH?
↓ ANNUALIZED CHANGE: **3.5%**

FEB. 9, 1966-AUG. 12, 1982
↓ ANNUALIZED CHANGE: **1.5%**

SEPT. 3, 1929-APRIL 28, 1942
↓ ANNUALIZED CHANGE: **10.6%**

JAN.19, 1906-AUG. 24 1921
↓ ANNUALIZED CHANGE: **1.1%**

Note: Chart is logarithmic, with vertical scale compressed to show changes in percentage terms. A rise from 100 to 110 takes the same space as a rise from 10000 to 11000, since both are 10% changes.

SOURCES: NED DAVIS RESEARCH; WSJ MARKET DATA GROUP

The first three secular bear markets lasted 15 years, 13 years, and 16 years, respectively. Our current rut of market swings with no aggregate progress has only lasted 8 years, a potentially discouraging sign for investors. But, investors can still make money during secular bear markets by rebalancing during major cyclical declines and looking for value in individual companies whose share prices are unfairly punished.

Last week we ended with some good news and we will do so again. First, this world-wide government stimulus is unprecedented, but similar historical measures appear to have been effective. Next, smart investors can continue to rebalance their accounts throughout heavy market sell-offs by dollar-cost-averaging into positions that are tattered. We believe this is best done through individual stocks, adding to companies that you believe in when their prices are down. Investing in individual securities is the best way to spot these opportunities. And finally, look for stocks with low P/E ratios (even single digit), companies selling around their book or liquidation value, and firms with low debt levels and solid cash positions. Not only can this help protect on the downside, but it can also offer great upside potential. If a few of these stocks move against us, but we are still committed to them, we buy more. We also believe in taking profits when a stock jumps too fast, too quickly, even when we still believe in the company. No doubt, in this environment, you are best served with a transparent, understandable approach to investing.

05

THE GREAT UNWINDING

W hy is the market so volatile right now, with huge negative and positive intraday swings that most often end on the downside? Market volatility is not only at an all-time high, but far above any previous record levels. It all seems to make no sense. We need to look to the chaos as a way to find order.

There are two forces working against stocks that help to explain current volatility.

The first has to do with valuations, or what someone is willing to pay for a stock. The preferred valuation metric for stocks is the price-to-earnings ratio (P/E). Unfortunately, the "E" part of this equation, corporate earnings, is a huge unknown. With the economy continuing to deteriorate rapidly and unemployment undoubtedly on an upward trend, earnings are as precarious as ever. Given this missing component, the market does not have a North Star to follow. The uncertainty is intense.

The second force and the driver over the past week is "The Great Unwinding," or forced selling. Hedge funds, Wall Street firms, and mutual funds are being compelled to sell securities, including positions that they do not want to sell. This is happening for two primary reasons: deleveraging and redemptions. To explain deleveraging, remember how wildly irresponsible Wall Street became. Bear Stearns, Lehman Brothers, Goldman Sachs, Merrill Lynch and Morgan Stanley functioned very much like giant hedge funds, borrowing huge pools of money to undertake speculative investments. In many cases, these and many other firms borrowed to the tune of $30 or $40 for every $1 in real assets. Much of this leveraged money contributed to the housing, commodity, and foreign currency booms. Now all of these positions are being unwound, effectively being reversed through selling. Investment strategist Ed Yardeni referred to forced selling by the $1.7 trillion hedge fund industry as "the greatest margin call of all time."

Redemptions represent the second element of "The Great Unwinding." A recent report from J.P. Morgan estimates that investors in hedge funds-of-funds have requested redemptions totaling roughly $100 billion for the fourth quarter of 2008. According to TrimTabs Investment Research, U.S. mutual fund redemptions totaled $75 billion in September alone. When investors ask for their money back, hedge funds and mutual funds are forced to sell securities. This helped cause the horrific performance compiled by many asset managers

Here are some further examples of forced selling:

• According to Bloomberg News on October 27th, the Japanese currency (the Yen) has risen to a 13-year high against the dollar as investors have unwound carry trades. The carry trade occurs when a trader borrows money in a currency with a low interest rate (Japan's interest rates have hovered at or close to zero for many years) and uses the funds to purchase an investment in a different currency with a higher expected return. Many fund managers borrowed in Yen to purchase U.S. assets. The Yen's recent strength is a sure sign of deleveraging.

- The California Public Employees' Retirement System, or Calpers, has had to sell stock to meet cash obligations, according to the Wall Street Journal on October 25th. The $188 billion state pension fund is raising cash to fulfill commitments to private equity and real estate investments. Because credit has dried up and their alternative investments are fairly illiquid, stocks represent the first asset class to be sold.

- In early October, Chesapeake Energy (CHK) CEO Aubrey McClendon joined the ranks of corporate executives who have been forced to sell company stock. According to a press release, McClendon involuntarily sold substantially all of his shares of Chesapeake common stock from October 8th through October 10th in order to meet margin loan calls. McClendon sold over 31 million shares at prices ranging from $12.65 to $24 per share. CHK's 52-week high was $74.

It is important to remember that these market events are interrelated. The vast number of chain reactions occurring throughout the system causes extreme volatility and unintended market manipulation. For example, as investors fearfully sell mutual funds in their 401(k) plans, the mutual fund managers sell stocks to meet the redemptions. This drives down stock prices, which triggers margin calls. Margin calls lead to more forced selling and the stock market tumbles even further. Hedge funds exercise "put" options that they purchased to provide downside protection. The party on the other end of the "put" option contract satisfies its cash obligation by selling more securities. This domino action is powerful and completely unpredictable.

In our opinion, a major mistake that investors have made in recent years is not knowing what they are buying—everything from mortgage-backed securities to exotic insurance-based options to certain emerging market funds. We are determined to avoid this mistake. For the equity allocation in our client portfolios, this leaves us with only one viable strategy. We are slowly and steadily buying understandable and transparent individual companies based on earnings prospects and fair valuations. Like everyone else, we have no idea where the bottom is, but we do know that all great long-term investors resist financial engineering and make understandable investments...We are committed to doing just that.

06

THE COLLAPSE
OF CHROME

B ack in 2000, Jim Cramer appeared on the financial network CNBC as a guest host of the morning television show Squawk Box. He was recommending a stock called General Motors (GM), which sold for around $90 per share. Cramer famously touted GM as "a bank in the metal bending business." Well, as it turns out, its banking operations have been disastrous and its metal bending business might be even worse. Today GM trades for approximately $3 per share with a market capitalization of $1.9 billion (in comparison, the market capitalization of Exxon Mobil is $376 billion). It is also becoming doubtful that GM can even survive without a probable government bailout.

Just last week, we learned that industry-wide car sales plummeted 32% in October, the twelfth straight month of decline, to 10.5 million vehicles. GM was hit particularly hard, with sales falling 45% in October. In the third quarter, GM lost $4.2 billion ($7.35 per share) and burned through $6.9 billion in cash, leaving the company with $16.2 billion in cash. GM says it needs at least $11 billion in cash to appropriately operate its business. This led GM to strongly imply that it will be difficult to make it through the year without major assistance.

GM's Detroit neighbor, Ford (F), also had an arduous quarter. Its sales plunged 30% in October, third-quarter losses amounted to $2.7 billion, and the company blew $7.7 billion in cash during the quarter. The mildly good news for Ford is that it has $30 billion in cash remaining on its balance sheet, so it can survive a little longer than GM.

Much like the U.S. banking industry, Detroit will most likely get an additional meaningful bailout. It is worth noting that when Congress passed the recent financial rescue package, it included $25 billion in loans to the auto industry. The Energy Department, which is responsible for doling out the funds, has not yet disbursed a single cent. But, in any event, this amount would merely serve as a Band-Aid for the automakers.

The U.S. has lost over one million jobs so far in 2008. The Center for Automotive Research estimates that the failure of GM alone would directly or indirectly result in the loss of over two and a half million jobs within one year—jobs that are essential to the health of our economy. While the Treasury has struggled mightily in orchestrating its equity-based bank bailout, the government has a true opportunity in how it handles the auto industry.

In our opinion, the U.S. auto industry's problems are two-fold:

1) The companies have been atrociously managed for more than twenty years. They have been late with every major innovation, in particular the move toward higher-quality vehicles. The Wall Street Journal recently quoted an unnamed long-time Detroit auto executive who said: "Since the mid-Seventies, I have sat through umpteen meetings describing how we had to beat the Japanese to survive. Thirty-five years later we are still trying to figure it out."

2) Organized labor's stranglehold within the industry leads to unrealistic wages and benefits, making it difficult for Detroit to compete against foreign automakers with lower labor costs.

While America's manufacturing prowess has diminished in favor of a bloated services sector, we have a unique opportunity to reform a major portion of our slumping productive capacity. To achieve this goal, an investment in Detroit should be designed to incentivize the creation of energy-efficient cars that will lead the world in innovation, style and quality. Instead of fueling our cars with Saudi Arabian and Iranian oil, we could be putting those dollars to work in the United States. Emergency economic times can often present opportunities to innovate in a way that will payoff for generations...after all, America is still using the Hoover Dam productively.

The second aspect of a Detroit aid package may be reasonable concessions on the part of labor unions and management. Most American workers are not afforded the wages and benefits enjoyed by autoworkers. The harsh reality is that these costs are economically unsustainable. And, if the average assembly line employee takes a cut, senior executives must also be asked to bite the bullet as a result of management's failures.

Many market pundits believe we are experiencing the worst economic conditions since the Great Depression. As the government spends taxpayer money to revive the economy, its programs should be geared toward improving our economic structure, not maintaining the status quo. Our current economic malaise could just be the opportunity we need to take the wheel and drive the global economy in the 21st century.

THE AMERICAN CONSUMER

M ark Twain is often credited with the quip, "The reports of my death have been greatly exaggerated." For many years, this has been the case for the American consumer. But this time, the consumer faces a truly daunting challenge. Economists have now confirmed that the current recession began in December 2007, already making this longer than the average recession since World War II. According to Allen Sinai, president of Decision Economics, "We will rewrite the record book on length for this recession. It's still arguable whether it will set a new record on depth. I hope not, but we don't know."

As we turn the corner each year from Thanksgiving into the holiday shopping season, the stock market examines the mood and spending plans of the American consumer. At around 70% of Gross Domestic Product (GDP), consumer spending is by far the largest contributor to the growth of the U.S. economy. This year, concern over weak holiday spending is heightened due to a waning global economy. According to the Commerce Department, personal consumption spending fell at an annual, inflation-adjusted rate of 2.7% in the third quarter. This represented the largest annual decline since 1980. On a positive note, though, last week's "Black Friday" retail sales actually jumped 3% from 2007, according to ShopperTrak. While this represents the smallest increase in three years, any rise is still great news in this environment. Further, "Cyber Monday" sales rose 15% over last year, with sales hitting $846 million versus $733 million, according to comScore.

ShopperTrak anticipates 9.9% fewer traditional shoppers this entire holiday season. A few analysts, however, point to significantly lower energy prices as a possible boost to those who do venture to stores or to retailers' websites. As you can see in the chart below, gasoline, which reached a peak average price of $4.17 per gallon in July, recently dropped below $1.87 per gallon. This is a significant 55% price decline and should function much like a "stimulus" for struggling consumers. In many ways, this is effectively a major tax cut for consumers.

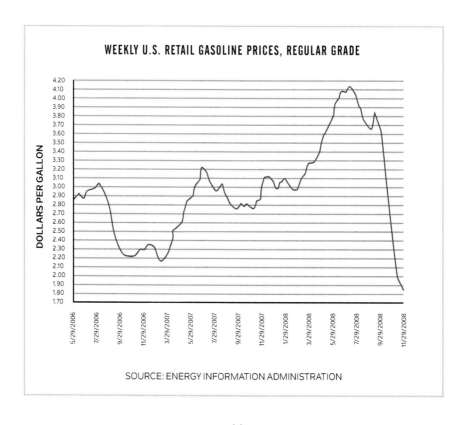

WEEKLY U.S. RETAIL GASOLINE PRICES, REGULAR GRADE

SOURCE: ENERGY INFORMATION ADMINISTRATION

On the other hand, consumers face increasing pressure on home equity lines of credit as house values plummet. As of the end of the third quarter, the S&P / Case-Shiller Home Price Index had declined 16.6% versus the third quarter of 2007 and most economists predict this figure will deteriorate further in the fourth quarter. Consumers must also confront the tightening of credit card lines as banks pull back on their risk exposure. According to the November 20th *Wall Street Journal*, "many big banks reported weak credit card results for the third quarter, with 'charge-offs'—reflecting loans considered to be uncollectible—rising to over 5% of total credit card balances and poised to deteriorate further." To mitigate their credit card portfolio risk, banks are taking action by raising interest rates, implementing new fees and tightening lending standards. To further compound consumer gloom, 401(k) and other investment balances have been hit hard by a more than 40% year-over-year drop in the S&P 500 index.

Repeatedly, the American consumer defies the odds. As Franklin Roosevelt once said, "When you come to the end of your rope, tie a knot and hang on." But, can consumers hang on this holiday season? Look for several indicators over the next few weeks. First, memories can be short, so a sizable bear market rally in stocks over the coming week or two could create a more secure perception of economic stability. Second, Friday will bring the next major employment report and news that is not disastrous will offer support to consumers during this vital season. A month ago, unemployment hit 6.5% and is expected to post an increase to 6.8%. Third, aggressive promotions by retailers on "Black Friday" and "Cyber Monday" proved effective, so look for continued creativity and smart merchandising to drive revenues. A resilient consumer could provide the market with some holiday cheer until late-January when a comprehensive fiscal stimulus package passes Congress and is signed into law by President Barack Obama.

08 FEAR & LOATHING ON THE INTERNET (AND EVERYWHERE ELSE)

t is difficult to go through a day without reading or hearing the word "depression" in the media. As far back as February 28th of this year, the Business and Media Institute said "historically negative media coverage has taken a turn for the worst, shifting from reporting on 'recession' to all-out 'depression.'" While economic conditions are undoubtedly treacherous, the media has a simple motive for exaggeration. Take the cable financial news network CNBC as an example. With the financial crisis gaining additional steam last month, CNBC had its most successful November ever; a 36% increase in viewers over November 2007.

It is beginning to appear that, although the fundamentals of the economy are certainly weak, the media's continued dire predictions of another Great Depression are compounding the problem. In many ways, this is the ultimate self-fulfilling prophesy. We can only hope that as time passes, people unplug from the media feeding frenzy and a renewed optimism sweeps America.

The great investor Sir John Templeton once said, "The four most expensive words in the English language are, 'This time it's different.'"

46

Most reporters and market pundits are certain that this economic downturn is different than the 8 prior recessions since the Great Depression. This extremely negative sentiment could imply that Americans' worst expectations are already priced into the stock and credit markets. However, the fundamentals of the economy must stabilize or improve over the next several months, or a massive snowballing phenomenon could turn into an avalanche.

The fear in the market is best exhibited in the U.S. 30-day Treasury bill. As *The New York Times* reported last Wednesday, "Investors accepted the zero percent rate in the government's auction Tuesday of $30 billion worth of short-term securities that mature in four weeks. Demand was so great even for no return that the government could have sold four times as much." The conclusion, many investors are so fearful and skeptical they are willing to park their money safely with the U.S. government in exchange for no return. Right now, the 30-day T-bill is figuratively the world's largest mattress.

In his December 8th *New York Times* column, David Carr said, "Every modern recession includes a media séance about how horrible things are and how much worse they will be, but there have never been so many ways for the fear to leak in. The same digital dynamics that drove the irrational exuberance—and marketed the loans to help it happen—are now driving the downside in unprecedented ways. The recession was not actually declared until last week, but the psychology that drives it had already been e-mailed, blogged and broadcast for months."

All the negativity makes us again recall Mark Twain, who once said, "When the end of the world comes, I want to be in Cincinnati because it's always twenty years behind the times." If the media keeps up its handiwork, we will all want to be in Cincinnati.

47

09

DEAR MR. PRESIDENT

T he following is a fictitious letter to President Obama from a responsible bank CEO.

DEAR MR. PRESIDENT,

Congratulations on your exciting inauguration day. Although the job will undoubtedly get tougher from here, there is significant optimism that your election will bring change to America. While I am skeptical as to whether we are truly entering an era of post-partisan politics, we are certainly entering a post-mega-bank society. The path of your presidency will depend on your acknowledgement of this fact.

Over the last several weeks, with earnings announcements from Citigroup and Bank of America, it has become painfully apparent that the "super major" or "money center" financial institutions in this country are insolvent. If they truly recognized the market value of their assets, these losses would lead to ratios short of the existing capital requirements.

We now know that Merrill Lynch, presently part of Bank of America, is polluted with toxic assets much like Citigroup. Citigroup is currently our worst offender, and also currently on life-support. It took $45 billion of taxpayer cash in their pockets and about $300 billion in guarantees on some of their bad assets just to keep the doors open. They even had to sell 51% of their most profitable business, SmithBarney, for a pittance.

Your predecessor and his former Treasury Secretary Henry Paulson made two crucial mistakes during this financial crisis. The first was letting Lehman Brothers fail. This set off a crisis of confidence and began to define the government's approach to fixing the financial system: inconsistency. Why transition Bear Stearns, Washington Mutual, and Wachovia; prop-up Citigroup and Bank of America; nationalize Fannie Mae, Freddie Mac and AIG; but allow Lehman to go bankrupt?

The second mistake revolved around the Troubled Asset Relief Program (TARP). TARP began as a plan to purchase distressed assets from ailing banks, which was a good idea. However, TARP quickly morphed into a program to purchase preferred equity stakes in America's financial institutions on behalf of U.S. taxpayers. The Treasury haphazardly threw varying amounts of money at some banks, while rejecting others: more inconsistency.

The good news is that you now control the second half of TARP ($350 billion). The best way to spend this money is to purchase distressed assets at market value from suffering institutions. Yes, TARP was originally supposed to do that, but it didn't. This will start to cure the root ailment whereas the first $350 billion was a poorly manufactured Band-Aid. Allowing a bottomless pit of bad assets to stay on bank balance sheets simply led to more write-downs and more capital injections as Citigroup and Bank of America illustrated.

In developing standards for purchasing these toxic assets, please be more consistent than your predecessor. Financial markets hate surprises. All banks need a level playing field. We need clearly articulated standards for determining which banks will benefit from your programs, which types of assets you are buying, and how you will value

49

them. There are many solid financial institutions like ours that did not partake in reckless lending and excessive securitization.

Buying bad assets from banks at market value will result in a final round of bank write-offs and, therefore, a final round of recapitalization. To recapitalize the banks, your administration needs to purchase common equity so that those with the most bad assets will have their equity holders diluted proportionally by the government's stake. Therefore, for the first time in this rescue, the reckless banks will face punitive measures and their capital ratios will be brought in-line. To date, this has truly been a bailout, and now you need a program with consequences for those banks that were most incompetent.

You would also serve taxpayers well to develop a plan for all the banks you will partially own as a result of a cohesive plan. If a "smaller"

> "IT WAS SO EASY FOR THE WALL STREET TITANS TO MAKE MONEY THAT THEY CONVINCED THEMSELVES OF THEIR OWN SUPREME INTELLIGENCE."

bank has become insolvent but does not pose a systemic risk, you should close it and coordinate a sale of the "good" assets. The bad assets would reside with the government where they would be held to maturity or sold when the economy recovers. As for the mega banks, use your ownership to split these companies up. Make them smaller. As Citigroup and Bank of America have conclusively proven, the "supermarket" approach to banking is unworkable. First, it creates giant institutions that are too big to fail. Second, it creates inherent conflicts of interest and breeds total irresponsibility.

Congress passed Glass-Steagall during the Great Depression (1933) to try and avoid a second Great Depression down the road. But in 1999, the Wall Street Gods determined that they could quantify risk and assured President Bill Clinton and Congress that they should be left alone to "innovate." It only took ten years for them to completely ruin the economy...It was so easy for the Wall Street Titans to make money that they convinced themselves of their own supreme intelligence. They constantly raised the stakes through excessive leverage. In the end, the inevitable economic downturn hit and now the entire system is spiraling out of control.

Putting these irresponsible banks and financial innovators in their place will take a strong political will. To leave these institutions in place is to postpone the inevitable. So, let me remind you of a line from your sobering inaugural speech: "...[O]ur time of standing pat, of protecting narrow interests and putting off unpleasant decisions—that time has surely passed."

Very Sincerely,
John Q. Banker, Chief Executive Officer
N.E. Responsible Bank
One Reasonable Place
Reserve Capital, USA 00001

10

CLASSIFYING THE CONTRACTION

The December 30, 2008 issue of *The Economist* relays this story: "In 1978 Alfred Kahn, one of Jimmy Carter's economic advisors, was chided by the president for scaring people by warning of a looming depression. Mr. Kahn, in his next speech, simply replaced the offending word, saying 'We're in danger of having the worst banana in 45 years.'" Today, there is no such semantic bias in favor of fruit. The word depression is profuse in the media and among a growing handful of highly respected economists and some less respected politicians.

Given the chance, Yogi Berra might have said that "a depression is not a lot of fun." Of course, rampant pessimism and feelings of hopelessness abound in most economic contractions, but what exactly is a depression? The answer to this question is elusive, but here is some perspective nonetheless.

The Business Cycle Dating Committee of the National Bureau of Economic Research is the official American arbiter for identifying recessions. This group "determined that a peak in economic activity occurred in the U.S. economy in December 2007." The Committee defines a recession as "a significant decline in economic activity spread across the economy, lasting more than a few months, normally visible in production, employment, real income, and other indicators." The Committee further believes "that domestic production and employment are the primary conceptual measures of economic activity."

Among economists, the popular definition of a recession is two consecutive quarters of negative economic growth, as measured by Gross Domestic Product (GDP). The U.S. economy reached this popular definition after a 0.5% annualized drop in third quarter GDP, followed by a further 3.8% annualized decline in the fourth quarter of 2008. Throughout the Great Depression, GDP fell about 30% from 1929 to 1933, according to *The Economist*. *The Economist* also writes that in Japan's "lost decade" of the 1990's, GDP fell 3.4% during the most severe peak-to-trough decline. Under current circumstances, if GDP fell by over 5.0% for a rolling one-year period, we think many would term this a depression, albeit far less severe than that of the 1930's. In our current climate, where absolute negativity prevails, a continued severe shrinking of GDP no longer seems impossible.

Employment is the Dating Committee's other crucial indicator. In January 2009, the national unemployment rate rose to 7.6%, which is the highest rate since unemployment reached 7.8% in June 1992. In the overall post-World War II period, unemployment peaked in November and December of 1982 at 10.8%, according to the Bureau of Labor Statistics. From September 1982 through June 1983, the unemployment rate remained above 10% for ten months. During America's Great Depression, unemployment peaked at 24.9% in 1933. In our current economic malaise, an unemployment rate surpassing the 1982 high of 10.8% would certainly lead many economists to begin declaring an economic depression. Given the current snowballing scenario, where fear begets more fear, such a circumstance is foreseeable over the next twelve months.

A final consideration, in addition to GDP and employment measures, is the events leading to a recession versus a depression. Our post-World War II recessions have been, for the most part, spurred by high interest rates that were designed to tame inflation. Much like the United States in the 1930s and Japan in the 1990s, this recession has some of the characteristics of a depression. Specifically, we have a bursting real estate bubble, a massive fifty-year debt bubble, a severe banking crisis and many initial signs of deflation.

To summarize, we believe the key indicator in measuring our current economic contraction will be employment and that GDP will be a major, but secondary consideration. We are experiencing a long and painful economic drought, and if unemployment exceeds 11% and GDP contracts in excess of 5% over a full year, some analysts will define this as a depression.

However, this is not a foregone conclusion. As we have seen before, confidence can return as quickly as it left. The investment philosopher Benjamin Graham wrote that "In the short-run, the market is a voting machine—reflecting a voter-registration test that requires only money, not intelligence or emotional stability—but, in the long-run, the market is a weighing machine." Therefore, if business and personal confidence can creatively seize the upper hand, this will derail the demagoguery of politicians, economists and analysts who have completely discounted the American spirit.

Based on the knowledge that the stock market has historically been a leading indicator of economic conditions, we are taking two important steps to protect our client portfolios. First, we invest in high-quality individual companies rather than opaque, expensive, overly diversified mutual funds. We can take comfort in owning stakes in solid long-term businesses, regardless of the "noise" in the broader market. Second, we spend a great deal of time discussing true risk tolerance and determining the appropriate asset allocation for our clients. And when appropriate, we use dollar-cost averaging to build equity positions gradually.

After all of these sobering statistics, we will once again leave you with a few optimistic thoughts. First, as we mentioned above, the stock market has historically soured prior to recessions and improved ahead of economic recoveries. While the stock market crowd is usually irrational in the short-term and subject to misleading "bear market rallies," it is typically ahead of the curve when it comes to identifying long-term economic recoveries. Secondly, all the talk before the economic tailspin was about "decoupling." This theory said that America could undergo a recession while many other countries worldwide would continue to thrive. We are actually experiencing the opposite phenomenon. The U.S. economy's deterioration is proving to be less severe than in many other countries, particularly some emerging markets. This means that capital is continuing to flow toward the United States. And third, whether you agree with the economic stimulus or not, it still means that hundreds of billions of dollars will be injected into the American economy. Some form of bank rescue (the most important dynamic in all of this) will ultimately contribute at least another $1 trillion to the U.S. banking system. Finally, we continue to see tremendous long-term value in good companies with reasonable valuations. When you directly own a piece of an American business you have the transparency and freedom to see this through.

11

COULD IT BE?

A s investors, we are constantly asking ourselves tough questions. Lately we have been grappling with the unthinkable.

COULD IT BE THAT THE MAJOR CREDIT RATING AGENCIES WILL CONTINUE THEIR ABYSMAL PREDICTIVE RECORD?

Standard & Poor's, Moody's and Fitch are the three primary bond rating agencies and have enormous influence over Wall Street. The highest rating they bestow is Triple-A. As enablers of the great financial crisis that we are now facing, these agencies rated sub-prime mortgage-backed securities and collateralized debt obligations as Triple-A based on the ridiculous models that their firms created.

These firms once rated The American International Group (AIG) as a Triple-A credit, all the while AIG piled on mind-boggling obligations through credit default swaps (CDS), which last quarter led to the largest loss in American corporate history—$61.7 billion.

Without these colossal errors, our economy would be in a much better position. But, Standard & Poor's, Moody's and Fitch are not

56

new to overlooking the elephant in the room. Remember Enron and WorldCom? Enron was rated an investment grade credit right up until the day it declared bankruptcy. WorldCom maintained its investment grade rating until three months before its bankruptcy.

Now these rating agencies are on a downgrading spree, cutting the ratings of vast amounts of mortgage-backed securities, many insurance companies and many banks. In fact, they recently down-graded the debt of both General Electric and Warren Buffet's Berkshire Hathaway. If their track record holds, then they are likely to be wrong once again.

COULD IT BE TRUE THAT BEARS MAKE MONEY, BULLS MAKE MONEY AND PIGS GET SLAUGHTERED?

Wall Street banks, the rating agencies and the regulators all embraced the concept that thousands of bad mortgages bundled together as one security were transformed into a good security; after all, it was "diversified." In an already overleveraged economy, faith in the all-encompassing power of broad diversification pushed us over the edge as the Wall Street banks leveraged their balance sheets thirty-to-one and bet the farm on these bogus mortgage-backed securities. Much of this was based on the misguided belief that housing prices could not decline.

Just as speculators participated on the way up to unsustainable heights, we now have others trying to push us down to new lows. The latest game in town is to drive fear about the prospects of certain companies by manipulating the credit default swap market. Credit default swaps are unregulated insurance that will theoretically pay if a company's bonds default. The higher the premium on a credit default swap, the higher the implied risk that a company will fail. However, the market for these instruments is just small enough that unscrupulous players can create fear. Traders are shorting certain stocks (betting the stock's price will fall) and then bidding up credit default swaps in an effort to fool the market into thinking that these companies are in irreparable trouble and then profiting handsomely from their short positions.

For example, according to a Merrill Lynch report issued on Friday, March 6th, the credit default swap market was indicating that Warren Buffett's Berkshire Hathaway had a greater risk of default than the country of Vietnam and that General Electric was at greater risk of default than Russia (a country that actually did default on its debt in 1998).

If the track record of outrageous greed holds, then these scare tactics should ultimately fail. Just this week, many of the stocks that have been victims of this strategy have rebounded strongly. Let us hope that this is a sustainable stock market rally.

COULD IT BE THAT INDIVIDUAL INVESTORS ARE AS WRONG AS EVER?

The American Association of Individual Investors released its most recent survey of investor confidence. The survey is the most negative in its twenty-two year history, with 70% of the respondents bearish about the market's prospects. The last time that 70% of the respondents agreed on something, it was in January of 2000, near the top of the technology stock bubble. At that time, 70% of respondents were bullish on the market's prospects. Again, let's hope their track record holds.

COULD IT BE THAT THERE ARE TWO TIERS OF FINANCIAL INSTITUTIONS, THE AWFUL AND THE OK?

The assumption before this week was that every financial institution was fatally flawed. Perhaps this is an overstatement. Of the Wall Street banks, we have thus far found that Bear Stearns, Lehman Brothers and Merrill Lynch were among the awful, but it appears that Morgan Stanley and certainly Goldman Sachs are among the OK. In terms of the super-banks, we know that Citigroup is awful, that Bank of America is perhaps somewhere between awful and OK, but it is increasingly appearing that perhaps Wells Fargo and J.P. Morgan are OK.

If our country truly has a large contingent of OK, i.e. well managed financial institutions, then there will be the opportunity for many positive surprises in the weeks and months ahead, much like we've seen this week.

COULD IT BE THAT STOCKS ARE PRICED APPROPRIATELY FOR A BEAR MARKET BOTTOM?

According to a recent Goldman Sachs study that analyzed the twelve previous bear markets beginning in 1929, assuming a March 2009 end to the present bear market, we are at very normal levels for a bottom. The historical average peak-to-trough price decline was 38%. We reached 56%. The average peak price-to-earnings ratio was 25.6. We reached 22.4 back in October of 2007. And finally, the historical average trough price-to-earnings ratio was 13.9. We reached 13.4.

Only time will tell, but there are numerous questions worth considering. The counter punch is that our economy and our markets are weakening at unprecedented rates with much of the rest of the world in even worse shape. Is this time different?

12

THE REARVIEW MIRROR

The first decade of the twenty-first century was one of the worst in modern history for U.S. equity markets.

Princeton University Professor Paul Krugman, a Nobel Prize winning economist and New York Times columnist, who has become a perennial pessimist, summed up what many are thinking: "...from an economic point of view, I'd suggest that we call the decade past the Big Zero. It was a decade in which nothing good happened, and none of the optimistic things we were supposed to believe turned out to be true." In conclusion, Krugman wrote "...let's bid a not at all fond farewell to the Big Zero—the decade in which we achieved nothing and learned nothing."

The overwhelming consensus among economists, market analysts, business journalists and academics appears to be that the next decade will be, like the decade past, an utter failure. Richard Tedlow, a professor of business administration at Harvard Business School, says, "It's been a decade of delusion...In many ways, we're worse off than the 1930s, we've created problems of moral hazard and we're faced with an astounding public debt."

60

The best summation of the collective conscious comes from Pacific Investment Management Company (PIMCO), the manager of the world's largest bond fund, Total Return. In May 2009, PIMCO management issued its secular (or long-term) forecast for a "new normal." PIMCO describes the "new normal" as an economy comprised of slow growth, increased regulation and a diminishing role for the U.S. in the global economy.

PIMCO is not alone. Many others are downright bearish about the U.S. economy and absolutely giddy about emerging markets like Brazil, Russia, India, and China. But could this be a rearview mirror phenomenon? After all, the Morgan Stanley Capital International (MSCI) Emerging Markets Index is up an average 11.38% per year over the 10 years ending December 31, 2009. This is not dissimilar to the 1990s, where the average annual return of the MSCI Emerging Markets Index was 11.05%.

But in the 1990's, returns in the U.S. were actually better than those of the emerging markets. According to the book *Triumph of the Optimists: 101 Years of Global Investment Returns*, the U.S. stock market returned an average 14.4% each year from 1990 through 1999.

Perhaps this is why in 1999 and 2000 James K. Glassman and Kevin A. Hassett copyrighted the *BusinessWeek* bestselling book, *Dow 36,000*. On the book's cover is a quote from Knight Kiplinger, the Editor in Chief of Kiplinger Publications, who wrote about the book: "Rock-solid investment advice...Long-term investors can place it on an alter next to the works of Benjamin Graham and Peter Lynch, as well as Warren Buffet's annual homilies to his Berkshire Hathaway investors."

Well then, the opinions of today certainly stand in stark contrast to those of ten years ago. The reason is simple: It is human nature to predict the future based on the recent past.

Ironically, one of the few people who predicted the malaise of the 2000s was someone who ardently believes you cannot time the market. John Bogle, the founder of the Vanguard Group and the creator of the $92 billion Vanguard 500 Index Fund, foretold in 2001 of a prolonged period of poor performance for domestic stocks on the heels of the extraordinary

61

returns of the 1980s and 1990s. Such prognostications are pretty good for a guy who rejects the validity of market predictions.

Today, Bogle says, "The 1990s was the golden decade for stocks, the 2000s was the tin decade and the next 10 years will be the bronze decade...Stocks will rise 7 to 9 percent over the next 10 years, below the historical norm but better than the last 10."

The "tin decade" posted an average annual decrease of 0.9% a year for the S&P 500, including dividends. This is the first negative return for a decade since modern stock market data began in 1927. Without dividends, the index lost 24% of its cumulative price value over the last ten years. This compares to a 42 percent cumulative price loss during the 1930s. But, during the '30s, the dividend yield was substantially higher, resulting in an annualized 1% per year positive total return throughout the Great Depression decade.

Since we know many of the risks that the world economy faces—high indebtedness among developed countries, political instability in emerging nations, terrorism, aging populations, high unemployment, weak banks, a Chinese real estate bubble and tapped-out consumers, to name a few—let us examine some of the positive aspects that nobody wants to openly discuss.

As we have examined in this essay, the simple idea that markets run in cycles of outperformance and underperformance is a powerful one. Over time, markets, specifically equity markets, have produced robust returns. The previously cited *Triumph of the Optimists* calculated the total return of U.S. stocks from 1900 through 2000, 101 years, at 9.9% on average each year.

Another positive force is worldwide population growth, which Switzerland-based UBS AG predicts will increase by 3 billion over the next three to four decades. Presently the world houses approximately 6.7 billion people. Population expansion is a reliable driver of economic advancement as additional people lead to expanded consumption.

Technological progress is another major force of economic breakthroughs. Make no mistake; there has been no slowdown in new discoveries. Our guess is that ten years from now we will all be amazed at where we stand.

Finally, at the most fundamental level, earnings drive stock prices. Over the last decade, many businesses got lazy because capital was easy to raise through newfangled debt instruments and lax lending standards. In order to raise new capital going forward, businesses will need to be friendlier to shareholders. This will mean running with greater efficiency, which will result in stronger earnings.

As we move into this new decade, remember what government regulators require in all investment disclosures, "Past Performance is No Guarantee of Future Results."

13

NOT A NEW NORMAL, JUST NORMAL

Over the last several weeks, the stock market has suffered a setback. So, are we on the cusp of the dreaded double-dip recession and another market crash? History indicates that we will avoid both, and that we are on a bumpy path to a normal recovery.

According to the well-regarded stock market historians at Ned Davis Research, Inc., "the recession ended in June 2009, so 2010 would likely mark months six to 18 of the expansion. Historically, the odds of a 10% correction in the S&P 500 between six and 18 months into an expansion are 77%." Therefore, the present correction should not be unexpected. Rather, as the economy regains its footing, it is ordinary to experience a market pullback.

Not only is the stock market bound to experience temporary down-drafts as the economy improves, but high unemployment can also be a stubborn adversary that persists well into a budding recovery.

The last time unemployment reached today's level was the early 1980s. From March 1982 through September 1983—a period extending 19 months—the national unemployment rate stayed above 9%, peaking at 10.8% in December of 1982.

64

The economy experienced sluggish growth rates of 2.2%, negative 1.5% and 0.3%, as measured by gross domestic product (GDP) in the three consecutive quarters leading up to the December 1982 peak in unemployment. However, the economy started to grow in the subsequent three quarters at rates of 5.1%, 9.3% and 8.1%, respectively, while unemployment remained above 9%. In other words, the economy began to grow aggressively even when unemployment was high.

Thus far in our present employment quagmire, the peak of unemployment was 10.1% in October of last year. Unemployment has been in excess of 9% since May of 2009, a total of 9 months so far. In the past three quarters, GDP has registered growth rates of -0.7%, 2.2% and 5.7%, respectively. If unemployment has indeed peaked and if history is any indication, the next three quarters could auger respectable economic growth even while unemployment remains elevated.

The early 1980s and what we are observing today clearly suggest the potential for renewed economic growth despite high unemployment, and the relatively mild recessions of 1991 and 2001 also indicate the same pattern. In 1991, payrolls did not increase for about a year and in 2001, it took two years, according to Albert Bozzo writing on CNBC.com. Each of the past three recessions, including the one we just experienced, indicate that employment is indeed a lagging economic indicator.

The 2000s was a "lost decade," both for the U.S. job market and stock market. Today there are only about 100,000 more jobs in America than there were ten years ago. This compares unfavorably to the creation of 20 million new jobs throughout the expansion of the 1990s, also according to CNBC.com.

As for the stock market, the S&P 500 posted an average annual decrease of 0.9% a year from 2000 through 2009, including dividends. This was the first negative return for a full decade since modern stock market data began in 1927. Without dividends, the index has lost 24% of its cumulative price value over the last ten years. This compares to a 42%

cumulative price loss during the 1930s. But, during the '30s, the dividend yield was substantially higher, resulting in an annualized 1% positive total return throughout the Great Depression decade.

Based on the funk of the last decade, it could be easy to perceive that the 2010s will be no different. In fact, Pacific Investment Management Company, the manager of the world's largest bond fund, has gone so far as to predict a "New Normal" economy that features a dismal employment picture, crushing budget deficits, and lackluster economic growth. But, it is human nature to project the recent past into the foreseeable future. To the contrary, we believe the malaise of the past decade is one compelling reason to feel optimistic about this new decade. In fact, over the last century, the U.S. economy has never endured two consecutive "lost decades."

Markets and capitalist economies can be surprising beasts. For example, if someone predicted several years ago that Toyota Motor Corporation of Bunkyo, Japan would today be engulfed in a quality crisis, while Ford Motor Company of Detroit, Michigan would be engaged in a relative boom, you might have laughed them out of the room. But markets often derail even the most widespread expectations.

The simple idea that economies and markets run in cycles of boom and bust and outperformance and underperformance is a powerful one. It is sensible to heed the advice of the great investor Sir John Templeton who famously intoned, "The four most dangerous words in investing are 'This time it's different.'"

14

THE BUSINESS OF BEARS

O ver the last two years, the press has obsessed over stories about and interviews with the experts that "predicted" the financial crisis. In most cases, "predicted" is a relative term. After all, many of these forecasters were anticipating a financial crisis for five, ten or even twenty years. The analogy that "a stopped clock is right twice a day" is apropos.

Presently, it is interesting that many of these same commentators have not changed their views. They are now predicting a double-dip recession, a debt crisis, persistently high unemployment, a governmental breakdown, and unsustainable national debts and deficits.

Because markets and economies generally move in cycles of boom and bust, it would seem likely that our economy will recover, just as it has historically done over and over again. More importantly, the majority of the economic evidence is showing stabilization or growth, which has been the trend for more than six months.

So, why would a cadre of analysts remain so vocally negative and bearish? The answer: it pays. Let us take a look at two of the most prominently negative commentators.

The *Atlantic Monthly's* website in early February reported on the perks enjoyed by one of these economists. "Nouriel Roubini...was christened 'Dr. Doom' by no less an authority than *The New York Times*. The notorious nickname has helped Roubini become a global economic rock star, recently seen partying with models in St. Barts."

When not painting the town red with fashion models, Roubini works with economic models as a Professor of Economics at New York University's Stern School of Business, as a columnist for Forbes.com and as the cofounder and Chairman of economic consultancy RGE Monitor.

According to a March 30, 2009 article in the now defunct *Portfolio Magazine*, RGE Monitor successfully monetizes its prognostications: "Subscription prices range from $10,000, for 'reading rights,' to more than $100,000, which includes personal meetings and consultations with Roubini or his staff."

So, is the persistently negative Roubini more right than wrong? That is difficult to ascertain, but a review of his many predictions indicates to us that his record is highly spotty.

The *London Times* reported on October 4, 2008, during the height of the financial crisis, that he "told a London conference that hundreds of hedge funds are poised to fail as frantic investors rush to redeem their assets and force managers into a fire sale...He said: 'We've reached a situation of sheer panic. Don't be surprised if policymakers need to close down markets for a week or two in coming days.'"

In hindsight, neither of these predictions materialized. Very few hedge funds failed and markets across the world remained open throughout the crisis.

Another persistent naysayer is Nassim Taleb, the author of two highly successful and critically acclaimed books, *Fooled by Randomness* and *The Black Swan*.

The fundamental point of Taleb's Black Swan framework is that highly improbable and unforeseen events happen more frequently than experts acknowledge and that these events have a disproportionate impact on outcomes. Therefore, according to Taleb, predictions are nothing more than a fool's game.

In August of 2009, on the cable financial news network CNBC, Taleb predicted that "choking debt, continued high unemployment and a system that rewards bad behavior will hamstring an economic recovery," according to CNBC.com.

Recently, Taleb had an interview published in *ai5000 Magazine*, where he revealed a fabulous calculation about investor Warren Buffet: "George Soros has 2 million times more statistical evidence that his results are not chance than Buffett does. Soros is vastly more robust. I am not saying that Buffet does not have skill—I'm just saying we don't have enough evidence to say Buffett isn't doing it by chance."

Like any other successful person, Mr. Buffet has had luck on his side, but we are doubtful that Mr. Taleb can quantify such good fortune. This made-for-media comment just happens to (randomly) correspond to the launch of the paperback edition of *The Black Swan* and also helps to promote Taleb's next book, for which he has received a multi-million dollar advance.

In *The Great Crash 1929*, John Kenneth Galbraith astutely observes, "It requires neither courage nor prescience to predict disaster...Historians rejoice in crucifying the false prophet of the millennium. They never dwell on the mistake of the man who wrongly predicted Armageddon."

Our current view of the market and the economy happens to coincide with that of hedge fund manager Barton Biggs, who described his framework in a recent Bloomberg interview: "I am often wrong, always in doubt." But Mr. Biggs presently feels that "People are nervous and apprehensive...and if you are an optimist, as I am—that things are going to work out—that's what provides an opportunity." And as a professional "go anywhere" hedge fund manager, Mr. Biggs has a significant financial incentive to be correct, not just blindly optimistic.

Oscar Wilde believed that, "The basis of optimism is sheer terror." While Wilde viewed the glass as half empty, Winston Churchill expressed a similar sentiment when he said, "I am an optimist—it does not seem to be much use being anything else."

15

A SNOWBALL HEADED FOR HELL?

> "I WISH A BUCK WAS STILL SILVER. IT WAS, BACK WHEN THE COUNTRY WAS STRONG...WHEN A MAN COULD STILL WORK, AND STILL WOULD. IS THE BEST OF THE FREE LIFE BEHIND US NOW? ARE THE GOOD TIMES REALLY OVER FOR GOOD? ARE WE ROLLING DOWNHILL LIKE A SNOWBALL HEADED FOR HELL?"
>
> MERLE HAGGARD
> (1981, *DOW JONES INDUSTRIAL AVERAGE: 870*)

We have just endured six straight weeks of stock market losses, the longest such streak since the fall of 2002. Since reaching a recent high on April 29, 2011, the S&P 500 has fallen 6.8%.

In the spring of last year, the market underwent a similarly frightening slide amidst below-consensus economic data and heightened European debt concerns. Over roughly 10 weeks, the market dropped 17% and stocks were not for the faint of heart. In the words of Yogi Berra, "It's like déjà vu all over again."

70

A Washington Post-ABC News poll released on June 7, 2011 shows that 9 in 10 Americans continue to rate the economy in negative terms, while 6 in 10 say the economy has not started to recover. According to a CBS News survey released June 8, 2011, 31% of Americans believe the economy is actually getting worse and 79% say the economy is downright bad. The American Association of Individual Investors weekly survey of investor sentiment finds only 24.4% of participants bullish.

The litany of economic problems is no less than intimidating. The Conference Board's Index of Leading Economic Indicators is slowing; the Standard and Poor's Case-Shiller Home Price Index has reached a new low; high gasoline prices are constraining the consumer; the tragedy of the Japanese earthquake and tsunami increased economic stress; the European debt crisis is getting worse with Greece looking increasingly imperiled; the Middle East is in revolt; U.S. employment is moribund; Congress is playing Russian Roulette with the debt ceiling; and the Federal Reserve plans to end its second round of quantitative easing this month.

In Warren Buffett's 2004 letter to shareholders, he wrote that "Investors should remember that excitement...[is] their [enemy]. And if they insist on trying to time their participation in equities, they should try to be fearful when others are greedy and greedy when others are fearful."

If the stock market is a barometer of general sentiment in the country over long periods of time, then it is instructive to look at historic rolling 10-year performance of the Standard and Poor's 500 Stock Index.

The Great Depression made negative rolling ten-year performance a reality. By the late 1930s, stock investors had experienced 10-year average annual losses of 5% per year. Due to the force of compounding, this equates to a cumulative loss of nearly 40% over this period. But as it turns out, buying equities in the late 1930s would have been a highly profitable endeavor both ten and twenty years later.

Buying stocks would have required nerves of steel as 1939 was a horrible time. World War II was breaking out in Europe with the beginnings of unchecked Nazi aggression, including the invasion of Poland and the bombing of Great Britain. Meanwhile, the Soviet Union was invading Finland. Back in the United States, the Northeast was facing its worst ever drought and the unemployment rate was 17.2% (it stands at 9.1% today).

Conversely, everyone and their brother wanted to buy stocks in 1929. The famous financier Bernard Baruch later described the scene before the Great Crash: "Taxi drivers told you what to buy. The shoeshine boy could give you a summary of the day's financial news...An old beggar who regularly patrolled the street in front of my office now gave me tips...My cook had a brokerage account and followed the ticker closely. Her paper profits were quickly blown away in the gale of 1929."

Similarly, a stock market craze permeated in 1999. James K. Glassman and Kevin A. Hassett published the best-selling book *Dow 36,000: The New Strategy for Profiting from the Coming Rise in the Stock Market*. They wrote, "the single most important fact about stocks at the dawn of the twenty-first century: They are cheap....If you are worried about missing the market's big move upward, you will discover that it is not too late. Stocks are now in the midst of a one-time-only rise to much higher ground—to the neighborhood of 36,000 on the Dow Jones Industrial Average." Twelve years later, the Dow now stands at 11,952.

In March of 2000, Cisco Systems (CSCO), the manufacturer of the Internet's guts, its routers and switches, sold for over $77 per share. Today it sells for about $15 per share. Perversely, it was more tempting for the average investor to buy CSCO for $77 than it is for $15—such is the fabric of human emotion.

In 2006, David Bach, the personal finance personality and New York Times best-selling author, published *The Automatic Millionaire Homeowner: A Powerful Plan to Finish Rich in Real Estate*. In the introduction, he wrote, "What if I told you the smartest investment you would ever make during your lifetime would be a home?" Interestingly, this proved to be about the worst time in American history to purchase a home.

So, as we write this, what is the best-selling business and investment book on Amazon.com? *Reckless Endangerment: How Outsized Ambition, Greed and Corruption Led to Economic Armageddon* by New York Times reporter Gretchen Morgenson. Couple this with the most hyped invest-ment paradigm, the "new normal," an environment of slow economic growth and meager investment returns promoted by Pacific Investment Management Company, and you get the sense that not only is the general public pessimistic, but so are most experts.

Historically, when rampant pessimism pervades, it is a good time to make long-term investments in equities. The next few weeks and months could be rough, and we will surely face cyclical bear markets along the way. But as the earlier-referenced chart would indicate, today's defeatism should result in long-term opportunity.

PRINCIPLES OF
CONTRARIAN INVESTING

16

THE DISCIPLINED CONTRARIAN

> "MANY SHALL BE RESTORED THAT NOW ARE FALLEN AND MANY SHALL FALL THAT ARE NOW IN HONOR."
>
> FROM HORACE'S ARS POETICA

In our experience, a strict investment discipline is the number one contributor to investment success. Changing strategy with the prevailing winds is the number one contributor to investment failure. Many individual investors, and even many institutions, are susceptible to chasing a moving target. We have shared the Dalbar, Inc.[1] and the American Association of Individual Investors (AAII) statistics with you before, but they are so telling that we cannot help but present them again.

In a study by Dalbar, Inc. from 1985 to 2004, the average mutual fund investor achieved a 3.7% annualized return while the S&P 500 achieved a return of 11.9%. The Dalbar Inc. study found that the reason for the average mutual fund investor's low return was that these investors chose to purchase the hottest of mutual funds at the end of bull markets, then became frightened and withdrew money from the market toward the end of bear markets.

In March of this year, when AAII released its investor confidence survey, it was the most negative in its twenty-two year history, with 70% of the respondents bearish about the market's prospects. The last time that 70% of the respondents agreed on something, it was in January of 2000, near the top of the technology stock bubble. At that time, 70% of respondents were bullish on the market's prospects.

Intuitively, it is clear that the AAII numbers reinforce the Dalbar study. Individual investors tend to make poorly timed decisions, but what about institutional investors?

In Warren Buffett's 1978 Berkshire Hathaway Chairman's Letter he pointed out "an irresistible footnote" about how even institutional investors act. He writes "in 1971, pension fund managers invested a record 122% of net [inflows] in equities—at full prices they couldn't buy enough of them. In 1974, after the bottom had fallen out, they committed a then record low of 21% [of net inflows] to stocks." Today, things are no different.

Bloomberg News reports that "Equity assets in the U.K. fell to 41 percent of holdings at the end of 2008, according to data compiled by New York-based Citigroup. The last time British pension funds held so little in equities was in 1974..." This is not only a British phenomenon. "The $181 billion California Public Employees' Retirement System... lowered its equities target to 49 percent from 56 percent..." and "Four of the world's seven largest pension funds...have cut their equity target allocations, data compiled by Bloomberg show."

Doing the opposite of the herd at market extremes is the definition of contrarian investing. Being a contrarian is not about disagreeing with everything in the marketplace, nor is it about being perpetually gloomy. Rather, it is about trying to recognize when most of the available money is either in or out of the market. In other words, when everyone is wildly optimistic, then you can surmise that very little money is left to flow into the market to further boost prices. The opposite is also true, when negative sentiment is running rampant, there is major money on the sidelines ready to take the field and boost equity prices. And this phenomenon is not just limited to the broader market as a whole. Keen investors can also pinpoint times when individual securities are in or out of favor with the crowd.

In light of this information, you might want to think about your investment philosophy. In other words, what is your discipline? Here is ours.

As investors, it is easy to get caught up in fads, headlines, paralyzing fear and unreasonable optimism. However, those investors who buy solid businesses at reasonable prices can profit handsomely over the long-term. Benjamin Graham, the father of "value investing" and a mentor to Warren Buffett, once posed the following question: "Ask yourself: If there was no market for these shares, would I be willing to have an investment in this company on these terms?" If we genuinely believe in the long-term business prospects of a company that we own at a fair price, the day-to-day fluctuations of the company's stock price should factor little in our investment decisions. The essence of investing is to know what you own and why you own it.

We consider the contrarian point of view in each investment decision that we make. When the stock market is gripped by fear and pessimism, we remain confident that stock prices will eventually reflect the long-term viability of the underlying companies. When the stock market experiences unjustified and excessive enthusiasm, we become cautious of overvalued stock prices.

We believe the most significant risk-reward decision in investing is the allocation to stocks versus bonds and that this simple determination overwhelmingly dictates portfolio volatility. We do not invest our clients in stocks unless we conclude that an allocation to stocks is appropriate, given each client's risk tolerance and time horizon. Our discussions of risk tolerance include both (1) financial ability to absorb short-term investment losses and (2) psychological ability to handle market fluctuations. For client assets that are not suitable for the stock market, we invest in individual fixed income securities for safety of principal and a steady source of income.

Finally, we pride ourselves on our commitment to active and substantive communication during both bull and bear markets.

As you consider the merits of our philosophy, we will leave you with another parting thought on yet another investment concept—reversion to the mean. Mean reversion, according to InvestmentWords.com, is "The theory that a given value will continue to return to an average value over time, despite fluctuations above and below the average value. This theory can be applied to any measurable value, including interest rates and the return on a certain investment."

A fair number of investment experts, including us, are forecasting an environment of lower returns than what we are historically accustomed to, but it is certainly worth remembering another Bloomberg report: "Equities appreciated an average of 12.91 percent a year from 1900 to 1999, while bonds returned 4.69 percent annually, according to data from the London Business School and Credit Suisse. Since the start of the new century, bonds gained 6.36 percent, compared with a loss of 2.27 percent for shares."

Over the longer-term, if we see even a modest reversion to the mean, pension funds and individual investors will once again have been incorrectly cautious at a market extreme.

1: Dalbar Inc. is a financial services and market research company that performs various ratings and evaluations of practices and communications that are committed to raising the standards of excellence in the financial services and healthcare industries.

17

SEVEN CONSENSUS OPINIONS

> "WE ARE STANDING BY A WISHING WELL / MAKE A WISH INTO THE WELL / THAT'S ALL YOU HAVE TO DO / AND IF YOU HEAR IT ECHOING / YOUR WISH WILL SOON COME TRUE."
>
> SNOW WHITE,
> *FROM SNOW WHITE AND THE SEVEN DWARFS (1937)*

Today we are examining what we perceive to be the most widely held consensus opinions among business journalists, economists, analysts, and investment managers. Below are seven thoughts that nearly everyone seems to agree on regarding the present market and economy:

1) "The American consumer will never be the same."

Clearly, the average American's personal balance sheet has taken a significant hit over the last couple of years with lower home values and diminished investment accounts. Americans have also accumulated bloated home equity and credit card debt, and now a rising unemployment rate is adding insult to injury. But, it is also true that many Americans have now deferred substantial spending for nearly a year. Consumers have cut clothing purchases and vacations, neglected to update household necessities, haven't replaced aging cars or upgraded housing. It is difficult to quantify this pent-up demand, but it could uncoil like a spring.

We would also venture to say that spending has become ingrained in our national culture, for better or worse. While a higher national savings rate would be a healthy long-term phenomenon, you can't change a zebra's stripes and we are not convinced that Americans will sustain high savings.

2) "A 'V' shaped recovery will not happen."
As the United States has emerged from previous recessions, GDP growth has gone from a negative reading to an above-average annual reading because many people and businesses defer purchases during a recession and manufactures and retailers permit inventories to deplete. When we begin feeling more comfortable, we tend to start buying again. But after this recession, most observers predict that we will emerge with below-trend GDP growth, i.e. less than 3% annual growth in the year after the recession; whereas a "V" shaped recovery would lead to annual GDP growth of 5%-plus during the ensuing year, which is more in-line with other post-recession periods. There will undoubtedly be a struggle between the competing forces of postponed purchases and the need to save more.

3) "The federal deficit is out of control and will only get worse and worse and worse."
The prospects are certainly dim, but with an improved economy

and structural changes on the revenue and expenditure side, hope is not lost. Many people do not fully understand the federal budget. The vast majority of federal expenditures can be attributed to Medicare, Medicaid, Social Security and national defense. Moderate, but intelligent, structural changes in these four areas can go a very long way toward changing our long-term fiscal outlook. Couple this with improving GDP growth, which leads to an expanding tax base, and the federal budget takes on a different complexion. Don't forget, ten years ago, the Treasury was running budget surpluses and even "retired" the 30-year bond as a funding mechanism. Unfortunately, this turned out to be a Brett Favre-like retirement.

4) **"The stock market has rallied too far, too fast, and September is historically the worst month for the market. Watch out below!"**
We are somewhat skeptical because nearly everyone thought and still thinks that the market will lose substantial ground in the near-term (i.e. a 20% correction). Investors most likely withdrew funds from the market in anticipation of this predicted swoon. If decent economic news prevails and asset managers think they are missing something, they will undoubtedly flood more money into the market.

We agree that the market rally is overdone for certain specu-lative stocks. But, in our view, quality is still underpriced in this market. There are many legendary franchises "on sale" with price-to-earnings ratios below fifteen times and dividend yields is excess of 3%.

5) **"Problematic inflation is nearly inevitable as a result of the immense fiscal and monetary stimulus."**
This viewpoint is wildly inconsistent with the other opinions on this consensus list, but many people hold them in concert

nonetheless. If a weak economy were to prevail for the foreseeable future, the probabilities favor a deflationary environment,
not an inflationary one. Post-bubble periods are indicative of
deflation, i.e. the United States in the 1930s and Japan in the
1990s.

The Federal Reserve and other central banks around the world
have the tools at their disposal to fight rising core inflation, as
long as the political will exists. However, if we do experience a
more robust recovery, we believe that commodity-driven inflation is a distinct possibility. We foresee inadequate capacity in
world commodity supplies to support even modest worldwide
economic growth.

6) "Unemployment will exceed 10%."

This is certainly looking highly probable. But in a note to clients
at the near-term market bottom on March 9, 2009, we wrote:
"While it is impossible to predict the precise future of labor
markets, we can all but guarantee that the unemployment rate
is going to get worse, probably considerably so, before it gets
better. But what does this imply for the markets? As Mark
Twain said, "History doesn't repeat itself, but it does rhyme."
Our last truly dire economic situation was in the early 1980s
when unemployment was not only high, but inflation was also
rampant. In November of 1981, the unemployment rate crossed
the 8.0% mark to land at 8.3% (similar to today [March 9, 2009]).
At that time the Dow was trading around 850. Over the next
14 months, unemployment continued to rise, finally peaking
at 10.8% in November and December of 1982. While the Dow
temporarily dropped to around the 800 level, the stock market
took off while unemployment continued to rise. By the end
1982, an awful year for employment in the U.S., the market
was over 1,000 and it never looked back."

If history does indeed rhyme this time around, we would not expect a market decline strictly as a result of a rising unemployment rate. However, if unemployment does continue to rise over the next 6-12 months, it will inevitably be a roadblock to a sustainable economic recovery.

7) "Commercial real estate is the next shoe to drop."

We find it amusing that only a small handful of market pundits were able to predict the first shoe that dropped (residential real estate), but now, all of the pundits believe they can predict the next shoe to drop.

Contrarian investing does not mean disagreeing with every opinion in the marketplace. Without a doubt, we expect some of the above consensus predictions will come to fruition. But, we are highly skeptical that all of these will ultimately materialize. Overall, our reading of sentiment is that many people continue to be very negative on the economy and the markets. To us, this means there is still opportunity to make smart, long-term investments that precede future money flows into the stock market.

18

IS SAFETY THE ANSWER?

Despite the robust stock market rally from the March 9th lows, most investors have been enamored with what they perceive to be "safe" investment alternatives in today's economy and market environment. Bonds and gold, therefore, have become the investments du jour while stocks have largely been ignored.

Morningstar reports that, year-to-date through September, investors have made net contributions of over $197 billion into taxable bond funds and almost $57 billion into municipal bond funds. U.S. stock funds, on the other hand, have attracted net inflows of less than $4 billion and international stock mutual funds have seen net contributions of less than $11 billion. In other words, for every dollar investors put in stock funds, they placed nearly seventeen dollars into mutual funds that invest in bonds. But, we advise caution to bond fund investors for several reasons.

Keep in mind the inverse relationship between interest rates and bond prices. As interest rates rise, bond prices typically fall, and vice versa. For example, if you purchase a Treasury bill today with a 3% yield and, subsequently, similar Treasury bills are paying 4%, the market price of your original bond will drop. The price declines in order to compensate a potential purchaser of the original bond for the lower income stream. The same phenomenon occurs with mutual funds that invest in bonds. If interest rates rise, the bonds held by the mutual fund would likely lose value, causing the fund net asset value to suffer.

When using a mutual fund to gain exposure to bonds, the decisions of other fund shareholders can also have a detrimental impact on returns. For example, when interest rates creep upward and the bonds held by a mutual fund begin to lose value, bond fund shareholders will probably begin withdrawing their money. (As we have seen time and time again, individual investors generally chase performance.) This leaves the fund managers without fresh cash to purchase new bonds at higher rates, further compounding an already difficult situation.

It can also be dangerous to base investment decisions on a past trend. The preceding 27 years have seen a secular bull market for bonds thanks to a declining interest rate environment. In 1982, the U.S. fed funds rate reached 20% to battle runaway inflation. Since then, interest rates have declined rather steadily and with few interruptions to a current fed funds target rate of zero. Clearly, policy makers cannot force interest rates any lower. And if the global economy continues to show signs of improvement, then central banks will likely raise rates to curb the inflation threat that the market perceives in loose fiscal and monetary policy.

Beyond the bond market, gold has been another hot asset class in 2009. According to Fortune, the SPDR Gold Trust (GLD), the world's largest gold exchange traded fund, has drawn over $12 billion in net assets this year. Amazingly, this fund alone has attracted roughly three times the total net assets that all U.S. stock mutual funds collected through the first nine months of the year. Even 1990s rap music sensation MC Hammer has gotten into the mix, touting "Cash 4 Gold" in one of numerous television commercials that gold recycling companies are running to cash in on the fever.

During the past decade, the spot price of the "yellow metal" has climbed from under $300 per ounce to over $1,000 today. But, it is difficult to gauge the intrinsic value of an ounce of gold because it does not produce a profit, pay a dividend, or create value in any real way. As Warren Buffet once quipped, "[Gold] gets dug out of the ground... Then we melt it down, dig another hole, bury it again and pay people to stand around guarding it. It has no utility. Anyone watching from Mars would be scratching their head."

These money flow statistics are instructive, not because they offer any real clues to the upcoming short-term trajectory of stocks, bonds, or gold, but because they reveal that investors appear to be succumbing to fear, perhaps at the expense of investment discipline.

One of the simplest and most effective investment strategies is to periodically rebalance a portfolio. While it can sometimes require intestinal fortitude, systematic rebalancing serves to increase exposure to "riskier" securities following big losses and helps investors buy low and sell high; the ultimate goal of investing. If investors were rebalancing, one would expect to have seen more money flowing into stock funds this year. Instead, dollars are continuing to favor safe haven investments while many investors have already missed a healthy and rapid rally in stocks.

Any experienced investor has undoubtedly felt the temptation to stray from a disciplined investment policy. But, in the words of Hindu Prince Siddhartha Gautama, better known as Buddha, "Endurance is one of the most difficult disciplines, but it is to the one who endures that the final victory comes."

19

THE NOT-SO-GOLDEN DOLLAR

Recently there has been much media attention around the deteriorating status of the U.S. dollar and the surging price of gold. As a result of these headlines, many clients have asked us about the investment implications of the dollar and of gold.

Since its March highs, the U.S. dollar has tumbled more than 40% against the Australian dollar. It has also dropped by about 18% versus the euro and the Canadian dollar.

However, the fall in the U.S. dollar has had a silver lining for the U.S. economy as the products that we export are now more competitive globally. Many large cap U.S. companies with international operations have been and will continue to be well-positioned to profit from the dollar's troubles. Many of the businesses in the S&P 500 generate over half of their revenue overseas, so when these companies convert their international revenues from a foreign currency to U.S. dollars, they are able to purchase more dollars and thereby enhance their profitability.

The dollar has "suffered" relative to other currencies for several reasons. The Federal Reserve is maintaining its policy of a near 0% federal funds rate. Central banks overseas, in many cases, have higher interest rates, so investors have a motivation to sell dollars in favor of higher-yielding currencies. The Federal Reserve also has created large amounts of "new money" by purchasing Treasury securities, agency bonds, commercial paper and mortgage-backed securities.

Additionally, President George Bush and President Barack Obama and their Congresses enacted policies that have created great chasms between revenues and expenditures that led to budget deficits and record increases in the national debt. Overall, our monetary (the Federal Reserve) and our fiscal (the executive and Congress) institutions have fostered policies that lead to a weaker currency.

We believe that the dollar has made an orderly and appropriate decline based on the above-mentioned monetary and fiscal policies. Contrary to many commentators, we do not believe the dollar is in a fundamental crisis. The proof is in the pudding. During the height of the worldwide financial crisis in late 2008 and early this year, the dollar actually gained ground when investors flocked to the world's safest currency. Even as recently as November 27th, Black Friday, when news began to spread about Dubai's debt crisis, fearful investors across the globe fled back to the dollar.

As the U.S. and world economies continue to recover and employment in the U.S. starts to rebound, the Federal Reserve will undoubtedly begin raising interest rates, which will inevitably boost the dollar. The U.S. is still the largest economy in the world and we continue to lead the world in innovation. Fundamentally, the U.S. system of government (no matter how ugly the political process can sometimes be) is superior to that of any other major economic power. The checks and balances built into our representative democracy are the world's greatest and a fiat currency is only as good as the government that issues it.

It is our view that the present readjustment in the dollar's value is a healthy one. But make no mistake, as the economic crisis wanes, our leaders will need to take steps to raise our nation's revenues and cut its expenses, thereby moving toward a balanced budget with lower deficits. An improving economy should naturally help reduce deficits as gross domestic product rises and the federal tax base expands, resulting in higher tax revenues. But, a balanced budget will be unlikely without the political will to either raise taxes or cut spending.

The government's proliferative spending, the Federal Reserve's loose monetary policy, and the weakening dollar are all historically inflationary in nature. Hence, many investors have moved money to gold. During the past decade, the spot price of the "yellow metal" has climbed from under $300 per ounce to over $1,200, seemingly setting new nominal record highs daily. However, inflation-adjusted, Fidelity Management & Research Company reports that gold reached its peak of $2,321 per ounce back in 1980. From this historical perspective, gold is still relatively cheap.

But, gold euphoria is widespread. According to *Fortune Magazine*, the SPDR Gold Trust (GLD), the world's largest gold exchanged traded fund, has drawn over $12 billion in net assets this year. Amazingly, this fund alone has attracted roughly three times the total net assets that all U.S. stock mutual funds collected through the first nine months of this year.

It is true that gold does not have many industrial uses, but it is perception that matters. Over centuries, people have widely recognized gold as a safe haven store of financial wealth. According to Fidelity Management and Research Company, this imperishable asset is still "the largest component of foreign exchange reserves in central banks around the world."

Gold's 300% rise over the past decade contrasts quite starkly with the performance of U.S. equities. According to a December 1st, 2009 *Business Week* article, "The total return for the S&P 500 since New Year's 2000 has been negative 10.8%." This enormous performance differential may be one reason why there are so many gold bulls in the world. After all, it is only human nature to follow the winners. As contrarian investors, we find the endless headlines about gold and the swarms of "gold bugs" unnerving.

We continue, though, to like the odds for U.S. equities, an asset class that continues to climb a "wall of worry," with countless analysts predicting a major correction and retail investors exhibiting deep skepticism. The 2000's have been one of the worst decades for U.S. stocks over the last century, rivaling the 1970's and the 1930's. Fidelity Management & Research Company looked back at these two dismal decades for equities and found the future promising. The subsequent 10-year average annual return for stocks from the 1939 low was a robust 9.3%. From the 1974 low, stocks' subsequent 10-year annualized return was 15.2%.

Clearly, it has been a challenging decade which began with the technology stock bubble and ended with a financial crisis that rivaled the Great Depression. Our country suffered through September 11, 2001 and we continue two costly wars in Iraq and Afghanistan. But as Abba Eban, an Israeli politician and diplomat observed, "Men and nations behave wisely once they have exhausted all the other alternatives."

20

COMMODITY CRAZE

Commodity prices are on a tear.

Since touching a 52-week low on May 25, 2010, the Standard and Poor's Goldman Sachs Commodity Index has risen more than 40% (first chart). This broad index represents a diversified group of commodities including energy, industrial metals, precious metals, agricultural goods and livestock (second chart).

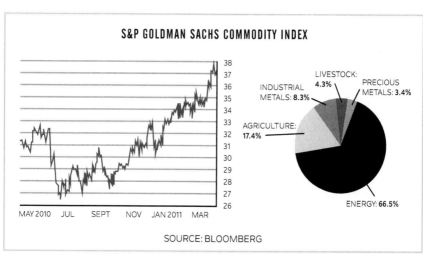

S&P GOLDMAN SACHS COMMODITY INDEX

SOURCE: BLOOMBERG

Oil prices have skyrocketed on unrest in the Middle East and North Africa to trade at over $106 per barrel on Monday and Tuesday before dropping back to around $100 today following the devastating earthquake and tsunami in Japan.

However, the only real oil supply disruption so far has been a reduction of 1.1 million barrels per day from Libya, CNBC reported on Thursday. This interruption amounts to just over 1% of daily supply. Of course, unrest could continue to spread throughout the region.

Many industrial metal prices spiked in 2010 on the back of a global economic recovery. For example, the Standard & Poor's GSCI North American Copper Index surged by over 29% last year.

On the precious metal front, news of gold's rise in value over the past few years has been unavoidable. Many analysts attribute gold's spike to fears of runaway inflation or economic collapse or, while highly uncommon, a combination of both. Perhaps proof of this thesis: viewers of Glenn Beck on Fox News are bombarded with commercials for gold companies enticing them to profit from the yellow metal's rise.

And agricultural prices have flourished too, including grain, corn, wheat, soybeans and sugar, partially driven by news of droughts in Russia and China, flooding in Australia and a wet crop in Canada.

But, interestingly, there have been no reports of an actual shortage of any mainstream commodity.

Many would argue that because markets are forward-looking, they are simply anticipating the shortages that will result from supply shocks and robust global demand. This may well be the case, only time will tell.

More likely, though, what we are really witnessing is the international trading community chasing "fast" and "easy" money.

With interest rates in the United States, Japan and the European Union hovering near zero and with all three major economies having engaged in some form of "quantitative easing" (buying bonds on the open market to inject cash into the financial system), the markets are awash in liquidity.

This pile of cash should ideally serve to bolster bank lending and help companies of all sizes raise equity and debt to fund acquisitions and research and development. The good news is that to some extent this is happening, but there is still a vast amount of money on the sidelines that has not been committed to long-term ventures.

A great deal of this short-term money rests in the hands of traders who are chasing commodity prices in an effort to make a quick buck. The argument that commodity prices are rising based on the legitimate inflation worries of long-term investors is oversubscribed. We believe the recent commodities boom is primarily a short-term trading phenomenon.

As evidence, the ten-year U.S. Treasury Bond closed today yielding 3.40%. If underlying inflation were a genuine fear, investors would be unwilling to tie-up their money for ten years in exchange for such a wretched interest rate. In other words, there is an extreme disconnect between Treasury yields and commodity prices.

Another indicator of inflation expectations can be found in Treasury Inflation Protected Securities, or TIPS. These U.S. government debt instruments receive automatic principal adjustments commensurate with the rise in the consumer price index, thus protecting investors from the erosive effects of future inflation.

The spread between the yields on a traditional Treasury and corresponding TIPS can then be used as a proxy for inflation expectations. As the table below indicates, the TIPS market is indicating subdued inflation over the next five, ten and even thirty years, particularly when compared to a CPI-based inflation rate of 3.23% since 1914.

	U.S. TREASURY	TIPS	INFLATION EXPECTATION
5 Year	2.05%	-0.57%	2.62%
10 Year	3.40%	0.92%	2.48%
30 Year	4.55%	1.87%	2.68%
		Long-Term CPI =	3.23%

Absent further supply shocks (no small assumption), here is our best guess for commodity prices over the next year.

Because it is hard to stop a runaway train, commodity prices are likely to continue their surge in the near-term, but a pullback becomes more likely as the weeks and months pass.

The economic pressure from higher commodity prices will slow global growth projections sufficiently to weaken speculative demand and subdue the commodity craze. In other words, high commodity prices in and of themselves will cause the rally to reverse course.

An additional downside risk to commodity prices could come from larger than expected supply. For oil, this could mean greater stability in the Middle East and North Africa. For agriculture, bumper crops could materialize in coming harvests.

On the policy side, a less accommodative Federal Reserve that discontinues quantitative easing or begins gradually raising interest rates would also provide a substantial headwind to commodity prices.

We believe paltry bond yields are too cool and overpriced commodities are too hot, whereas certain equities seem just right, despite the potential for temporary setbacks along the way. If the market enters a legitimate correction here, which is more likely than not, we will most certainly look for buying opportunities.

21

THE HIJACKING
OF BEN BERNANKE

The commodity market is holding Ben Bernanke hostage. Exploding gasoline and food prices might force the Federal Reserve Chairman to raise interest rates despite his fears that the economy is too weak to stomach it.

The Standard and Poor's Goldman Sachs Commodity Index, an energy-heavy measure of commodity prices, is up about 43% from a May 25, 2010 lull and has risen approximately 17% from one year ago. The price of gold, a component of the index, has advanced more than 29% year-over-year.

Many analysts and economists believe that this rise in commodity prices—particularly in the areas of energy and agriculture—will lead to widespread inflation among all goods and services. After all, American commerce depends heavily on oil and gasoline to move people and products from destination to destination. It is only common sense that more expensive oil will ultimately drive up prices as businesses pass on their higher costs to consumers.

However, we disagree with some analysts who anticipate continued commodity inflation as far as the eye can see. We fear that a sustained rise in food and gas prices will stall the nascent recovery, leading to another economic slowdown that would itself drive down commodity prices. Just think back to June of 2008, when $147-per-barrel oil helped spark the ensuing financial crisis and Great Recession.

Now more about Ben Bernanke...Before entering government service, Mr. Bernanke was a professor of economics at Princeton University. As an academic economist, Mr. Bernanke studied the Great Depression. This area of emphasis made the Chairman particularly sensitive to deflation, or a decrease in price levels.

In the 1920s, the United States experienced a rapidly expanding economy and as the nation boomed, so did our ability to create goods and services. Unfortunately, our debt levels also began to swell. When economic activity came to a crashing halt late in 1929, the devastation left the country with enormous under-utilized productive capacity and loads of debt.

Today, the U.S. faces a debt problem, but we face a more immediate dilemma stemming from improving capacity utilization.

Capacity utilization averaged 80.5 percent from 1972 to 2010 and is presently hovering at 77.4 percent. Although this number is somewhat low, it has recovered markedly from the 2009 bottom of 68.2 percent. When a nation has greater capacity to create goods than it has demand for those goods, deflation is a possibility.

And the current unemployment predicament is preventing demand for goods and services from keeping pace with productive capacity. With the March 2011 unemployment rate registering at 8.8%, compared to an average rate of 4.6% in 2006 and 2007, one can hardly argue that jobs are plentiful.

Bernanke is highly sensitive to this overcapacity because deflation can be an unrelenting problem that is harder to solve than inflation.

World War II broke the back of the deflationary spiral of the Great Depression in the United States. But Japan has been unsuccessfully battling deflation for more than 20 years, whereas even the Weimar Republic was able to eventually tame its runaway inflation.

As such, Bernanke's overwhelming goal with the federal funds rate (which is nearly zero) and with quantitative easing (parts one and two) is to provide easy money as the cure for deflation.

But, this extra supply of money has led speculators to commodities as a way to make a quick buck.

So here is Bernanke's conundrum. If commodity prices continue to rise, he will need to weigh the harmful repercussions of higher interest rates within a fragile economy against the damaging impact of higher oil prices on the American consumer.

When you fill up your gas tank, Bernanke's decision doesn't seem too complex. If higher interest rates can contain rising commodity prices, then what is Bernanke waiting for?

Well, many investors believe the commodity craze is transitory—that when some of the supply concerns ease (Middle East unrest, for example) prices will fall. The bond market is the best illustration of this widely held conviction.

According to John Lonski at Moody's Capital Markets Group, the 10-year Treasury yield has averaged 7% since 1980, but today stands at a mere 3.42%. And when we analyze the implied inflation rate by subtracting the current yield on 10 and 30 year Treasury securities from their equivalent Treasury Inflation Protected Securities, we find that the bond market anticipates inflation at just 2.62% over the next ten years and only 2.77% over the next thirty years.

The commodity market is indicating runaway inflation while the bond market sees subdued inflation over the long-term. No doubt, Bernanke has found himself in quite a quandary.

We can offer Bernanke the advice of one of our favorite Yogi Berra quotes: "When you come to a fork in the road, take it."

22

NO PAIN, NO GAIN

> "THE KEY TO MAKING MONEY IN THE STOCK MARKET IS NOT TO GET SCARED OUT OF IT."
>
> PETER LYNCH, FIDELITY MAGELLAN MANAGER (1977-1990)

Since the Standard and Poor's 500 reached its near-term bull market high on April 29, 2011, we have experienced highly volatile trading on a day-to-day basis. Through it all, the result is a loss of 14.4% for the index. Interestingly, the market is down 7.4% year-to-date, but the dramatic volatility has made it feel much worse.

It is nonsensical, distracting and scary to see the market plummet 5% one day and rebound 4% the next. But, after the worst recession since the Great Depression and two spectacular bear markets within recent memory, one cannot expect the market to peacefully progress higher.

Bespoke Investment Group[1] tracks volatility in the form of "all or nothing days." These are trading sessions where 400 out of the

500 stocks in the S&P 500 go up or go down. In other words, these represent days when stocks largely move in unison and with no direct connection to the underlying fundamentals of each individual company.

As you can see from the chart below, these herd events have been quite common over the last five years. During the strong bull market of the 1990s, such days were rare. They were even infrequent during the tech crash of 2000 to 2002 because that bear market was more specific to one sector and more isolated to the largest of the S&P 500 stocks.

According to a study that The New York Times performed, since the beginning of 2000, "price fluctuations of 4 percent or more during intraday sessions have occurred nearly six times more than they did" from 1960 to 2000.

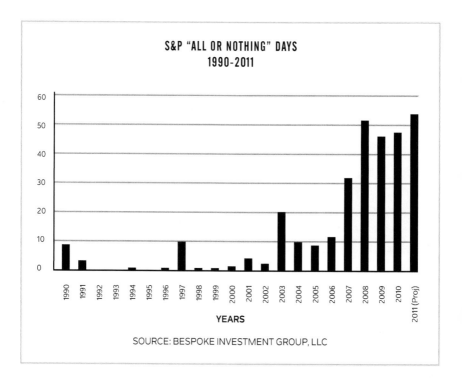

S&P "ALL OR NOTHING" DAYS 1990-2011

YEARS

SOURCE: BESPOKE INVESTMENT GROUP, LLC

100

Yet another measure of the inordinate volatility in recent years comes from Andrew Lo, a finance professor at the Massachusetts Institute of Technology. He found that 10 of the 20 biggest daily upswings and 11 of the 20 largest daily declines from 1980 through August 2011 have occurred in just the last three years.

And the volatility is not just in the United States. Over the last three months, the Morgan Stanley Capital International (MSCI)

> "HISTORICALLY, THE VOLATILITY ASSOCIATED WITH STOCKS HAS COME WITH AN UPSIDE IN THE FORM OF HIGHER RETURNS. IN OTHER WORDS, 'UNCERTAINTY' IS YOUR FRIEND."

Europe, Asia and Far East Index of developed markets and the MSCI Emerging Markets Index have correlated 96% and 97%, respectively, with the S&P 500, reports CNBC.com.

Many commentators blame high-frequency trading—where computers buy and sell the same stock in seconds or less—for the extreme volatility. This argument has merit as experts estimate that about 60% of today's volume represents high-speed trading. Suffice it to say, such trading is not helpful or productive.

However, the "uncertainty" that exists in today's economy is the prime culprit for the crazy gyration of stock prices. After all, according to a recent Bloomberg National Poll of Americans, only 9% are confident that the U.S. will not slide back into a recession, while 72% of participants say that America is on the wrong course. And for the first time since early September 2010, sentiment gauges from both the American Association of Individual Investors and Investors Intelligence are registering more bears than bulls.

Further, the Conference Board reports that consumer confidence in August fell to a reading of 44.5, the lowest since 40.8 in April 2009. But, don't let "uncertainty" fool you. According to Haverford Trust, consumer

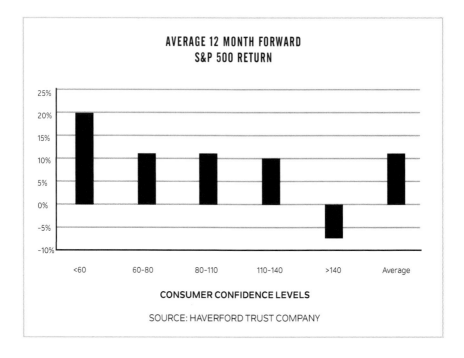

AVERAGE 12 MONTH FORWARD
S&P 500 RETURN

CONSUMER CONFIDENCE LEVELS

SOURCE: HAVERFORD TRUST COMPANY

confidence is a contrarian indicator. As the below chart exhibits, extremely low readings bode well for future stock returns, while very high readings are a harbinger of negative performance.

Fidelity Investments found that from June 30, 1981 through June 30, 2011 the S&P 500 posted an average annual return of 8% in terms of price appreciation (not including dividends). But, investors who missed the best 5 days during this 10,950 day period saw their returns drop to 6.4%. If they missed the best 20 days (1.8% of the time period), their returns were reduced to 3.7%.

Although market volatility is heightened, it is not a new phenomenon. According to Ned Davis Research, going back in market history to 1928, the market swings in one direction by at least 10% once a year, by at least 20% once every three and a half years and by 30% once every six years.

Historically, the volatility associated with stocks has come with an upside in the form of higher returns. In other words, "uncertainty" is

102

your friend. Think back to the spring of 2009, by most measures the last time investors were this gloomy about the future. Since closing at 676.53 on March 9, 2009, the S&P 500 has rallied a whopping 72% to close at 1,167 yesterday, excluding dividends.

Looking ahead, the present earnings yield (earnings divided by price) on the S&P 500 is nearly 8%, based on profits achieved in a difficult economic environment over the last twelve months. Compare that to the yield on a ten year U.S. Treasury bond of 1.875%. In locking-up our money for the next ten years, we know what our choice is .

1: Bespoke Investment Group is a research and financial services company.

23

NIRVANA

With stocks displaying tremendous volatility and with bonds yielding next to nothing, it is no wonder that investors are looking for a state of perfect happiness beyond these traditional asset classes.

In 1991, the grunge rock band Nirvana made alternative music mainstream with their album Nevermind. Today, in the world of investments, alternative asset classes are becoming conventional. When the esoteric enters the mainstream, like alternative music topping the pop charts, you have an oxymoron. When this happens in the world of economics, you have a problem.

Take home ownership as an example. In October of 2004, President George W. Bush was publically celebrating a new era of prosperity, in which nearly every American had the opportunity for home ownership: "We're creating... an ownership society in this country, where more Americans than ever will be able to open up their door where they live and say, welcome to my house, welcome to my piece of property..."

You may remember seeing neighbors and wondering how that person could afford their house. But, unsustainable trends like the

U.S. housing bubble only become crystal clear through hindsight.

Few people, including the President of the United States, saw disaster on the horizon. Rather, the vast majority of Americans, thought more widespread homeownership was a panacea.

In 2000, David Swensen, the Chief Investment Officer of the Yale University Endowment, published the book, Pioneering Portfolio Management: An Unconventional Approach to Institutional Investment. At the time, Swensen had already been transitioning Yale's portfolio toward alternative assets—real estate, timber, hedge funds, non-dollar-denominated securities, etc.—for nearly 15 years.

As such, Swensen was a pioneer; he was ahead of his time. His strategy of allocating the vast majority of Yale's endowment to alternatives continued to work all the way to 2008.

But now, everyone from retail stock brokers to bank trust departments are pushing alternative strategies, sometimes utilizing expensive mutual fund products or exchange-traded funds to mimic Swensen—albeit twenty-six years later.

Just the other day our office received a package advertising the Nationwide Alternatives Allocation Fund. The fund's intent is to "provide investors with exposure to several categories of alternative investments with investment performance that may have a low correlation to the performance of more traditional investments (i.e., stocks of U.S. and international developed-country issuers and investment-grade bonds issued in the U.S.)." A division of Nationwide Insurance distributes the product, but Goldman Sachs Asset Management, L.P. manages the investments.

Interestingly, just last month Goldman Sachs announced it would close its most high profile hedge fund, Global Alpha. In other words, Goldman's super-rich Global Alpha clients are getting refunds while Nationwide's retail investors are being aggressively marketed another Goldman-run vehicle. Theoretically, high net worth clients are perceived to be more sophisticated than the average retail investor, making this the kind of anecdotal contrarian sign for which we need to be attuned.

The natural human inclination in investing is to look at recent trends and project the same conditions into the next ten years. This is nearly always wrong.

Thirteen years ago, in 1998, newsletter writer and best-selling author Harry S. Dent, Jr. penned the book, *The Roaring 2000s: Building the Wealth and Lifestyle You Desire in the Greatest Boom in History*. As it turned out, the decade of the 2000s let out a whimper rather than a roar. But, a booming stock market was the most recent trend when Dent wrote the book in 1998. Perhaps foreshadowing another untimely prediction based on recent events, Dent's newest effort, published just last month, is entitled, *The Great Crash Ahead: Strategies for a World Turned Upside Down*. And believe it or not, even Harry has gotten into the alternative investment game, promoting his own alternative exchange-

> "THE NATURAL HUMAN INCLINATION IN INVESTING IS TO LOOK AT RECENT TRENDS AND PROJECT THE SAME CONDITIONS INTO THE NEXT TEN YEARS. THIS IS NEARLY ALWAYS WRONG."

traded fund since September 2009 called the Dent Tactical ETF.

And we believe we are seeing yet another development that nobody predicted. Coming into 2011, strategists were nearly universal in their opinion that emerging market stocks would thrive and that U.S. multinationals would likewise benefit from their exposure to emerging market growth. "BRIC" countries, i.e. Brazil, Russia, India and China, were the place to go for gains.

Well, year to date, Bespoke Investment Group finds that U.S. companies that get more than half of their revenue domestically have drastically outperformed their Standard and Poor's 500 brethren who get more than half of their revenue internationally.

Furthermore, the alternative investment that looked invincible until about a month ago was gold. On August 19th, 2011, the most popular gold exchange-traded fund (GLD) surpassed the largest S&P 500 exchange-traded index fund (SPY) in value. Since then, even gold has tumbled.

Many of the hedge fund managers who invented the alternative investment category have recently hung up their spurs, citing outsized stress and a lack of investment opportunity. Stanley Druckenmiller closed Duquesne Capital in 2010 after 29 years, George Soros in July of this year returned investors' money after 41 years and Carl Icahn followed a similar path in 2011 after 43 years.

These retirements present a dichotomy in the world of alternative investments. The innovators are getting out and the imitators are getting in.

24

FEAR ITSELF

> "SO, FIRST OF ALL, LET ME ASSERT MY FIRM BELIEF THAT THE ONLY THING WE HAVE TO FEAR IS FEAR ITSELF—NAMELESS, UNREASONING, UNJUSTIFIED TERROR WHICH PARALYZES NEEDED EFFORTS TO CONVERT RETREAT INTO ADVANCE."
>
> FRANKLIN D. ROOSEVELT

We believe that Americans' expectations about the future are low. Therefore, we conclude investors are assigning a higher likelihood to negative outcomes and, as such, are underestimating the odds of optimistic scenarios.

According to Fidelity's Millionaire Outlook for 2012, the average U.S. millionaire has $3.05 million in assets. Of these respondents, 35% are negative about the current economic environment, 34% are neutral and only 31% are positive.

This general pessimism has exhibited itself in mutual fund flows over the last twelve months as investors have pulled more than $170 billion out of stocks while contributing more than $200 billion to bonds.

The present cliché is that investors are not so much looking for a return on their money as a return of their money. This mentality can lead to interesting investment decisions.

For example, investors are so desperate for safety that they are reaching for the obscure. Norway is an oil-rich democracy with 3% unemployment and a budget surplus. Traders, by assigning the lowest premiums to Norway's credit default swaps of any sovereign nation, have declared the country to be the safest in the world. With a 10-year bond that yields 1.8%, foreigners now own 70% of Norway's outstanding government debt.

The New York Times reports that the safety trade is so intense that Norway's largest bank, DNB, has engineered a new kind of instrument, "...so-called covered bonds, which are backed by Norwegian mortgages. These were first made available in the United States in 2010, and $10 billion of them have already been sold. This year, the bank began placing its own bonds privately with American investors, raising $10 billion this way."

In the late 1920s, a time when people were seeking return on investment, banks, like Goldman Sachs, were designing investment trusts to make stock investing more accessible to the common man. At that optimistic juncture, just a few years before the Great Depression wreaked havoc on our nation, stocks were so popular as to elicit a "scarcity value."

As the Norway example helps illustrate, what is scarce today is the idea of a "safe" investment. Another such case is the two-year German note which has carried a negative yield for the past 30 days (it presently yields -0.02%). This means that investors are paying the German government to hold their money for twenty-four months simply because they believe the government will eventually give it back.

Perhaps the most notable concept of a "safe investment" with a monster premium is the 10-year U.S. Treasury Bond, which yields 1.8%

today. If you think of that valuation in terms of a stock, you are paying about 55 times "earnings" for peace of mind. In 1999, you could have paid a similar multiple for Microsoft (MSFT). Now Microsoft is a company that sells for about 15 times its earnings and pays a dividend of 2.7%. Just as people now cannot imagine the economy ever picking-up, in 1999, when Microsoft carried the same approximate valuation as today's 10-year bond, they couldn't imagine the economy ever slowing down.

It is not only bank product ingenuity and fixed income valuations that imply a fear flight, but it is also investor surveys. Last summer was bitter for the market and coming off its lull from August 2011, the S&P 500 is actually up about 25%. What is fascinating is that investors are less optimistic now than they were then, despite (or maybe because of) the market's gains.

> "JUST AS PEOPLE NOW CANNOT IMAGINE THE ECONOMY EVER PICKING-UP, IN 1999, WHEN MICROSOFT CARRIED THE SAME APPROXIMATE VALUATION AS TODAY'S 10-YEAR BOND, THEY COULDN'T IMAGINE THE ECONOMY EVER SLOWING DOWN."

Consumer confidence and surveys by Investors Intelligence and State Street Investor Confidence are all lower now than one year ago. The most bullish of these contrarian indicators is that Wall Street Investment Strategists are now recommending the lowest equity allocation in five years. These surveys are fickle and normally rising stock prices boost confidence, but people are so distraught that even a market rebound has not cheered them.

In addition to the surveys, accepted expert opinion is less than optimistic. The stories of Jeremy Siegel and Bill Gross illustrate this point.

Looking back to 1994, Professor Jeremy Siegel of the Wharton School of Business at the University of Pennsylvania published a well-received book entitled *Stocks for the Long Run* (he published a "Second Edition, Revised and Expanded" in 1998). In the book, Siegel meticulously documents more than 100 years of historical stock market returns. His conclusion: stocks generate nominal returns of 9% to 10% per year. The public at-large and the investor community widely accepted his view, especially in 1998. And, for several years after publication, it appeared that Siegel was even low-balling equity returns.

Then disaster came to pass, first with the dot-com bubble, then 9/11 and finally the financial crisis and the Great Recession.

Now, accepted expert opinion has swung to the other extreme. Bill Gross, the widely respected manager of the world's largest bond fund, PIMCO Total Return, recently authored a commentary entitled "Cult Figures." In it, he predicts that long-term nominal stock returns will be 4%. He also speculates that long-term nominal bond returns will be 2%. In his analysis, then, a balanced portfolio will return 3% (and if you assume inflation of 3%, then the real, inflation-adjusted return will be 0%). Gross gives seemingly valid reasons behind his logic. After all, he is an intelligent, rich man (Allianz, the German insurance giant that owns PIMCO, pays him a reported $200 million per year).

But, 18 years ago, Siegel filled an entire book with profound reasons why stock returns would average 9% to 10% per year and Siegel is also smart and wealthy (he is a founder of WisdomTree ETFs).

In his four page commentary, Bill Gross pokes fun at the "rather ill-timed" publication of Stocks for the Long-Run. Ironically, perhaps Gross' note will prove just as "ill-timed" as Siegel's book?

25

SAFETY IS POPULAR

> "AVOID POPULARITY: IT HAS MANY SNARES,
> AND NO REAL BENEFIT."
>
> WILLIAM PENN

With the Dow Jones Industrial Average reaching a new all-time high, market participants remain skittish. This is evidenced in frequent investor surveys from the American Institute of Individual Investors and Bespoke Investment Group, which both indicate that bears outnumber bulls. Many people seem to be waiting for the market to unravel.

Fear and greed drive financial markets, particularly when fundamentals are unclear. Given the widespread news coverage of today's global uncertainty, from the fiscal cliff to sequestration, angst about the European debt crisis to flash crashes, it is no wonder that investors are particularly worried these days.

Adding insult to injury, the last twelve years have brought two historic drops in stocks prices. First was the tech bubble from 2000 to 2002, followed by the financial crisis from 2007 to 2009. Investors watched riches turn to ruin twice, with many buying and selling at inopportune times only to cement these monumental losses.

The volatility of the market over this period (2000-2012) has been startling as well. Over the last twelve calendar years, the Standard and Poor's 500 Index was down more than 2% on 179 different days. To put this in perspective, during the prior 52 years from 1947 to 1999, the market only traded down over 2% on 174 different days.

Professors Daniel Kahneman, University of California at Berkeley, and Amos Tversky, University of Michigan, study behavioral finance, people's psychological reaction to money matters, and have found that their subjects feel loss more profoundly than they do gain.

For example, the researchers asked study participants if they would accept a 50% chance of losing $100 with a 50% chance of gaining $150. From a statistical standpoint, this is a good deal. Your expected return on each bet is $25. So, if you play the game enough times, you will ultimately end up with a $25 gain for each bet you place.

Interestingly, most study participants refused the bet. A majority would accept the offer only when the researchers raised the potential gain to $200 from $150. People needed a potential gain of twice their chance of loss to acquiesce to the deal.

Given the news cycle, the volatile nature of financial markets and people's general desire to avoid losses, it is no wonder investors have shunned the stock market. The result of this flight is tangible.

Since March of 2009, an almost four year period of exceptional performance for the S&P 500 stock index, investors have only placed about $91 billion into equity mutual and exchange-traded funds while pouring more than ten times as much, $1.2 trillion, into bond mutual and exchange-traded funds, according to information that Fidelity Investments compiled.

If you take these money flows back to the beginning of 2008, Bernstein Global Wealth Management calculates that investors have pumped more than $1 trillion into U.S. domiciled bond funds, while yanking $250 billion from U.S stock funds.

Meanwhile, retail investors have moved money into "alternative investment" vehicles at an alarming rate. These nontraditional investments range from baskets of commodities to mutual funds utilizing complex trading schemes. The appeal of these funds is the claim that they are non-correlating to stocks. According to McKinsey & Company, individual savers have more than doubled their exposure from $312 billion in 2008 to $712 billion in 2012. Not surprisingly, these types of investments dramatically underperformed in 2012.

Abraham Lincoln said, "Avoid popularity if you would have peace." So what are the implications of fear and the flight from traditional stocks? Largely the money from core equities has flowed to bonds and dividend-paying stocks. Let us take a look why we should be wary of these popular asset classes.

We will examine bonds first. Fixed income has a place in portfolios because it provides current income and helps lower volatility. Bond prices have surged and yields have fallen dramatically during the past five years as investors sought safety in high-quality bonds and as the Federal Reserve lowered its benchmark interest rate to zero.

Even though bonds serve a purpose in many portfolios, it is important to realize that the income earned from bonds is far less than average. For example, the 10-year U.S. Treasury currently yields 1.92%. The iShares Core Total U.S. Bond Market ETF, which includes government, mortgage and corporate bonds and has a weighted average maturity of 6.5 years, has a twelve-month yield of 2.55%. At these paltry interest rates, it is hardly conceivable that bond income will even keep pace with inflation over the long-term.

Similarly, low bond yields limit price appreciation, a major component of bond funds' strong returns since interest rates began to fall from lofty levels in the early 1980s. For bond prices to keep rising, yields need to fall even further. And with bond yields near all-time lows, it is difficult to envision major declines in interest rates going forward.

In addition to bond funds, another flight to safety for investors has been dividend-paying stocks. Additional research from Bernstein

Global Wealth Management indicates that high-dividend-yielding stocks (defined as the 100 stocks in the S&P 500 with the highest dividends) are overvalued. Going back to 1965, the long-term average weighting of these 100 stocks in the S&P 500 (a market cap-weighted index) is 34.7%. In 2012, their weighting was 44%.

Unfortunately, timing the peak for dividend stocks is impossible. These trends toward overvaluation can go on and on. For example, when technology peaked in 2000, that sector was almost 30% of the S&P 500 from its long-term average of 12.5%.

Now let us look at an anecdotal example using two particular stocks, one that investors view as safe and one that suddenly seems speculative. Both are solid companies, but investor perception dictates price in the short-term.

As we all know, The Hershey Company (HSY) makes chocolate, which is a fairly steady business, and for this reason investors presently view it as a safe investment. Hershey trades for 29.3 times trailing earnings and 21.2 times estimated forward earnings. Compare this to Apple (AAPL), which is a cyclical business that is dependent on innovation, traits that investors presently fear. Apple sells for 9.5 times trailing earnings and 8.3 times estimated forward earnings. From a price-to-earnings standpoint, Apple is less than half the price of Hershey.

The crazy thing about the stock market is that even if nothing changes about the fundamental businesses of Hershey and Apple, investor sentiment could swing from fear to greed, and the valuation of these companies could easily flip-flop. Apple could double and Hershey could be cut in half. Presently, investors need to be suspicious of the popular and crowded safety trade.

26

LONG-TERM PERSPECTIVE

The stock market is off to a rough start in 2014. After the S&P 500 fell 3.52% and the Dow dropped 5.27% in January, a poor U.S. manufacturing report sent equities lower in the first trading day of February.

Many investors are once again scared, and for good reason. Since the beginning of a secular bear market in 2000, stocks have seen tremendous volatility including two major declines of 49.1% from 2000-2002 and 56.4% from 2007-2009. And although some disciplined investors did reasonably well with a balanced stock and bond portfolio during this time, many others have jumped in and out of the market at precisely the wrong times and suffered lousy returns as a result.

To help keep a longer-term perspective, the below chart examines a period where interest rates were in a generational upturn, which could theoretically resemble the current environment as the Federal Reserve begins to tighten monetary policy by tapering its quantitative easing program.

Beginning in 1941, interest rates started a long upward trend, with the ten-year Treasury yield rising from 2% to a peak of 16% in 1981.

116

WORST TOTAL RETURNS OVER VARIOUS HOLDING PERIODS, 1941-1981

PERIOD OF RISING RATES	
10-YEAR TREASURY YIELD	
1941	2%
1981	16%

ANNUALIZED TOTAL RETURN

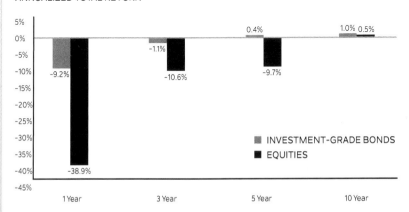

PERCENTAGE OF HOLDING PERIODS WITH NEGATIVE RETURNS				
	1 YEAR	3 YEAR	5 YEAR	10 YEAR
BONDS	18%	3%	0%	0%
STOCKS	25%	8%	5%	0%

Past performance is no guarantee of future results. You cannot invest directly in an index. See appendix for important index information. Based on rolling monthly holding periods. Bond returns represented by the performance of a composite of the IA SBBI U.S. Intermediate-Term Government Bond Index (67%) and the IA SBBI U.S. Long-Term Corporate Bond Index (33%) from Jan 1941 through Dec 1975, and by the Barclays Aggregate Bond Index from Jan 1976 through Dec 1981. Stocks represented by the S&P 500 Index. Source: Morningstar EnCorr Fidelity Investments (AART) as of 9/30/13.

This was a difficult time for bond investors because, as interest rates rise, bond prices decline. And on the equity side, investors were fearful with the Great Depression still in the rearview mirror and the country enduring wars, political turmoil and economic hardships, including a secular bear market that lasted from around 1968 through 1981.

During this 41-year period of rising interest rates, major wars, the civil rights movement, a President's assassination and another's resignation, stagflation, and countless other nerve-wracking developments, both stocks and bonds had some awful years.

But, investors who held on for three years had equity losses just 8% of the time and bond losses only 3% of the time. With a five-year time horizon, equity investors lost money just 5% of the time and bonds

> "SUCCESSFUL INVESTORS ARE NOT THE ONES WHO PICK THE HOT STOCK OR WHO PREDICT WHEN THE BEAR MARKET IS COMING. RATHER, THEY ARE THE ONES WHO AVOID PANICKED, EMOTIONAL DECISIONS AND INSTEAD STICK TO A DISCIPLINED LONG-TERM PLAN."

never saw losses. And over ten-year holding periods, neither stocks nor bonds ever registered a decline. Remember too that portfolios balanced between stocks and bonds would have seen considerably less volatility during the period.

While it can be difficult to maintain a long-term perspective when the market becomes disagreeable, it is immensely important to do so. Successful investors are not the ones who pick the hot stock or who predict when the bear market is coming. Rather, they are the ones who avoid panicked, emotional decisions and instead stick to a disciplined long-term plan.

27

CONSENSUS
FAILS—AGAIN

n fixed income investing, duration is a measure of the sensitivity of a bond's price to a change in interest rates. The higher the duration of a bond portfolio, the more value that portfolio is expected to lose as interest rates rise.

Although duration is a slightly different concept than average maturity, the two are closely tied. And as such, the overwhelming consensus among investors has been to keep fixed income duration (and average maturities) short to protect against rising interest rates. Most money managers, therefore, have favored the purchase of bonds that yield less and mature sooner to protect principal when interest rates begin to rise.

But, alas, there is a problem. Portfolio duration assumes a parallel shift in the yield curve. In other words, that rates will rise proportionately across all maturities—3 month, 6 month, 1 year, 3 year, 5 year, 10 years, etc.

Over the last six months, though, as experts begin to speculate that the Fed will raise rates in 2015, the yield curve has not risen proportionally. Rather, rates on shorter maturity bonds have increased

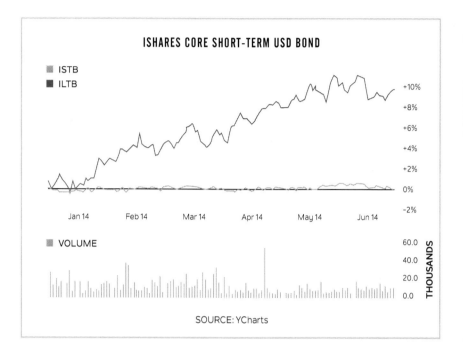

ISHARES CORE SHORT-TERM USD BOND

ISTB
ILTB

+10%
+8%
+6%
+4%
+2%
0%
-2%

Jan 14   Feb 14   Mar 14   Apr 14   May 14   Jun 14

VOLUME

60.0
40.0
20.0
0.0

THOUSANDS

SOURCE: YCharts

while longer-term bond yields have not. In other words, the yield curve has flattened.

Short-term rates have risen because the Federal Reserve indicated that it may raise rates in 2015. Meanwhile, investors are still questioning the longer-term health of the economy, which is suppressing rates at the long end of the yield curve. As a result, many bond investors have been caught flatfooted.

The chart below shows the iShares Core Short-Term U.S. Dollar Bond ETF, with an effective duration of 2.7 years, versus the iShares Core Long-Term U.S. Dollar Bond ETF, with an effective duration of 13.1 years. Amazingly, the short-term fund (blue line) has underperformed dramatically.

This is yet another example of the dangers of following the crowd. We manage the bond portion of our client portfolios using an intermediate laddering approach, fairly equally weighted among various maturities. This technique avoids the pitfalls of trying to predict the direction of interest rates, let alone the shape of the yield curve.

28

COMMODITY FUNK

On March 11, 2011, we wrote an essay entitled "Commodity Craze," which argued that the pricing of most commodities—from gold to oil to wheat—was too high. The crux of our argument was the disconnect between inflation (especially inflation expectations) and the prices of commodities.

We didn't predict a collapse in commodity prices, which has since occurred, but we did argue for a correction in prices. In 2011 this was a contrarian opinion because commodity bulls (especially gold bugs) were everywhere.

The prices of commodities, over the long-term and in the aggregate, cannot outpace the rate of inflation. Commodities tend to be plentiful and markets price them on the margin. Therefore, if demand far outpaces supply for a period of time (and prices rise materially), the market will create substitutes or alternative ways to produce a commodity. Oil is a prime example—the marketplace invented more fuel-efficient engines, battery-powered cars, natural gas fleet vehicles, horizontal fracking, etc.

Investors tend toward the manic, and this is certainly the case with commodities. One day the consensus is that central banks oversupplying the world with fiat money will spur inflation and drive the price of real assets (namely commodities) skyward. A mere four years later, and pundits now argue that the oversupply of commodities and slowing growth in China will forever depress commodity prices.

Surely, the truth lies somewhere in between.

As of this writing, oil has tumbled about 55% over the past twelve months; from their 2011 highs, gold is off more than 40% and iron ore is down about 70%; and silver, copper and natural gas are all well into bear market territory. The Standard and Poor's Goldman Sachs commodity index, which we highlighted in our "Commodity Craze" article, has collapsed more than 50% since 2011.

Interestingly (and not coincidentally) the crash in commodity prices has been concurrent with a rally in the dollar.

Although we were quite early, we published a piece on December 7, 2009 "The Not-So-Golden Dollar" about the consensus bearishness toward the U.S. dollar relative to gold prices. We predicted stocks would outperform gold and that the dollar would ultimately stabilize. Since then, the S&P 500 has surged and the dollar has undergone a powerful rally.

Because the U.S. dollar is the world reserve currency, commodities trade in dollars. Hence the stronger the dollar, the weaker commodity prices (i.e. you can buy more of a commodity with $1.00).

This week is a great example of the power of currency over commodity prices. China, which pegs its currency to the dollar, decided to devalue the yuan. Because the Chinese artificially manage their currency, this devaluation requires them to purchase dollars, ultimately buying U.S. Treasury securities, the only market large enough to accommodate the required volume. This action drove the 10-year Treasury yield down to 2.0982%, and oil prices, in the face of additional dollar strength, plummeted over 4% on Tuesday alone.

We are beginning to get the sense that the commodity rout is overdone. Outside of the doomsday set—those who believe the U.S. is headed for an economic and currency collapse—it's difficult to find anyone who is bullish on commodities. A lot of people see a buying opportunity coming, but few are recommending an investment now.

Obviously, it's impossible to identify market bottoms, so we aren't attempting that, but we most certainly see long-term opportunities in diversified integrated oil stocks and U.S.-based industrial exporters. For example, investments in Exxon Mobil, Royal Dutch Shell, Caterpillar and Cummins are presently compelling.

We do not believe the dollar must fall in order for these investments to ultimately prosper. Rather, the companies simply need time to adjust to the strong dollar. After all, a strong dollar has historically been good for equities and bonds because it lowers input costs for companies—from raw materials to labor. For now though, the equity

> "OUTSIDE OF THE DOOMSDAY SET—THOSE WHO BELIEVE THE U.S. IS HEADED FOR AN ECONOMIC AND CURRENCY COLLAPSE—IT'S DIFFICULT TO FIND ANYONE WHO IS BULLISH ON COMMODITIES."

market is thinking short-term about how the strong dollar will affect earnings over the next several quarters and reacting negatively.

One final thought about the increasing strength of the dollar and the continuing collapse in commodities...The fears about rising interest rates in the U.S., which would add fuel to the dollar's fire, are overblown.

Although we believe that the Federal Reserve is committed to raising rates in 2015 and ending its zero interest rate policy, we expect the Fed to move at a snail's pace. The world economy faces deflationary pressures from poor demand, aging populations, technological advancements and a wide variety of structural challenges. U.S. interest rates should not get too far ahead of the rest of the developed world.

The Fed seems determined to move off of zero, but it probably won't aggressively raise rates while the rest of the globe eases policy.

We believe now is the time to make additional investments in value-adding companies that the market has punished because of the fall in commodity prices and the strong dollar.

29

THE FUTURE OF INTEREST RATES

With most market participants predicting a Fed rate hike in December, "lift off" for interest rates is nearly upon us. For years there have been two overwhelming consensus opinions in the fixed income world:

- First, bond portfolios should be short duration (a measure of bond price sensitivity to rising rates), which most often means keeping the average maturity shorter than the index.
- Second, once interest rates start to rise, they will continue to rise, albeit slowly over the long-term.

Because a sustained rise in rates has yet to occur, these consensus opinions have largely led most managers to underperform. With "lift off" potentially just around the corner, is now finally the time for these views to pay off for investors?

Maybe...The answer will lie in the yield curve.

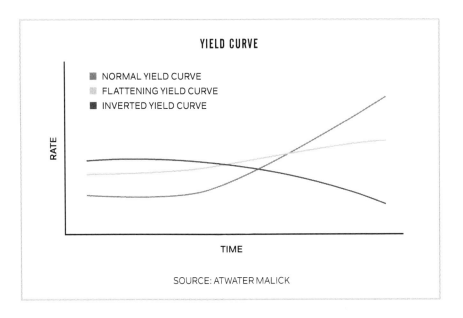

YIELD CURVE

- NORMAL YIELD CURVE
- FLATTENING YIELD CURVE
- INVERTED YIELD CURVE

RATE

TIME

SOURCE: ATWATER MALICK

A yield curve is a simple graph that illustrates the level of interest rates at various years to maturity. The y-axis displays the interest rate and the x-axis shows the time to maturity. While the Federal Reserve controls short-term rates by setting the Fed Funds Rate, the rest of the yield curve has a mind of its own.

The U.S. Treasury yield curve is normal today; meaning rates are lowest at the short end and higher as you extend the maturity date (see yield curve examples above). Put differently, bond investors can earn a higher interest rate by waiting longer to get their money back. By "locking-in" a rate of return for a longer period of time, bond investors also accept greater inflation risk and interest rate risk.

Most experts expect that when the Fed raises the Fed Funds Rate, the curve will remain normal and undergo a parallel shift—all rates across all maturities will generally move up proportionally.

In our view, this is a risky assumption (and most likely incorrect). Rather, as the Fed pushes up short-term rates, the yield curve will likely flatten over time. This would occur if the economy slows because of the rise in short-term rates. A slower economy would imply lower long-term inflation (or even deflation), which would push longer rates down.

In a worst case scenario, the Fed could push rates to the point where the curve inverts. This means, most likely, that they have engineered a recession. An inverted yield curve preceded each of the last seven recessions, on average twelve months before each recession began.

If the Fed raises short-term rates very slowly, and if the resulting damage to the economy is minimal, the yield curve may indeed remain normal. We have our fingers crossed for this outcome, which would increase the odds that this long-lived bull market continues to plug along.

But, don't be surprised if the yield curve flattens and longer duration fixed income continues to perform satisfactorily. And, as for a sustained and persistent rise in rates, remember, the yield curve will constrain the Fed. If longer rates don't keep up with the rise in shorter rates, the Fed would need to halt rate increases or possibly even reverse them to attempt to avoid an inverted yield curve and a recession.

30

WHAT TO EXPECT

There is extreme danger in relying on the accuracy of any prediction. The future is much too unknowable to venture guesses on how the economy will grow, what will become of interest rates and inflation or how profitable corporations will be.

That said, with investing we need to make some baseline assumptions about how various securities will perform in order to create retirement income plans for clients. Others in our profession need to make guesses about how endowments will perform to determine how much to distribute to support charitable enterprises or what returns a pension fund needs to achieve in order to pay its retirees.

Recently there has been considerable literature about diminishing future investment returns. Much of this stems from four legitimate concerns: 1) a very low interest rate environment which, in and of itself, is indicative of lower forward bond returns; 2) a low rate of inflation; 3) poor economic growth and 4) full equity valuations. The graphic below is from a recent McKinsey Global Institute study that suggests future returns will be significantly lower than the historical average of the last 30 years.

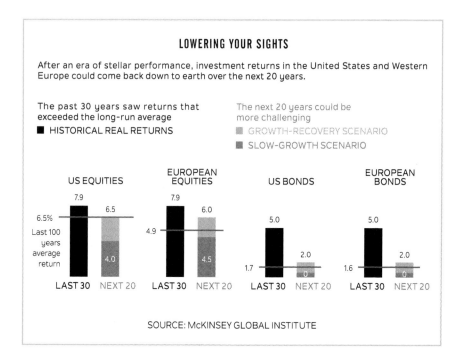

LOWERING YOUR SIGHTS

After an era of stellar performance, investment returns in the United States and Western Europe could come back down to earth over the next 20 years.

The past 30 years saw returns that exceeded the long-run average
■ HISTORICAL REAL RETURNS

The next 20 years could be more challenging
■ GROWTH-RECOVERY SCENARIO
■ SLOW-GROWTH SCENARIO

SOURCE: McKINSEY GLOBAL INSTITUTE

We are somewhat heartened at the continued pessimism about financial markets. As contrarian investors, we believe that skepticism is the perfect environment for the market to produce healthy returns.

Just for fun, let's accept two of the above headwinds—low interest rates and low inflation, which are linked phenomena—and reject the other two, poor economic growth and full equity valuations. Let's assume that the economy can get back to trend growth simply on the basis of pent up demand and that equity valuations in a low interest rate world can expand significantly, while technological advancement and globalization keep inflation and interest rates low. This would lead to anything but below average future returns.

Again, there are too many variables to know with any certainty what will happen, but the continued pessimism about investing in general and future returns specifically makes us believe the reality could be different than the expectations. It is fascinating to note that we have not seen a single research piece since we started our firm in 2008 to suggest that future investment returns will be higher than average—nobody thinks such a fantasy is even possible.

Regarding the retirement income planning we do, for clients, the implied return on a 65% stock and a 35% bond portfolio (a "balanced" investment approach) that we tested for a client in a "poor" market scenario is 4.76% per year over the next forty-plus years. Our software uses a 2.5% inflation assumption, meaning real returns would be just 2.26% per year. Using McKinsey's numbers, their "growth-recovery scenario" for U.S. stocks and bonds at a 65% stock and 35% bond allocation is 4.925% over the next twenty years, or 2.525% real returns net of 2.4% inflation. In McKinsey's "slow-growth scenario," they show the same portfolio returning 3.3% per year over the next twenty years with 1.6% inflation for a real return of 1.7%—this strikes us as unreasonably low.

Although the current pessimism has a potentially optimistic result, when making projections for clients, we will continue to be cognizant of a "poor market" scenario and do everything we can to prepare clients accordingly. However, we can't help but be encouraged by the almost unanimous forecasts for lower future returns.

31

THREE THINGS WE ARE TERRIBLE AT

Obviously, this is not an exhaustive list of our flaws, merely a short summary of our three most significant investment deficits. We will note, however, that all investors share these handicaps. Being aware of these weaknesses is half the battle, while avoiding them is the other half. Although we have succumbed to all these mistakes before, we work hard to avoid making them again.

MACRO INVESTING

A trader following a macro strategy bases decisions primarily on an overall view of economic and political environments, i.e. macroeconomic theories. When we started Atwater Malick eight years ago, the most popular macro stance was the idea easy monetary policy would create rampant inflation. To date, this view has been wrong. Since 2009, core CPI inflation has been a mere 1.7% annualized. The failure of this thesis points to the fact that macro investing is simply guesswork. The world is too big, complicated and uncertain to accurately predict the future macroeconomic environment.

As another example, many investors, especially professionals, have been unwilling to commit to fixed income (bonds) over the last several years for fear of higher interest rates, which hurt bond prices. Anecdotally, we have seen institutional investors consistently underweight bonds for years, instead opting for alternative asset classes. Yet just this week, yields on the 10-year German bund and the 30-year Swiss government bond turned negative as global interest rates continue to plummet and as bonds extend their multi-decade bull market further than anyone ever predicted.

Bottom line, it is far better to have a comprehensive financial plan that informs your investment decisions rather than trying to make sense of a highly unpredictable world. Owning individual stocks and bonds is invaluable as well-run companies adapt to constantly changing environments and high-quality individual bonds provide steady cash flows and a hedge against stock market volatility.

BIG AND/OR QUICK PROFITS

The potential upside of any investment idea—a hot new technology, a "proven" trading strategy, an incredibly cheap security or a fast growing stock—is almost always trumped by the potential downside. But in the fog of excitement and perceived certainty, the pitfalls are difficult to process. Put another way, investments that have the potential for huge upside also have the potential for huge downside.

In our stock selection discipline, we should feel confident estimating a company's long-term rate of return based on dividend yield, earnings and dividend growth rates, and price-to-earnings multiple changes. Using this technique, we look for companies that we anticipate can increase in value over the long-term at an 8% to 12% average annual rate. Therefore, we aim to avoid "hot stock" ideas where we speculate that we can make a quick or outsized profit.

In one of our more egregious mistakes, after an exhaustive due diligence process, we purchased shares in a company that we believed was worth two or three times its share price. Although we might have been correct if not for the collapse in oil prices, the investment turned sour. This error made us even more aware of the importance of getting on base versus swinging for the fences. Strikeouts hurt a lot worse in investing than in baseball.

MARKET TIMING

After more than fifteen years of investing for clients, we have seen two brutal bear markets (the dot com crash and the financial crisis). We have also seen two robust bull markets (late 2002 through 2007 and 2009 through today). In the process, we have read a myriad of expert opinions, forecasts and analysis. We have come to the conclusion that, much like meteorologists, stock market forecasters are sometimes right and often wrong. But the accuracy of their forecasts is overwhelmingly driven by pure luck. It is no accident that the most famous stock market forecasters are either permanently bullish or permanently bearish—after all, as the saying goes, a stopped clock is right twice a day.

The next bear market could begin with stocks trading at twenty times earnings or with stocks trading at fifty times earnings. It could start for any reason and at any time. It could come tomorrow or we may not see it for many years. We would never even consider trying to time the next bear market by selling stocks and going to cash. Rather, we plan to stick to a discipline of setting appropriate asset allocation targets, reevaluating these targets as clients age and personal circumstances change, reinvesting cash in underperforming securities and rebalancing after major multi-year moves in the market.

The most important thing you want from an investment advisor is an experienced and disciplined approach to investing—a process that slowly evolves based on experience, not based on overconfident market predictions. Furthermore, you want an advisor that focuses on doing the little things right and being aware of the pitfalls of doing big things wrong.

32

BREXIT, ELECTION, AND SO ON

M arkets always face uncertainty. Whether it is international upheavals like "Brexit" or the constant barrage of negativity that accompanies a Presidential election cycle, we never know what the immediate future will hold. Investing, therefore, requires a firm acceptance that volatility is inescapable. Following the Brexit vote, the Dow Jones Industrial Average lost over 883 points in two trading days and panic gripped investors. Just four days later, on July 1st, the Dow had already recovered these losses. Since then, we've seen day-to-day ups and downs.

Equities don't always recover their losses in such short order. But history shows that investing becomes less risky over longer periods of time. Staying in the market reduces the probability that an investor will lose money. From 1926 through 2015 there were 88 rolling three-year periods for the market and in only 15 of those were returns negative. Over the same time period, there were 81 rolling ten-year periods and only 4 had negative returns. All the while, stocks returned an average of 10% per year. Adding a 25% bond allocation would reduce your chance of having a negative return over a rolling ten-year period to less than 1%, while only trimming your average annual return to 9.2%. Bottom line, as the saying goes, investing is about time in the market, not timing the market.

Another example of time in the market comes by way of dividends. While a 2% or 3% dividend may not seem consequential when stock prices can swing by 2-3% in a single day, the reality is that collecting and then reinvesting dividends is a fundamental driver of returns. From January of 1988 through last week, reinvesting dividends doubled the cumulative return of the S&P 500, from 722% to 1,451%. The little things matter.

We are committed to every detail of our investment strategy to maximize your opportunities. Regardless of the headlines, patience has historically been a profitable investment attribute.

33

INCREMENTALISM

The January 23, 2017 issue of *The New Yorker* contained an excellent article on "The Heroism of Incremental Care" as it relates to the practice of medicine. The author, Dr. Atul Gawande, a surgeon, made a strong argument for the concept of incrementalism and tied it by analogy to infrastructure. In reading the piece, we felt it was further analogous to investment management and financial planning, particularly the approach we take with clients.

Incrementalism is about lowering expectations, understanding that progress takes time and that success is gradual. Often when telling someone that we manage investments their first inquiry is about a hot stock or what the market will do this year. Frankly, we don't know any hot stocks, nor do we know where the market is headed in the short-term. Instead, successful investing is about taking small, unglamorous, methodical, and contrarian steps with as much consistency as possible.

The public is attracted to boastful prognostications about how the market is going to boom or bust, or to heroic solutions to problems or opportunities. We've seen many examples of advisors concocting a story about how to cope with runaway inflation, the collapse of the dollar, the "guaranteed" protection of principal, the inevitable crash of the stock or bond market, etc. Invariably, these emotion-charged, all-or-nothing approaches end in poor returns (at best) and major losses (at worst).

We, as incrementalists, on the other hand, look to face problems before they occur versus being reactionary to a crisis. We want to take a long-term view and work to reduce unavoidable issues, while accepting that we can't anticipate or prevent all problems. Because people's savings and their retirement are propositions that require relationships lasting years, we know that slow-and-steady is the best philosophy.

The reason this topic is vital right now is because we believe that at 25 times trailing earnings, the Standard and Poor's 500 is expensive (overvalued). Investors are paying too much money for a company's potential future dividends and profits. Furthermore, bonds continue to offer a paltry yield.

However, we aren't conceited enough to declare an end to the stock or bond bull markets. Timing the market in the short or intermediate-term continues to be a fool's errand. But, we are advocating an incremental approach to reducing equity exposure while purchasing high-quality bonds as a way to prepare for an eventual opportunity to rebalance stock positions at lower prices. An opportunity that may come in a day, a week, a month, a year or longer...

34

THE CASE OF THE
EXPENSIVE MARKET

I t's a real mystery. The market is expensive, yet stocks have never-theless been trending ever higher.

Bloomberg News reports that in a recent closed-door investment confab, the legendary hedge fund manager Paul Tudor Jones observed that the total market capitalization of U.S. stocks is currently about 125% of U.S. GDP. In other words, the aggregate value of American equities (which represents the economic output of only a fraction of the economy) exceeds the goods produced and services provided across the entire U.S. economy.

For perspective, before the financial crisis this number reached 110% and before the dot com bubble burst in March of 2000 this figure hit 151%. A measure of 125%, therefore, is expensive (the long-term average is 68%), but not unheard of.

Furthermore, the cyclically adjusted price-to-earnings (P/E) ratio (a measure of the index's price divided by its ten-year average infla-tion-adjusted earnings; also known as the Shiller P/E) of the Standard and Poor's 500 is more than 29 times.

This ratio has only been around these levels in two prior periods—1929,

139

just before the Great Depression and from 1997 until 2000, a period of market gains that ended with the S&P 500's bear market from March of 2000 to November of 2002.

The Shiller P/E was just over 44 at its December 1999 dot com peak. So, again, at 29 times, stocks are expensive (the long-term mean is 16.75), but not as expensive as the dot com days.

Such rich valuations are no guarantee that the market will fall imminently.

A recent Yale University survey of professional money managers found that 99% of us believe that the Dow Jones Industrial Average will be higher one year from now. However, over half of those same managers say the market is expensive.

This disconnect is a bit disturbing because financial markets always revert to the mean eventually.

Said differently, if stocks are now expensive, at some point the pendulum will swing and equities will be cheap again. If managers see the market as too expensive but also anticipate further gains, they are counting on a major pick-up in corporate earnings and, therefore, economic growth. But, what happens if news disappoints, do stocks then disappoint? Herein lies the mystery.

Because timing the market is impossible, we can't solve the mystery of the ever-ascending market. Rather, we must enjoy it, manage it and prepare for a day when things aren't so simple. Here's how we are proceeding:

ENJOY IT WHILE WE CAN...Valuations are a poor market timing tool. Stocks can stay expensive for a long time. Momentum is a powerful force in investing. In the final leg of a bull market, investors will look for any reason to keep the rally going.

Keeping an appropriate allocation to stocks, even when we know equities are expensive, is necessary so that we can participate in rallies like the current one. No expert or pundit knows when the market will stall. Hence, we'll never make an all-or-nothing bet for or against stocks. Otherwise, there is the possibility of missing strong periods.

REBALANCE ALLOCATIONS AND REEVALUATE GOALS...Very simply, rebalancing means bringing your allocation back to your long-term target. If your target is 60% stocks and 40% bonds and, given the outperformance in stocks, you now have 70% in stocks, then rebalancing back to 60% stocks is prudent. We've been actively doing this for clients.

Additionally, because the market has been robust for a long time, many of our clients don't need to be as aggressively invested to meet their goals (they actually have a higher probability of meeting their retirement spending needs with a lower stock allocation). Specifically, for some clients, it is more optimal in our retirement income projections to have more exposure to bonds (a lower volatility portfolio) to more consistently fund retirement outlays.

SEEK SHELTER GRADUALLY...Due to the impossibility of timing the market, implementing subtle changes may involve selling aggressive, expensive holdings and trying to replace them with more defensive-oriented stocks.

For example, we recently sold our position in Coach, the fashion brand, and we have been gradually adding a position in CVS Health, the pharmacy benefit and retail behemoth. Still more subtle is our normal discipline of rebalancing within our equity portfolio, which dictates that we add to underperforming and out-of-favor names that will ultimately rotate back into the market's good graces as circumstances evolve.

Bottom line, it is best not to "fight the tape." We will happily participate in the present rally. But, we will do it with our eyes open.

THE INVESTMENT INDUSTRY

35

MADOFF AND HIS
MANAGER OF MANAGERS

An overwhelming trend in the investment management industry over the last ten years has been the "manager-of-managers" approach. This method, often labeled "fund-of-funds," has been heavily promoted by many institutional investment consultants and private wealth managers that cater to high net worth investors. The concept is to employ a variety of middlemen—brokers, financial advisors, private banks, hedge fund-of-fund managers, etc.—who charge a fee to select multiple third party managers to invest their clients' money. One of those third party managers was Bernard Madoff. But before we go there, let us revisit the middlemen and the purported justifications for their extra layer of fees: 1) diversification, 2) access to the "best" managers available and 3) due diligence.

First, one cannot argue against the benefits of diversification. When done right, diversification can reduce the impact a few badly performing investments will have on your overall portfolio. But in the current broad market decline, owning investments managed by ten, twenty or even thirty different managers in every imaginable category has not cushioned losses one iota. Broad diversification without transparency

144

can be a recipe for disaster. One of our clients recently asked us to define investment transparency. Our definition is the ability to know what you own and why you own it. A manager-of-managers process makes it difficult to know what securities you own and even tougher to contemplate why you own them.

Second, the broad market decline has rendered access to the "best" managers much less useful. Many managers whose exemplary funds were closed not so long ago now have plenty of capacity to accept new assets under management. It can also be difficult to define the "best" managers without focusing on short-term investment results, which frequently leads to performance chasing. Not to mention that several experts surely considered Mr. Madoff a "best in class" manager.

Now for the due diligence part...

According to a Bloomberg News story about Tremont Capital Management, a hedge fund-of-funds company, "Tremont's Rye Investment Management unit had $3.1 billion, virtually all the money the group managed, allocated to Madoff...Tremont, which manages a total of $5.8 billion, would have made roughly $62 million this year peddling funds that are solely run by Madoff...Hedge funds that invested with [Madoff] charged fees to their clients for the task of vetting the fund."

Another firm that marketed itself based on a thorough due diligence process was the Fairfield Greenwich Group, which reportedly had more than half of the firm's assets, about $7.5 billion, invested with Mr. Madoff. According to *The New York Times*, "Fairfield boasted about its investigative skills. On its Web site, the firm claimed to investigate hedge fund managers for 6 to 12 months before investing. As part of the process, a team of examiners conducted personal background checks, audited brokerage records and trading reports and interviewed hedge fund executives and compliance officials."

So what does Fairfield Greenwich Group have to say for itself? According to a company statement, "FGG, like so many other Madoff clients, was a victim of a highly sophisticated massive fraud that escaped the detection of top institutional and private investors, industry organizations, auditors, examiners and regulatory authorities." We question how FGG can label the oldest financial deception in the book—a Ponzi Scheme—as highly sophisticated. After all, such a scam simply amounts to repaying one level of investors with funds raised from the next group.

As Warren Buffet often says, "Only when the tide goes out do you discover who's been swimming naked." After about a forty percent drop in the Standard and Poor's 500 Index and an even greater calamity in most other investment classes, Mr. Madoff's firm was swamped with redemption requests from investors needing to create liquidity. But, of course, there was no money to be had. Bernie had lost it, squandered it, gifted it and stashed it.

> "YOU SHOULD BE ABLE TO SEE AND UNDERSTAND
> EXACTLY WHAT YOUR INVESTMENT MANAGER IS DOING."

The lessons are simple. First, do not invest with someone who promotes a "black-box" management methodology. You should be able to see and understand exactly what your investment manager is doing. Second, and you have heard this one before, if it sounds too good to be true, it probably is...Mr. Madoff claimed to consistently earn returns of about 1% per month over many years. He never had 30% gains or 30% losses, just 1% per month, 12% per year. No way, no how. That level of return is bound to come with commensurate volatility.

36

MUTUAL FUNDOSAURUS

For many years, stocks have been a common method of building financial wealth. When purchased at a fair price and sold at a full valuation, stocks can produce stellar returns. In fact, even after the recent equity bear market, the S&P 500 has returned 7.41% annually over the past 20 years ended March 31, 2009 with dividends reinvested in the index.

Because of strong potential returns, stocks have gained ever greater popularity over the years, and the financial services industry has responded by devising clever ways for the "average" investor to participate in the stock market. These include common trust funds, mutual funds, variable annuities, exchange traded funds (ETF's) and hedge funds. Along the way, the industry created countless other financial products as well. Some have stood the test of time and others have not.

As the famous investor Barton Biggs reminded us in a November 11, 2008 Fortune article, "there is no asset class too much money can't spoil." While he was referring to hedge funds, we think this adage also applies to mutual funds. The first mutual fund was organized in 1924 as a method

147

of pooling investors' assets together to purchase a diversified portfolio of individual stocks. Early mutual funds allowed "small" investors to own a diversified basket of equities at a time when it was not yet cost-effective for everyday folks to directly purchase and monitor individual stocks. In exchange for limited transparency and control, mutual fund clients gained diversification and professional oversight of their portfolios.

Over the years, there have been dramatic changes in both the mutual fund industry and the options available to individual investors.

While the mutual fund industry has grown exponentially, technology and the Internet have expanded the options available to individual investors. Through the advent of discount online brokerage sites, retail investors are now able to purchase individual stocks for modest commissions. And thanks to the free flow of information through the Internet, investors and independent investment advisors can more easily access vast amounts of pertinent data about publicly-traded companies, including all Securities and Exchange Commission regulatory filings. Therefore, the opportunity now exists for individual investors to directly own interests in the companies that mutual funds are frequently trading.

So why are mutual funds still so widely used? We think a clue lies in the flow of mutual fund assets. *Total assets* invested in mutual funds at the end of 2007 were roughly $12 trillion. But according to data from the 2008 Investment Company Institute Fact Book, *total sales* of mutual funds throughout 2007 were $24 trillion—almost *twice the level of assets*. Now that is salesmanship.

You can partially attribute this to the natural ebb and flow of money in the economy. Fortunes are accumulated and spent, funds are redeemed to pay for financial goals, and new millionaires are made each day. But in our view, the vast majority of this phenomenon can be attributed to (1) the transactional incentives built into the financial services industry and (2) performance chasing.

As you know, mutual funds are the tool of choice for most financial salespeople. These funds often carry hefty expense ratios and sales loads

148

and can therefore be highly profitable when the salesperson closes a deal. Unfortunately, the profitability of a transaction sometimes ranks higher on the priority list than simplicity, transparency, and prudent advice.

According to a study called the Quantitative Analysis of Investor Behavior by financial research firm Dalbar, from January 1, 1988 through December 31, 2007, the average equity fund investor earned an annualized return of only 4.5%, while the S&P 500 returned 11.8%. We think this is attributable to "performance chasing," a common reason investors churn mutual funds. This occurs when an investor sells a poorly performing fund in favor of the hottest performing fund. Reversion to the mean and Murphy's Law dictate that the purchase of this "best of breed" fund will happen at exactly the wrong time, right before the fund starts to underperform.

We take a different approach to investment management. First, we provide a fee-only service which removes the incentives to sell financial products. Second, our portfolios are highly transparent, so our clients know what they own and why we make each investment. Third, our approach is straightforward. We make long-term investments in individual stocks with solid growth prospects and fair valuations. We complement our equity portfolios with high quality bonds. Finally, we are committed to maintaining active communication with our clients to ensure they understand the decisions we are making.

In a world of unscrupulous Ponzi schemes and convoluted mortgage-backed securities, simplicity and transparency reign supreme. We believe wise investors will continue to move toward independent investment advice, while rejecting opaque, complicated financial products. If recent experience is a good teacher, then overly complex investments that clients cannot see, understand, and quantify, should go the way of the dinosaur.

149

37

THE VALUE
OF INVESTING

I n the eyes of many people that we talk with, "investing" has become a commodity. As the financial services industry has grown exponentially over the past decade, so has the number of choices available to savers. Since 1995, the number of mutual funds has grown by over 54% and the number of exchange traded funds (ETFs) has expanded from 2 to a whopping 743, according to data from the 2009 Investment Company Fact Book. And the most recent Occupational Outlook Handbook reports that there were roughly 176,000 personal financial advisors in the U.S. in 2006. It is easy to see why so many people are confused and disenchanted by "investing."

An Internet driven stock bubble, followed by a crash, then a severe credit crisis and second stock market crash shortly thereafter, have also fed the belief among many that investing, specifically in stocks, is a fool's game. For the past decade, stocks have returned virtually nothing. In many cases, if investors made poorly-timed decisions, stock market investments actually lost money over the past 10 years.

But despite recent difficulties, equity investing remains vitally important, not only to individual savers, but to our society as a whole.

150

Over the past 100 years, stocks have created great wealth for Americans. There are common examples of individuals who amassed fortunes from stock investments, such as Warren Buffet. But there are anecdotal examples as well. One investor who we met several years ago turned a lucrative 1950's era sales commission of $5,000 into a $10 million nest egg through diligent investments in "blue chip" U.S. companies over 5 decades.

Professor Jeremy Siegel of the Wharton School estimates that the compound average annual real return (after accounting for inflation) of stocks has been about 7% since 1802. These are powerful returns for a 200-plus year period that includes a civil war, a Great Depression, two world wars, numerous recessions, and countless other impediments to economic growth and stability. Through it all, though, the U.S. economy has consistently delivered excellent results.

There are few other opportunities to achieve this kind of long-term growth. Sure, an enterprising individual who starts or purchases a business or invests in a lucrative piece of real estate can achieve hefty returns. But, this sort of investment requires a significant capital outlay and will carry the higher level of risk associated with a concentrated investment. Additionally, investors are limited in the types of investments that can be practically made in tax-advantaged accounts that are commonly used to save for retirement, such as IRA's.

When you view equities over very long periods, the advantages provided to individual savers from investing are obvious. Perhaps the more often overlooked beneficiary is our American society as a whole. In a broad sense, stock investing should serve to allocate capital efficiently to well-run businesses. Individual investors and their advisors help corporations raise capital to expand their operations, fund research and development efforts, create new and better products, and ultimately contribute to the growth of our economy. In other words, investment raises the capital that funds innovation. This is a vital component to an increasing standard of living for Americans.

This system is far from perfect, and capital is occasionally allocated to poorly-run businesses in times of heavy speculation—think Pets.com during the technology bubble or Countrywide Financial during the real estate bubble. But, eventually these problems work themselves out and capital is ultimately shifted to true innovators.

We strongly believe in this system, which is one of the many reasons we invest independently. In order to fully understand the value of investing, it is imperative to know what you own and why you own it. In our current "focus list" portfolio of stocks, we own companies in all kinds of businesses that improve our standard of living. For example, we have holdings that find new sources of oil and gas to fuel the engine of our

> "FOR MANY, THIS IS A NOVEL APPROACH TO INVESTING, AND WE CHALLENGE PEOPLE TO REORIENT THEIR THINKING IN THIS WAY, TO REALIZE THAT INVESTING CAN BE TRULY INTERESTING, MEANINGFUL AND EVEN PROFITABLE."

economy, that build medical diagnostic equipment to detect disease, that create software used to design roads and bridges, that provide families with the protection of life insurance, that engineer seeds so that farming is more productive, and the list goes on. A company can both profit the individual investor and contribute to improving people's lives—these are not mutually exclusive concepts.

One terrific example of what we believe to be a great investment that simultaneously works to benefit society is Johnson & Johnson (JNJ). JNJ is a diversified healthcare company, with 39% of sales from pharmaceuticals, 36% of sales from medical devices and diagnostics and 25% of sales from consumer products. Purely from an investment standpoint, JNJ is appealing due to modest trailing and forward price-to-earnings ratios, a healthy dividend yield, and a mountain of cash on its balance sheet.

On July 2, JNJ announced that it would put some of its cash to good use through a major $1 billion investment in Dublin, Ireland-based

Elan Corporation. In exchange for this investment, JNJ received an 18.4% interest in Elan and a controlling interest in Elan's Alzheimer's Immunotherapy Program (AIP). JNJ will invest an additional $500 million "to continue the development and launch activities of bapineuzumab, a potential first-in-class treatment that is being evaluated for slowing the progression of Alzheimer's disease," according to a statement from JNJ. The company also reports that, "In the U.S. alone, as many as 5.3 million people are living with Alzheimer's disease. The direct and indirect costs of this and other dementias to payers, including government programs, amount to more than $148 billion annually, according to the Alzheimer's Association." These are the kind of breakthroughs that have the potential to rescue our bankrupt healthcare system and greatly improve people's lives.

Elan and JNJ's commitment to research to slow the progression of Alzheimer's disease and to potentially even create a vaccine is amazing. Dr. Dale Schenk, the Chief Scientific Officer for Elan, describes it this way: "After twenty years of following the science and advancing this technology into the latest stages of clinical development, it is our responsibility to ensure that this therapy, upon further clinical and regulatory progress, may be made available to the broadest range of patients globally. The capabilities of Johnson & Johnson will help in achieving that goal."

This is certainly a noble pursuit, but it is also difficult to argue the potential profitability of such a venture. For many, this is a novel approach to investing, and we challenge people to reorient their thinking in this way, to realize that investing can be truly interesting, meaningful and even profitable.

38

WRESTLING WITH ALLOCATORS

For prudent investors, asset allocation serves as the cornerstone of a sound investment strategy. A sensible investment policy should consider factors such as investment time horizon, goals, future plans to save, potential for emergency expenditures, cash flow projections, and psychological tolerance for losses. These factors should be balanced with economic and market expectations to construct an appropriate mix between high-risk and low-risk assets. A portfolio with a larger allocation to high-risk assets should offer the potential for greater returns. On the other hand, a portfolio with more exposure to safer, low-risk investments should be expected to deliver stability and more modest returns.

Sounds easy enough...Unfortunately, this simple, effective concept has become lost on too many investors in favor of overly-complicated strategies that lead to performance-chasing, higher fees and, hence, lower returns.

"Wealth managers" have developed complex strategic asset allocation models in recent years and many have based these recommendations on a dangerous concept in investing: past performance. You

154

have undoubtedly read the standard investment disclosure that past performance is not indicative of future results. However, this adage is too often forgotten.

Take the recent survey released by Capgemini-Merrill Lynch and published in *Barron's* on September 21st (see pie charts below). The study compares the typical asset allocation strategy employed by wealthy investors in 2005, before the credit crisis and the "Great Recession," with today, as our economy and credit markets appear to

WHERE'S THE MONEY GOING?

Comparing Harris Bank's 2005 model portfolios to its 2009 version suggests how much more popular bonds have become in recent years; Capgemini-Merrill Lynch's survey of wealthy individual's portfolio also indicates that they are taking Wall Street's advice.

HARRIS BANK BALANCED TAXABLE
2005

CORP & GOVT BONDS — 35%
EMERGING MARKETS — 6%
U.S. MID & SMALL CAP — 8%
SHORT-TERM TREASURIES — 9%
DEVELOPED INTL — 11%
U.S. BIG CAP — 31%

2009

CASH - 1.1%
EMERGING MARKETS - 2.7%
COMMODITIES - 3.3%
ALTERNATIVES - 3.9%
INTL SMALL CAP - 3.9%
U.S. MID & SMALL CAP - 4.2%
DEVELOPED INTL — 10.6%
U.S. BIG CAP — 29.6%
CORP & GOVT BONDS — 40.7%

CAPGEMINI-MERRIL LYNCH WEALTH SURVEY
2005

EQUITIES — 30%
CASH — 13%
REAL ESTATE — 16%
ALTERNATIVES — 20%
FIXED INCOME — 21%

2009 (FORECAST)

FIXED INCOME — 30%
ALTERNATIVES — 7%
REAL ESTATE — 15%
CASH — 20%
EQUITIES — 28%

SOURCE: HARRIS BANK; CAPGEMINI

be recovering. Compared with 2005, the survey participants are now allocating less money to equities, real estate and alternative investments—the asset classes that have declined most through the crisis. To the contrary, the surveyed investors are parking more funds in cash and fixed income, which are the asset classes that have outperformed through the "Great Recession."

Morningstar, Inc. recently reported that "bond funds attracted net deposits of $209.1 billion in the first eight months of the year while stock funds drew $15.2 billion." They went on to state that "nine of this year's 10 best-selling funds buy bonds and only one, Vanguard Total Stock Market Index Fund, focuses on equities." These statistics represent further evidence that the vast majority of retail investors are showing a preference for fixed income. Regular readers of our commentaries know that the overwhelming response of individual investors is not normally a bullish sign.

The increase in fixed income from 21% to 30% in the Capgemini study is suspect when you consider the super-cycle bull market in bonds over the last 28 years. Bond prices move inversely to interest rates, so as rates have cratered, bond prices have boomed. Former Federal Reserve Chairman Paul Volcker boosted the federal funds rate to 20% in June of 1981 in order to break the back of inflation. Nearly three decades later, Federal Reserve Chairman Ben Bernanke has lowered the federal funds rate to 0%. The United States has experienced a steady decline in rates over nearly three decades.

Are the Capgemini results simply the consequence of investors neglecting to rebalance their portfolios? (Rebalancing would serve to increase exposure to "riskier" securities following big losses). Possibly, but the majority of "wealthy" investors receive professional advice, so either they have lost faith in the recommendations of their advisors, or the advisors themselves are basing their recommendations on past performance.

In recent years, wealth management firms have popularized the concept of "strategic asset allocation." According to Investopedia[1], strategic asset allocation is defined as "a portfolio strategy that involves periodically rebalancing the portfolio in order to maintain a long-term goal for asset allocation." On its surface, this is a great concept because it leads investors to buy low and sell high; the ultimate goal of investing. But, as the above-mentioned survey suggests, advisors may not be adhering to this strategy. So, when the concept would have been most potent, many have abandoned it.

In our experience, managers employing "strategic asset allocation" have increasingly followed a trend toward more asset classes and broader diversification. For instance, examine the model portfolio currently being recommended by Mohamed El-Erian, the well-known co-chief investment officer for Pimco (see the pie chart below). Mr. El-Erian is suggesting that investors commit funds to ten different asset classes, ranging from U.S. equities (simple enough) to special opportunities (your guess is as good as ours).

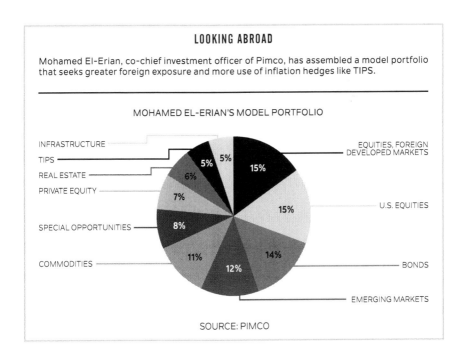

LOOKING ABROAD

Mohamed El-Erian, co-chief investment officer of Pimco, has assembled a model portfolio that seeks greater foreign exposure and more use of inflation hedges like TIPS.

MOHAMED EL-ERIAN'S MODEL PORTFOLIO

INFRASTRUCTURE — 5%
TIPS — 5%
REAL ESTATE — 6%
PRIVATE EQUITY — 7%
SPECIAL OPPORTUNITIES — 8%
COMMODITIES — 11%
EMERGING MARKETS — 12%
BONDS — 14%
U.S. EQUITIES — 15%
EQUITIES, FOREIGN DEVELOPED MARKETS — 15%

SOURCE: PIMCO

157

For the average individual investor, we see major problems with this approach. First, under most managers this portfolio would be very expensive. Investors would typically pay various fund managers to run each of the ten asset classes, and an additional fee for a financial advisor to "coordinate" the strategic asset allocation. Second, there is rarely communication among the ten fund managers, which dilutes the overall strategy. Third, the portfolio would ultimately contain a massive number of securities, making it extremely difficult to outpace market returns.

Although Mohamed El-Erian caters his recommendations to large, institutional investors, in reality, many individual investors apply a virtually identical strategy by building a portfolio of multiple mutual funds that invest in various asset classes. This strategy merely offers

> "WE DO NOT VIEW BROAD DIVERSIFICATION AMONG A NEVER-ENDING LIST OF SECURITIES AS AN EFFECTIVE MEANS OF MANAGING RISK."

investors the "special opportunity" to pay exorbitant fees for broad diversification, an approach that is much more likely to enrich an advisor than his or her clients.

We do not view broad diversification among a never-ending list of securities as an effective means of managing risk. Rather, our Investment Philosophy Statement, outlines our straightforward, transparent approach to managing risk through asset allocation.

We believe the most significant risk-reward decision in investing is the allocation to stocks versus bonds and that this simple determination overwhelmingly dictates portfolio volatility. We do not invest our clients in stocks unless we conclude that an allocation to stocks is appropriate, given each client's risk tolerance and time horizon. Our discussions of risk tolerance include both (1) financial ability to absorb short-term investment losses and (2) psychological ability to handle market fluctuations. For client assets that are not suitable for the stock market, we invest in individual fixed income securities for safety of principal and a steady source of income.

Today's world of investing can be daunting. Investors must navigate a sea of investment options running the gamut from stocks and bonds to structured notes and credit default swaps. But, when it comes to investing, complicated is not necessarily more effective. As Leonardo da Vinci once said, "Simplicity is the ultimate sophistication."

1: Investopedia is a for-profit website that focuses on investing education and financial news.

39

DECEMBER 16, 2009

THE FOUR HORSEMEN
OF PORTFOLIO RETURNS

As an investor, it can be easy to miss the forest for the trees. Fads, convoluted investment products, and the daily noise of the financial media distract us when we should be focusing on the basic principles that are the overwhelming determinants of long-term success. Unfortunately, ignoring the following four fundamental investment considerations can lead to apocalyptic returns.

FEES

High fees can be a threat to achieving competitive investment returns. Most investors are logically focused on net-of-fee returns, but over time, exorbitant fees are often the very cause of sub-par performance.

According to a 2007 speech by John Bogle, the founder of The Vanguard Group, the average equity mutual fund expense ratio in 1977 was about 1.0%. In 2008, three decades later, the average fee for a U.S. stock fund had escalated to 1.6%, according to Morningstar.

Albert Einstein is quoted as saying, "The most powerful force in the universe is compound interest." On the surface, this 0.6% fee differential may seem minimal, until you consider the effect of compounding. For example, let's review two hypothetical equity mutual funds that each generates before-fee annual returns of 8%: Fund A carries a 1.0% fee and Fund B charges 1.6%. At the end of 20 years, if you began with a $500,000 investment, Fund B's higher expenses would have destroyed over $200,000 of value.

Investors in individual securities should also contemplate trading costs. Thanks to the advent of online trading, ordinary investors now have the ability to trade individual stocks and bonds at reasonable costs. However, excessive trading can still rack up substantial expenses without actually improving performance, which takes us to our next headwind.

TURNOVER

Turnover is an indicator of how frequently managers buy and sell assets within a portfolio. According to William Harding, an analyst with Morningstar, the average turnover ratio for managed U.S. stock mutual funds is 130%. In other words, the average manager of a 100-stock mutual fund would sell and replace every stock, then liquidate 30 of the replacement stocks, all within a year. Viewed another way, the fund holds each stock for an average of just over 9 months.

This represents pure short-term speculation, not true investing, and should be a point of caution for mutual fund investors. When purchasing shares of a high-turnover mutual fund, it is nearly impossible to identify what you are actually buying. Rather than getting a diversified basket of sound long-term investments, you end up with a faceless trading vehicle.

Most mutual funds are under intense pressure to consistently keep pace with the broader market. If a fund experiences a few months of lackluster performance, investors will often withdraw their money in favor of competing managers. This leads many funds to a short-term mindset that drives high turnover and poor performance.

TAXES

Frequent trading can also drive taxes higher, further deteriorating "take-home" returns in taxable accounts. And the higher the turn-over, the greater the damage from taxes, because short-term capital gains, or the price appreciation of stocks sold after being held less than a year, receive worse tax treatment than long-term capital gains.

"The Securities and Exchange Commission says more than 2.5 percent of the average stock fund's total return is lost each year to taxes, significantly more than the amount lost to fees. The tax bite varies from zero percent for the most tax-efficient funds to 5.6 percent for the least efficient," according to a 2003 article from Bankrate.com. Once again, if you apply the impact of compound returns over many years, the results can be devastating.

Many investors do not realize that capital gains can occur even in a year when a fund loses value. Typically, as funds incur losses, sharehold-ers head for the doors and force fund managers to sell long-held posi-tions to meet redemptions. For example, the Dodge & Cox International Stock Fund, a popular fund with a solid long-term track record, incurred over $1.50 per share in capital gains distributions in 2008, a year in which the fund lost almost half its value.

MARKET TIMING

According to the folks at The Motley Fool, a popular investment website, "It's not timing the market that's key, but rather the amount of time you're in the market." In fact, Nobel laureate William Sharpe found that market timers must be right an incredible 82% of the time just to match the returns realized by buy-and-hold investors. Nevertheless, that has not stopped people from trying.

The Motley Fool calculates that between 80% and 90% of the returns realized on stocks occur between 2% and 7% of the time. To further illustrate this phenomenon, The Motley Fool also reports that, "Using data from Bloomberg, American Century Investments looked at the period from 1990 to 2005 and found that a $10,000 investment would have grown to $51,354 had you just sat tight from beginning to end. However, if you had missed the best 10 days in that 15-year period, your returns would have dwindled to $31,994; if you had missed the best 30 days, you'd be looking at a mere $15,730." Not only do these statistics explain the temptation to make a quick profit, but they also illustrate the dangers in missing the relatively few trading days that contribute the bulk of positive returns.

"THE DODGE & COX INTERNATIONAL STOCK FUND, A POPULAR FUND WITH A SOLID LONG-TERM TRACK RECORD, INCURRED OVER $1.50 PER SHARE IN CAPITAL GAINS DISTRIBUTIONS IN 2008, A YEAR IN WHICH THE FUND LOST ALMOST HALF ITS VALUE."

Former U.S. President Theodore Roosevelt once said, "With self-discipline most anything is possible." By undertaking disciplined research to avoid high fees, unnecessary turnover, excessive taxes and misguided market timing, investors will stay on the path to reaching their investment goals.

40

THE FIDUCIARY STANDARD

Ronald Reagan once quipped, "The most terrifying words in the English language are: 'I'm from the government and I'm here to help.'"

Today, an equally frightening pronouncement is, "I'm a financial advisor and I'm here to help."

You know this to be true. Think of yourself at a social function. When you meet a financial advisor, you nearly snap a tendon trying to move in the opposite direction. The presumption is that financial advisors are trying to sell you something that will fatten their wallet more than yours.

Just look to the recent civil fraud case that the Securities and Exchange Commission filed against the greatest financial advisor of all, Goldman Sachs.

Essentially, Goldman participated in the creation and marketing of a subprime mortgage derivative security that Goldman believed was likely to lose value. And then Goldman sold this product to its client. This alone was legally permissible.

The SEC, however, contends that Goldman went a step further and made a material misrepresentation about the security. The SEC

164

claims that Goldman failed to disclose to the buyers of the security that hedge fund manager John Paulsen, a notorious subprime mortgage bear, helped choose the mortgages that the security tracked. Paulsen was, all along, planning to bet that the security would lose value.

But why is Goldman Sachs, acting as a broker, legally allowed to sell an inferior security to its client in the first place?

As a broker, the legal standard that Goldman must follow is that of suitability. A product doesn't have to be all that good as long as it is considered suitable.

Goldman argues that its client was a huge, sophisticated German bank and, therefore, the product was inherently suitable. Effectively, the argument contends that the German bank knew what it was getting when it purchased the security in question. And while testifying before

> "THE PRESUMPTION IS THAT FINANCIAL ADVISORS ARE TRYING TO SELL YOU SOMETHING THAT WILL FATTEN THEIR WALLET MORE THAN YOURS."

Congress last week, several current and former Goldman employees suggested that the German bank purchased the low-quality asset to balance its risk profile by gaining exposure to the U.S. housing market.

Goldman Sachs says that the German bank's purchase of the security, in and of itself, proved suitability. The SEC, therefore, has to evidence a material misrepresentation; essentially establish that Goldman lied to sell the investment.

To offer an everyday example of the suitability standard, it is helpful to consider a more pedestrian product than a complex mortgage derivative-based instrument. Take variable annuities, which are often so complex in nature that the buyer and the seller don't understand the product. A variety of more straightforward investments may satisfy the buyer's goals with substantially lower fees. The fact that a variable annuity may be the worst option available does not mean it is unsuitable. Hence, wildly opaque and confusing financial products are legally sold every day.

In order then for the public to put aside suspicion and fear of financial advisors, there should exist a legal requirement for "all professionals who provide investment and financial advice or who hold themselves out as providing financial or investment advice, without exceptions and without exemptions" to act only in the best interest of their clients. Such is the goal of the Committee for the Fiduciary Standard, a group of financial professionals who are lobbying Congress to include a pro-

> "TODAY ONLY A MINORITY OF FINANCIAL ADVISORS ARE LEGALLY OR ETHICALLY REQUIRED TO ADHERE TO A FIDUCIARY STANDARD, BY WHICH, AT ALL TIMES, THEY MUST ACT FOR THE SOLE BENEFIT AND INTEREST OF EACH CLIENT."

vision in comprehensive financial reform legislation that would require a fiduciary standard.

The Committee for the Fiduciary Standard promotes five core principals to define a fiduciary standard: 1) Put the client's best interest first; 2) Act with prudence; that is, with the skill, care, diligence and good judgment of a professional; 3) Do not mislead clients; provide conspic-uous, full and fair disclosure of all important facts; 4) Avoid conflicts of interest; and 5) Fully disclose and fairly manage, in the client's favor, unavoidable conflicts.

Today only a minority of financial advisors are legally or ethically required to adhere to a fiduciary standard, by which, at all times, they must act for the sole benefit and interest of each client. It is wise to directly ask financial advisors to which standard they are required to comport, a suitability standard or a fiduciary standard. If they say a fiduciary standard, insist that the advisor acknowledge this claim in writing. After all, you want people working for your interests rather than their own.

All professionals rendering advice to others should think of the words of Albert Einstein who said, "Try not to become a man of success but rather try to become a man of value."

41

FINANCIAL ARCHITECTS

> "YOU KNOW I ALWAYS WANTED TO PRETEND
> I WAS AN ARCHITECT."
>
> GEORGE COSTANZA

It seems like the business of investing becomes more and more complicated as time passes. In a world of perplexing financial products and 24-hour streaming financial news, investing for important financial goals can seem like an incredibly daunting task, perhaps worthy of a whole team of money managers.

Today the vast majority of financial advisors employ an investment approach called open architecture, also referred to as manager-of-managers. Many extremely wealthy families, such as Rockefeller and Company, and huge endowments, like Harvard and Yale Universities, adhere to the approach of allocating capital to various third-party investment managers. For these enormous pools of capital, this approach can be effective. However, we doubt strongly that such a strategy is practical for most high net worth individual investors.

As the typical sales pitch goes, the financial advisor develops an overarching asset allocation strategy for the client, often to include domestic and foreign stocks, bonds, commodities, managed futures, private equity, and various other asset classes. The advisor then vows to seek out the industry's most talented portfolio managers in each asset class by investing in various financial products, often mutual funds.

On the surface, it is evident why the client may find this strategy appealing, as it promises to offer access to the best portfolio managers in the world, all delivered through a local professional who pledges to serve as the financial quarterback, sitting on the same side of the table as the investor.

The appeal to the advisors who promote open architecture, though, is slightly less apparent.

Much of the financial advisory industry has realized that hiring others to manage their clients' investments is a terrific way to 1) devote more time and effort to selling investments to new clients, while 2) escaping accountability.

Open architecture is generally easy to administer. Instead of diligently researching a select basket of individual stocks and bonds and explaining these specific investments in detail to clients, a manager-of-managers can simply choose a handful of financial products and put the account on autopilot. It is rare that a financial advisor is familiar with the largest holdings or the most current thinking of the various managers in a portfolio. This ease of administration frees more time to dedicate to marketing and sales.

By outsourcing the actual investment management responsibilities, open architecture shifts accountability to faceless third-party portfolio managers in faraway locales. For example, if a local advisor invests his clients in a large cap stock fund and the fund performs poorly, the advisor simply blames the manager and replaces the fund with the latest top tier manager. This passes as due diligence, but in practice it often leads to performance-chasing as advisors search for funds with robust short-term track records.

Truly understanding a manager's investment philosophy is vastly different than screening Morningstar's mutual fund database for appealing criteria. Amazingly, the trade publication *Investment News* reported in its June 25th issue that "Morningstar plans to offer advisers shorter summaries and bullet points of its fund research." Apparently the contents of the existing one-page reports are too daunting.

But, the vital question is, does run of the mill open architecture actually work?

> "IF A LOCAL ADVISOR INVESTS HIS CLIENTS IN A LARGE CAP STOCK FUND AND THE FUND PERFORMS POORLY, THE ADVISOR SIMPLY BLAMES THE MANAGER AND REPLACES THE FUND WITH THE LATEST TOP TIER MANAGER."

Unfortunately, open architecture generally fails for several reasons: inadvertent indexing, limited portfolio coordination and high fees.

When advisors purchase multiple financial products, often ten or twenty mutual funds in a portfolio, the strategy in reality owns hundreds, or even thousands, of underlying securities. Eventually the portfolio looks just like a broadly-diversified index fund—representative of the entire market and unable to outperform.

The simple fact is that the product managers do not communicate with each other. With so many stocks, when managers are not explicitly coordinating their efforts, your portfolio effectively becomes random. In other words, the right hand does not know what the left hand is doing.

Most importantly, the typical retail manager-of-managers approach eats into investor returns because it involves two layers of expenses: a top-level account fee and product-level fees within each asset class.

To be fair, open architecture can succeed when a highly sophisti-cated manager utilizes a limited number of high-quality, low-cost funds with complimentary and consistent philosophies and if the advisor is willing to stick with the funds through thick and thin.

But open architecture, as ordinary financial advisors practice it, is simply not a legitimate investment approach. Many successful investors from Peter Lynch to Warren Buffett to John Templeton advocate buying solid businesses for the long-term. Many well-known academics, such as Burton Malkiel and Jeremy Siegel, advocate various forms of low-cost indexing. But we are not aware of a single respected academic or esteemed investor that would recommend the average open architecture approach because it combines the worst traits of stock-picking and indexing.

42

BOND BONANZA

I n these dog days of summer, we are witnessing the continuation of a multi-year trend. Investors and their advisors are pouring dollar after dollar into fixed income funds while largely fleeing equities.

This year, stock funds have endured a net $1.1 billion in outflows while bond funds have enjoyed $177.6 billion in inflows, according to the Investment Company Institute. This is a carry-over of a theme from 2009, when investors piled over $284 billion into taxable bond funds and over $72 billion into municipal bond funds while yanking almost $26 billion from equity funds.

As evidence of this bond boom, Pacific Investment Management Company, or PIMCO, the world's largest manager of fixed income funds, has recently been attracting an astonishing $1 billion a week from investors, according to Bill Gross, the firm's co-founder and co-chief investment officer.

The average investor is clearly voting with his feet. But given the spotty track record of retail investors, this persistent trend makes us question whether stocks or bonds offer greater value in today's environment.

American corporations are responding to robust investor demand for fixed income by issuing new debt at very low interest rates. According to The Wall Street Journal, "this month has been the busiest July on record for sales by U.S. companies with junk-credit ratings. Asia's debt market is on pace for a record year, and European companies are also raising money apace."

Last week, McDonald's issued $450 million in 10-year debt at 3.5%, a record low yield for a large U.S. corporate issuance. And as one would expect, current yields on U.S. government debt are even lower, with the 10-year Treasury bill generating less than 3% and even the longer 30-year Treasury bond yielding about 4%.

In other words, interest rates are extremely low and unlikely to fall much further. While Federal Reserve Chairman Ben Bernanke recently reiterated his commitment to keeping the central bank's benchmark overnight rate around zero for an "extended period," continued stabilization in the U.S. economy over the coming months and years should eventually drive interest rates higher.

And as we have articulated in past market updates, there exists an inverse relationship between interest rates and bond prices. If and when rates rise, bond prices will surely fall. Even PIMCO's Gross, often branded "the Bond King," estimates that "bonds have seen their best days."

We know that bonds, in general, offer investors perceived safety of principal, but in exchange for wretched current yields. Throw in exposure to rising interest rates, and bonds appear to be a mediocre investment at best and a dangerous mirage at worst. On the other hand, stocks appear to offer a solid value by several measures.

Based on price-to-earnings (P/E) multiples, equities appear inexpensive. Thirteen of the 25 largest companies in the Standard & Poor's 500 now trade at or below 10 times estimated 2011 profits, including ExxonMobil, Microsoft, Intel, Merck, IBM and Hewlett-Packard.

The average P/E ratio among the entire S&P 500 stands at roughly 15 and U.S. companies are continuing to grow earnings at a rapid pace. About 80% of S&P 500 companies have released their second-quarter earnings so far, and 78% of them have beaten analysts' estimates, according to Thomson Reuters. On average, earnings per share are up 37% year-over-year, compared with the 27% growth analysts expected.

A stock's earnings yield, or the inverse of its P/E ratio, is often compared to bond yields to gauge the relative value of each. In a July 3rd Barron's article, Oppenheimer strategist Brian Belski noted that the present 8% earnings yield on the S&P 500 is five percentage points above the 3% yield on the 10-year Treasury note. Belski's research shows that, historically, when the gap has been this wide, the average one-year return on the S&P has been 26.7%.

Although we believe stocks offer substantially more value than bonds, fixed income should still play a vital role in many portfolios, even considering the high probability of a rising interest rate environment in the future. From 1941 to 1981, a period of escalating rates, government bonds generated a total annual return of 3.3%, according to Fidelity Management & Research Co. But when used to complement equities, "a 20% allocation to bonds shaved off more than one-fifth of the portfolio's volatility, yet only marginally lowered the overall return (from 11% to just below 10%)."

All bond investment strategies, though, are not created equal. When you invest in a bond mutual fund the decisions of other fund

> "THE AVERAGE P/E RATIO AMONG THE ENTIRE S&P 500 STANDS AT ROUGHLY 15 AND U.S. COMPANIES ARE CONTINUING TO GROW EARNINGS AT A RAPID PACE."

shareholders greatly affect you. For investors who need stability and a steady stream of income within a portfolio, we believe in the time-tested strategy of laddering a portfolio of high-quality individual bonds rather than investing in bond funds.

When constructing portfolios to match client risk and reward parameters, we arrive at an appropriate long-term asset allocation between equities and fixed income. Presently, when implementing these long-term allocations, we recommend a tactical slant favoring stocks over bonds.

When faced with overwhelming investor favoritism toward a certain asset class, it is advisable to follow the words of poet Robert Frost:

"Two roads diverged in a wood, and I— / I took the one less traveled by, / And that has made all the difference."

43

GLOBETROTTERS

Most investment strategies today include at least a modest allocation to foreign equity markets.

While specific percentage recommendations will vary among advisors, a logical starting point is the fact that the United States currently represents about 40% of the global stock market. This rationale would lead to 60% of a portfolio's equity exposure devoted to international markets, perhaps a bit too bold for most investors.

For a more realistic proxy of how managers allocate their clients' portfolios, Morningstar reports that the typical target date mutual fund allocates somewhere between 20% and 45% of its total equity holdings outside the U.S.

Why do so many investors look overseas?

For starters, many point to the potential diversification benefits from allocating capital to all corners of the globe. Theoretically, economies and stock markets around the world should not flourish or decline in tandem.

Furthermore, international investing has exploded simply because that is where the growth has been. While United States gross domestic product (GDP) contracted at a 2.6% rate in 2009, India expanded at a 7.4% clip and China grew by an impressive 9.1%.

As a result, emerging market mutual funds are now enormously popular—a contrarian indicator. According to Bloomberg News, "Individual investors are pouring money into emerging-market stocks at the fastest pace since 2007. The last time investors were this bullish, the MSCI Emerging Markets Index sank 11 percent in three months, data compiled by EPFR Global and Bloomberg show."

Overall we would not quibble with the notion that international diversification is favorable when constructing a portfolio. We do take issue, however, with the method by which most financial advisors seek access to global markets.

Readers of our past market commentaries are familiar with our distaste for "outsourced" investment management, i.e. financial products such as mutual funds, due to limited transparency, high fees and tax inefficiency. Yet in our experience, most portfolios rely heavily on international and emerging market mutual funds for exposure to companies that trade directly on foreign stock exchanges.

Drawing a distinction between domestic and foreign equity investing is hardly as black and white as one might think. According to the below chart from Ned Davis Research, of companies in the S&P 500 that report foreign earnings, 30.9% of their revenue and 54.4% of their profits were derived from overseas in 2009, a significant rise from 2000. Moreover, 507 non-U.S.-listed multinational companies currently trade on the New York Stock Exchange, as well as many thousands of American multinationals. In today's integrated world economy, an investor can strategically seek international diversification through individual companies.

MetLife (MET), for example, recently closed a $15.5 billion acquisition of Alico from the beleaguered insurance giant, American International Group (AIG). AIG sold Alico, an otherwise healthy

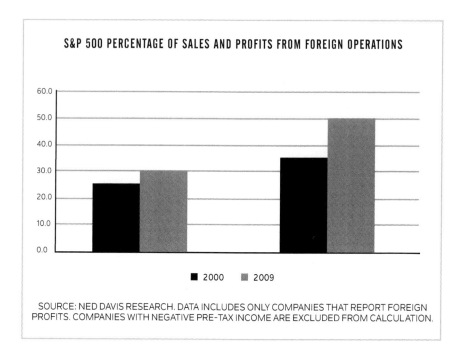

S&P 500 PERCENTAGE OF SALES AND PROFITS FROM FOREIGN OPERATIONS

■ 2000   ▨ 2009

SOURCE: NED DAVIS RESEARCH. DATA INCLUDES ONLY COMPANIES THAT REPORT FOREIGN PROFITS. COMPANIES WITH NEGATIVE PRE-TAX INCOME ARE EXCLUDED FROM CALCULATION.

business, to help repay its taxpayer-funded bailout. The deal allows MET, already the largest U.S. life insurer, to significantly expand its presence in Asia, Europe and Latin America. Nearly all of Alico's business is outside the United States. The company recently predicted that operating results would rise as much as 45% next year, helped by the acquisition.

A recent *Bloomberg Businessweek* article profiled Coca-Cola (KO), and its attempt to expand its African beverage business. "Coke has been in Africa since 1929 and is now in all of its countries; it is the continent's largest employer, with 65,000 employees and 160 plants. In 2000 about 59 million African households earned at least $5,000, which is the point when families begin to spend half their income on nonfood items, according to a recent McKinsey report. The study suggests that number could reach 106 million households by 2014. Coke plans to spend $12 billion in the continent during the next 10 years, more than twice as much as in the previous decade," according to *Bloomberg Businessweek*.

For Diageo (DEO), the British spirits maker, Africa was among its fastest growing regions last year, growing 10 percent and representing 13 percent of total sales. At a time when Diageo is shuttering factories in Ireland and Scotland as a meager European economy takes its toll, they intend to invest 100 million pounds ($158 million) to expand in Africa next year.

We have more confidence in Coke and Diageo's ability to uncover opportunity in Africa than we do in an emerging market mutual fund manager sitting at a desk in Minneapolis.

Among our portfolio of companies, perhaps Procter & Gamble (PG) maintains the most ambitious plan for international expansion. P&G has articulated a growth strategy of, "touching and improving the lives of more consumers in more parts of the world, more completely." Put in more measurable terms, P&G would like to sell its products to 5 billion consumers by 2015 and achieve $175 billion in sales by 2025. And the 173-year-old company appears to be on the right track, increasing its global household penetration—the percentage of households using at least one P&G product—nearly two percentage points in its most recent quarter, to 61%.

A significant contributor to international investment returns is often currency exchange rates. For example, let us consider an American investor who purchases shares of a mutual fund that invests in Mitsubishi UFJ Financial Group, the largest bank in Japan. In times when the U.S. dollar drops relative to the Japanese yen, this investor should prosper as the profits Mitsubishi UFJ earns in yen are repatriated to U.S. dollars. Obviously, the opposite holds true as a strong dollar hinders returns.

Yet by investing in individual companies that do business overseas, we benefit or suffer from the very same currency effects. For instance, Coach (COH), the New York-based maker of handbags and leather goods, booked 22% of its fiscal 2009 sales in Japan. In its most recent quarter, Coach's Japanese sales rose 13.8% to $173.1 million, which included a 10.6% positive impact from currency translation.

The most compelling argument in favor of multi-national American companies may be their track record for allocating capital overseas before most Wall Street strategists see an opportunity. For instance, Procter & Gamble began marketing its brands in China in 1988, long before emerging markets became en vogue among asset allocators. Today, P&G is the largest consumer products company in China, with about $5 billion in annual sales and a strong record of profit growth.

By owning individual businesses rather than investment products, an investor can essentially cut out the middle man and the commensurate extra layer of management fees. Individual, multinational companies offer the geographic and currency diversification that come from foreign investing, along with the transparency, tax efficiency and control that are so often lost in investment products.

44

VARIABLE ANNUITIES: A FALSE PANACEA

Variable annuities come with a variety of claims, when in reality these investments are frequently low returning, highly complex and extraordinarily expensive. In this essay, we will outline the commonly overhyped claims surrounding variable annuities.

CLAIM 1: "THE INVESTMENT IS GUARANTEED, YOU CANNOT LOSE MONEY."

Basically, a variable annuity is an investment account that includes a life insurance policy as a means of protecting the initial investment. In fact, the minimum death benefit of this insurance policy is often equal to the original investment.

Variable annuities also typically include an annual fee, normally 1% or more, and fees for various policy riders, which can easily reach another 1%.

So, think of the guarantee in these terms: Would you buy an insurance policy with a $200,000 death benefit for $200,000 today and an additional annual fee of $4,000 (2% x $200,000)? Of course you would not; such a proposition makes no economic sense.

Also, many variable annuities have surrender charges that begin at 10% the first year and decline incrementally over ten years until there is no longer a penalty. If, for example, you have an unforeseen emergency in year two of such a contract and you absolutely need the money in the annuity, you could lose 8% in a "guaranteed" investment.

CLAIM 2: "YOU WILL PARTICIPATE IN A RISING STOCK MARKET WITHOUT THE DOWNSIDE RISK."

The problems with this premise are twofold: fees and investor behavior.

We already talked about the 1% annual contract fee and the 1% rider fee, which we have found to be relatively standard in the industry. Now add another estimated 1% expense ratio for the underlying mutual funds. You are suddenly 3% behind the market each year before you even start, comparable to racing in the Daytona 500 with a hippopotamus strapped to your roof.

Furthermore, according to the research firm Dalbar, over the prior twenty years through December 31, 2009, equity mutual fund investors realized an average annualized investment return of 3.17% versus a return of 8.20% for the Standard and Poor's 500 stock index.

Dalbar attributes these subpar returns to "irrational behavior." Investors tend to leave underperforming funds in favor of outperforming funds at exactly the wrong time. There is no reason to expect a different phenomenon within variable annuities.

As such, when considering extraordinary fees and investor behavior, most variable annuity holders are going to realize below-average market returns.

CLAIM 3: "NO MATTER WHAT, YOU ARE GUARANTEED TO EARN AT LEAST 6% PER YEAR."

Please bear with us, as this explanation is convoluted. But, this is a very important reason why variable annuities are generally less than optimal.

Insurance companies frequently have a number which they refer to with varying terminology, but we will call this figure the "minimum guaranteed income benefit" (MGIB). According to the annuity sales-man, this is the minimum dollar value that will compound at 6% (or 5%, 7%, etc. depending on the annuity).

And the assertion is true, the MGIB does compound at a "guaranteed" rate, but often the rate is adjustable at the desire of the insurance company after an introductory period or if times get rough.

What becomes of the ultimate dollar value of the MGIB at the exer-cise or maturity date of the annuity? The insurance company deter-mines how much you will receive each month by annuitizing the MGIB (to annuitize means that you contractually agree to receive a series of certain payments for a set period of time).

It is vital to note that the interest rate at which the company will annuitize the MGIB is the truly important rate, one that is rarely advertised and often buried within the prospectus. This "annuitiza-tion rate" renders the MGIB much less meaningful.

In our experience, you are never actually permitted to withdraw the MGIB in a lump sum. Rather, you get a monthly benefit that the insurance company calculates based on its annuitization tables.

To fully appreciate why an insurance company cannot legit-imately guarantee 6% per year, you must understand that the investment pie is only so big. In other words, there are not enough investment returns to go around.

By statute, insurance companies' investment portfolios consist mainly of bonds with a small allocation to equities and other asset classes.

The insurance company needs to cover its overhead and turn a profit, so how could it earn the necessary return to cover its costs and generate positive earnings, while still leaving you with the advertised 6% guaranteed return? It simply could not.

Another reason why 6% guaranteed returns are not truly available to investors is because gross commissions to the sellers of variable annuities are often 5% to 10%. Selling a $200,000 annuity can gen-erate a gross commission of $10,000 to $20,000 for the salesperson.

The insurance company must also cover this copious payout with its investments and still maintain profitability.

CLAIM 4: "ANNUITIES ARE TAX-DEFERRED AND THEREFORE EXTREMELY TAX-EFFICIENT."

Once again, there is an element of truth to this statement. The interest, dividends and capital gains within the annuity are tax-deferred. But, when the money is eventually distributed, you get whacked with taxes.

Any appreciation within a variable annuity is taxed as ordinary income when cash is withdrawn after death. On the other hand, more conventional investments offer a step-up in cost basis at death, so that no income or capital gains taxes are due when you transfer stocks and bonds to heirs.

Amazingly, it is not unusual to see a variable annuity within an IRA, which is already a tax-deferred account. This approach is like wearing a belt and suspenders to keep your skinny jeans from falling off.

In debunking these common claims, we are generalizing based on a hodgepodge of variable annuities that we have analyzed for clients over the last ten years. Most annuities that large publically traded insurance companies sell are wildly complex and often have prospectuses that can run to a thousand pages, so a variety of details may be different from what we have described above.

That said, the famous admonition "if it sounds too good to be true, it probably is" still applies, particularly with the majority of variable annuities that we see.

45

A CROWDED TRADE

I n the world of investments, the phrase "crowded trade" is used to describe a security or an investment theme that has attracted an unusually large number of participants.

As an investment idea becomes more and more popular, it attracts greater inflows of capital, but the fun never lasts forever. As contrarian investors, we want to avoid being the last person to arrive at the party.

Over the past ten years, we have witnessed extraordinary turmoil in financial markets, caused by a tech bubble, a real estate bubble, two stock market crashes and a full-blown financial crisis. U.S. equity markets endured a decade of flat returns for the first time since the 1930s.

All of this has driven investors into asset classes that salesmen promote as "safe." Gold has surged. Bond mutual funds have delivered robust returns as interest rates have plummeted to the lowest levels on record. Alternative assets have become all the rage. And variable annuities, insurance-based investments that promise competitive returns with negligible risk, are experiencing vigorous sales. We believe that this phenomenon—the idolization of so-called safe investments—is today's most crowded trade.

185

The most adamant fear mongers are focusing their marketing efforts around concepts like asset preservation, retirement income strategies and tax reduction. These buzzwords tend to be harbingers of a "can't lose" sales pitch that promises absolute safety on the downside while still registering respectable returns on the upside. A detailed analysis of these alleged cure-all products can illustrate that they are contrary to the best interest of clients.

A prime example of advisors peddling such products comes in the story of a market prognosticator named Harry S. Dent, Jr., the producer of a newsletter geared primarily toward financial advisors who are part of his HS Dent Advisors Network.

Dent's predictions, which have swung 180 degrees from intense optimism to extreme pessimism over the past decade, are primarily

> "WE BELIEVE THAT THIS PHENOMENON—THE IDOLIZATION OF SO-CALLED SAFE INVESTMENTS—IS TODAY'S MOST CROWDED TRADE."

based on demographic trends. His present prophecy centers around the aging of the baby boomer population, which he theorizes will lead to a collapse in consumer spending, the largest component of the American economy. Yet just over a decade ago he used the same baby boom demographic arguments to predict a savings-induced economic windfall, which proved stunningly inaccurate.

Mr. Dent's track record indicates the he is an opportunist. Thirteen years ago, in 1998, Dent penned the book, *The Roaring 2000s: Building the Wealth and Lifestyle You Desire in the Greatest Boom in History*. Publishing a book about an imminent stock market boom during the sixth year of the biggest bull market in history undoubtedly helped Dent sell plenty of books. At the time, Dent's bullish outlook confirmed the underlying optimism that existed in America. It probably also helped his followers sell aggressive investment vehicles to clients eager to cash in on the dot-com phenomenon at precisely the wrong time.

Dent's most recent literary effort, published in September, is entitled *The Great Crash Ahead: Strategies for a World Turned Upside Down*. In our experience, financial professionals adhering to Dent today are often pushing variable annuities as they foretell doom and gloom. (Variable annuities come with a variety of claims, but in reality they are frequently low returning, highly complex and extraordinarily expensive.)

Another, albeit less egregious, example of industry salesmanship lies in "absolute return" mutual funds. Although Morningstar does not have a specific category for these vehicles, it has identified roughly three dozen funds that adopted the term, according to *InvestmentNews*. Of these funds, only ten existed just three years ago.

The name "absolute return" is clearly designed to imply positive returns regardless of the market environment. But a successful businessperson will attest, you can only garner meaningful gains when undertaking a degree of risk. Economic history has demonstrated again and again that there is no free lunch.

In the real world, where periodic losses are inevitable, *InvestmentNews* reports that just 4 of the 24 absolute return funds that were around on January 1, 2011 have produced positive performance through September. Once Again, the industry has mass-produced ineffective products to play on the current hysteria among consumers.

Another crowded "trade" is the financial planning profession itself. Today, a sea of advisors with countless credentials, affiliations and specialties seek clients with one ambitious marketing effort after another.

The market for investment advice is among the most confusing in existence for consumers. Our advice is simple—insist on two things—modest fees and a fiduciary standard.

The fiduciary standard, which does apply to registered investment advisors (RIAs) like our firm, requires that we only recommend investments that we believe are in the client's best interest. Furthermore, the fiduciary standard demands that we act with prudence, disclose all material facts (such as disciplinary records), disclose all fees and compensation, control investment expenses and avoid all material conflicts of interest. In the case that a conflict is unavoidable, it must be fully revealed.

Brokers and registered representatives, on the other hand, are subject only to a suitability standard. In other words, as long as a product or transaction is not considered unsuitable, they are generally permitted to put personal and firm interests ahead of the client's.

For example, a broker who recommends a variable annuity for a client is under no obligation to select the lowest-cost, most understandable product in the marketplace. In fact, the broker may choose the most complex product paying the highest commission as long as the variable annuity is considered suitable given the client's circumstances.

According to a survey of 502 RIAs conducted by TD Ameritrade in August, 90% said that they either added new clients or held steady in the past year. More importantly, 29% of these RIAs named the fiduciary standard as the primary reason why they earned the new clients' business, outweighing any other rationale.

In a congested profession with a less-than-stellar reputation, it appears that the fiduciary standard is catching on as a means of ensuring that clients come first.

46

INTEREST IN DIVIDENDS

> "DO YOU KNOW THE ONLY THING THAT GIVES ME PLEASURE? IT'S TO SEE MY DIVIDENDS COMING IN."
>
> JOHN D. ROCKEFELLER

In the world of investments, everything is cyclical. Hot trends inevitably cool off and passé ideas return to popularity. Today, stock dividends have become the latest investment theme to regain favor.

As the last secular bull market was surging in the late 1990s, dividends became a mere afterthought and many analysts even condemned them. Equities were easily achieving double-digit total returns year after year, making dividends seem relatively insignificant. Furthermore, many market professionals suggested that corporations were better served using cash to fund acquisitions and other growth opportunities, a sign of rampant optimism. The logic was that companies had superior internal investment opportunities and to return money to shareholders in the form of a cash dividend was actually a waste. It was the era of the celebrity CEO who could make no bad decisions.

The next twelve years, however, were an entirely different story. Equities entered a "lost decade" of relatively flat returns with the S&P 500 at roughly the same level where it peaked in 2000. And instead of the public considering CEOs to be celebrated allocators of capital, they have gradually become bemoaned fat cats.

Ironically, since 2000, a point in time when dividends were largely ignored, virtually the only return that buy-and-hold equity investors reaped were from dividends. This "reversion to the mean" phenomenon is not unusual, but always unexpected.

Today, dividends are experiencing renewed appeal throughout the investment community. In aggregate, U.S. equity mutual funds suffered $103 billion in redemptions in the 12 months ended January 31, 2012, according to Morningstar. But, nervous investors did not shun dividend stocks. Just last year, mutual funds that focus on dividends attracted $3 billion in inflows and dividend-themed exchange traded funds took in another $14.3 billion. There is often an inverse relationship between mutual fund flows and future performance—positive flows can predict underperformance, while negative flows can suggest outperformance.

Investment companies have identified the opportunity to appeal to yield-starved investors, launching 16 brand new dividend-oriented funds in 2011. Even the Fidelity Equity Income Fund II, which appointed a new manager and increased its exposure to dividend-paying stocks, changed its name to the Fidelity Equity Dividend Income Fund.

Perhaps an interesting sign of the general hunger for dividends is the March 2012 cover of *Investment Advisor* magazine with its headline, "Dividends, Dividends, Dividends!" The assumption among the punditry is that—given below-trend economic growth and, at the same time, strong corporate balance sheets- future returns favor companies that return cash to shareholders.

Despite general enthusiasm, sometimes a contradictory sign, there is actually very sound logic behind dividend stocks. According to

Morningstar, "Since 1927, high-dividend-paying stocks have returned 11% per year, beating the 8% return from nonpayers and resulting in an ending wealth that is 8 times larger. Better yet, they accomplished this feat while incurring less volatility."

Furthermore, Ned Davis Research finds that between 1972 and 2005, S&P 500 stocks that had consistently grown their dividends outperformed the nonpayers by 6%. And presently, the dividend payout ratio (the amount that a corporation distributes in dividends relative to its earnings) is at a historic low of 32 percent. In the past, the average payout ratio has been over 50 percent. This statistic implies that companies have plenty of room to raise their dividends in the years ahead.

Moreover, the tax rate on qualified dividend income—currently 15% for most taxpayers (now 20% for many and even higher for a few)—is at an all-time low.

> "IF THE MARKET PERFORMS WELL OVER THE NEXT SEVERAL YEARS, WHICH IS OUR EXPECTATION, INVESTORS WILL EVENTUALLY TAKE NOTICE AND START CHASING RETURNS. DIVIDEND STOCKS COULD EASILY TRAIL THE OVERALL MARKET IF SENTIMENT IMPROVES."

Finally, bond yields have become so paltry that dividends are an increasingly important source of income. As of today, the yield on the ten-year Treasury stands at 1.97% whereas the dividend yield on the S&P 500 is 1.93% and offers the potential for price appreciation.

Yet, after turning in stellar performance relative to other equities in 2011, dividend stocks have not fared as well through the first two months of 2012. According to Bespoke Investment Group, the stocks in the S&P 500 that pay no dividend have outperformed the 50 stocks in the index with the highest dividends by a whopping 12.03%.

In our opinion, dividend-paying stocks serve an important role in a diversified portfolio. In fact, our managed equity portfolio has a considerably higher average yield than the overall market. But dividends are not a cure-all for apprehensive investors. The consensus seems to be that dividend stocks are sure to hold their value, continue paying healthy yields and offer potential capital gains.

We urge caution that dividend-payers are still equities and carry the risk of loss. And stock dividends are not guaranteed—just ask shareholders in most financial companies during the crisis years of 2007-2009.

Of equal importance, if the market performs well over the next several years, which is our expectation, investors will eventually take notice and start chasing returns. Dividend stocks could easily trail the overall market if sentiment improves. This is an important reason to hold a mix of equities in different businesses and with varying market capitalizations, geographic footprints and dividend levels.

The bull market that began in March of 2009 is now the ninth longest bull market since 1928, but the retail investor has still not returned. For now, dividend paying stocks are the investor's training wheels to get back into the market. But if stocks have a big year of gains, greed can take over and folks may think they are riding in the Tour de France and toss the training wheels.

47

THE FUTURE OF BONDS

For the last thirty years, bond yields have fallen fairly consistently. Consequently, bond prices have risen over this period of time. It is often said that "what goes up must come down," and this is probably the case with bond prices. In an environment where the Federal Reserve has lowered short-term interest rates to zero and engaged in active bond buying (quantitative easing) to push down long-term rates, is the party over for bond holders? Are we about to enter a new super-cycle of rising interest rates that will leave bond investors licking their wounds?

It is interesting to note how stocks and bonds performed during prior super-cycles of rising and falling interest rates.

From 1982, after interest rates peaked, through 2012, the Barclays Capital Aggregate Bond Index returned an average of 8.82% per year. Stocks also did well during this period, with the S&P 500 returning 11.14% per year, but with far more drama, especially from 2000 until now. Therefore, purely from a "sleep at night" perspective, owning bonds for the last thirty years served investors well, even though stocks actually did better.

According to Craig L. Israelsen, an associate professor at Brigham Young University, the federal discount rate (which the Federal Reserve sets) was 1.34% in 1948, similar to today. Over the next thirty-three years, this rate climbed somewhat steadily to 13.42% in 1981—reflective of a prolonged and dramatic increase in interest rates. During this time, the Barclays Capital Aggregate Bond Index provided an average annual return of only 3.83%. Meanwhile, the S&P 500 returned 11% annually during this period of rising rates.

In other words, stocks did well during a prolonged period of rising rates (1948–1981) and falling rates (1982–2012). Bonds, however, delivered significantly lower returns when interest rates were on the rise.

Using a slightly different time period when interest rates increased dramatically, 1941 to 2009, Fidelity Investments calculated a 3.3% per year return for Treasury bonds. However, after backing out an average annual inflation rate of 4.6% over the period, the real return for Treasury bonds was -1.3% per year.

This does not mean, however, that bonds should be irrelevant to investors. The chart below shows that even in a rising rate environment (1941 to 1981), bonds lowered overall portfolio volatility (standard deviation). A 100% stock portfolio from 1941 to 1981 returned 11% with a standard deviation of 14%. Adding just 20% to bonds reduced overall return by about 9%, but volatility dropped by more than 20%.

Given the present depressed level of interest rates, we can infer three things from the last 70 years of history: 1) Bonds should experience below average returns and probably will not outpace inflation over the next several decades, 2) Bonds still have a place in the portfolios of risk-averse investors as a hedge against volatility and 3) Stocks will likely dramatically outperform bonds over the long-term.

48

THE ROAD TAKEN

> "TWO ROADS DIVERGED IN A WOOD, AND I—I TOOK
> THE ONE LESS TRAVELED BY, AND THAT HAS MADE
> ALL THE DIFFERENCE."
>
> *FROM THE ROAD NOT TAKEN,*
> *ROBERT FROST, 1916*

In the spring of 2011, inflation expectations were high with commodity prices soaring and gold spiking. At that time, Federal Reserve Chairman Ben Bernanke described these inflationary forces as transient. Not too many people believed him.

A large number of diversified investment managers that implement a tactical asset allocation strategy increased their exposure to commodities—an inflation hedge—around this very time.

The 2011 drift to "alternative investments," mainly commodity-centric ones, has been a regrettable asset allocation decision for many managers. The Goldman Sachs Commodity Index has plummeted nearly 20% from its April 4, 2011 near-term high; while the price of gold has collapsed by more than 25% since its August 29, 2011 peak.

As a matter of fact, the overall trend among professional investors to avoid traditional U.S. stocks for the last several years has been disastrous. Not only have managers emphasized commodities as an alternative investment, but they have also stressed "less volatile" vehicles because of an innate fear of markets. Lo and behold, the experts largely abandoned the most conventional investment vehicle at the wrong time.

Through the end of May, the Standard and Poor's 500, an index of essentially the largest U.S. companies, has gained an average annual return of 16.87% over the last three years. Compare this to the afore-mentioned Goldman Sachs Commodity Index (energy, agricultural, metals, etc.), which returned just 4.79% annually over the same period.

> "THIS IS ASTONISHING ONLY IN THAT A PASSIVE GROUP OF ORDINARY STOCKS DRAMATICALLY OUTPERFORMED COUNTLESS MIT PHDs AND HARVARD MBAs RUNNING HEDGE FUNDS."

Furthermore, the Hedge Fund Research International Fund Weighted Composite Index, a measure that includes about 2,200 constituent hedge funds of all varieties, returned 5.03% per year over these three years. This is astonishing only in that a passive group of ordinary stocks dramatically outperformed countless MIT PhDs and Harvard MBAs running hedge funds.

At the root of the mistake of underinvesting in the most traditional of asset classes (U.S. stocks) lay both sophisticated and simple reasoning.

Most basically, many investment managers looked at which asset classes performed the best in the five years prior to the financial crisis and assumed this outperformance would continue indefinitely, leading them to hedge funds, emerging markets, international bonds and commodities. This analysis lacked the intellectual firepower of the most sophisticated asset managers, but the conclusions were the same.

The complex reasons for a forecast of below average U.S. stock performance stemmed from five major themes, all interrelated, that have yet to manifest themselves. In our view, most major asset management organizations held these opinions and, as such, these views were the consensus forecast.

First, an expectation of inflation, and the repositioning of portfolios to reflect this anticipation, is the leading spoiler of investment performance for broadly diversified wealth advisors who implement a tactical asset allocation strategy. After much fretting over central bank money printing—Bloomberg calculates that there have been 511 easing actions by central banks since June 2007—inflation has yet to materialize.

Subdued inflation has allowed the United States Federal Reserve to keep short-term interest rates at 0%, while also purchasing $85 billion a month in long-term Treasury bonds and mortgage paper to suppress rates. The ten-year Treasury bond pays 2.161%, while a thirty-year mortgage fetches 3.53%—extraordinarily low rates. Therefore, the second prediction, which is part and parcel with the first, was that the Fed would not be able to maintain its amazingly accommodative policies this long, but they most certainly have.

Because most thought inflation would occur by now and because they then surmised the Fed would need to raise rates, experts have been broadly bearish on stocks. The third mistake then, rather than allocating more dollars to stocks, managers have instead pushed more and more money into alternative investments, which have lagged core U.S. stocks significantly.

Ordinarily such low interest rates and a highly accommodative Federal Reserve would typically result in a weak dollar, the fourth common prognostication. But, thus far, the dollar has strengthened—and markedly so over the last six months. As a result, foreign stocks and commodities (because you can buy more of them with fewer dollars) have been laggards.

And finally, the fifth misstep was the assumption that slow U.S. economic growth would result in lackluster stock market returns. Although seemingly logical, in reality there is little short or intermediate-term correlation between gross domestic product (GDP) growth and stock market returns. With the United States consistently delivering below-trend economic growth over the last three years, the U.S. stock market has produced above average returns—much of which the Federal Reserve has made possible with its aggressive actions. This takes us back to the first mistake...

19

FAUX-SOPHISTICATION

> "THAT'S BEEN ONE OF MY MANTRAS—FOCUS
> AND SIMPLICITY. SIMPLE CAN BE HARDER THAN
> COMPLEX: YOU HAVE TO WORK HARD TO GET YOUR
> THINKING CLEAN TO MAKE IT SIMPLE. BUT IT'S
> WORTH IT IN THE END BECAUSE ONCE YOU GET
> THERE, YOU CAN MOVE MOUNTAINS."
>
> STEVE JOBS,
> 1998 *BUSINESS WEEK* INTERVIEW

We have written extensively over the last five years about the effectiveness of a simple, understandable, transparent and low-cost investment philosophy. The way we invest, which we outlined for the first time in September 2008, stems from the discomfort we experienced while watching our industry slip into darkness. Luckily, our timing could not have been better.

For the five years ending September 30, 2013, the most basic index of American stocks, the Standard and Poor's 500, doubled the annualized performance of the Hedge Fund Research Incorporated Fund Weighted Composite Index—10.02% versus 5.01%. This means that a passive basket of U.S. stocks dramatically outperformed the sophisticated, "go anywhere" strategies that the most brilliant practitioners on Wall Street conceived.

Lately we have fielded several inquiries about alternative investment strategies as a way to manage risk. It seems to us that despite all the evidence to the contrary, investors are still searching for something that doesn't exist—a formula to sidestep market losses while also getting a better return than bonds currently offer.

> "DESPITE ALL THE EVIDENCE TO THE CONTRARY, INVESTORS ARE STILL SEARCHING FOR SOMETHING THAT DOESN'T EXIST—A FORMULA TO SIDESTEP MARKET LOSSES WHILE ALSO GETTING A BETTER RETURN THAN BONDS CURRENTLY OFFER."

And this impossible quest is not limited to individual investors. *The New York Times* recently reported that "so-called alternative investments now account for almost one-quarter of the roughly $2.6 trillion in public pension assets under management nationwide, up from 10 percent in 2006, according to Cliffwater, an adviser to institutional investors."

The Rhode Island pension plan, for example, has increased its investments in alternatives from zero to almost $2 billion, or 25% of its assets, in the last two years. The result has been poor performance and outrageous fees. Their investment expenses for the year ended June 30th were $70 million versus a prior estimate of $11.5 million, primary due to alternative investments that charge up to 2.5% annually of assets under management plus another 20% of profits.

In reference to individual stock investing, the legendary Fidelity Magellan Fund manager, Peter Lynch, said, "The simpler it is, the better I like it." We think this sentiment applies to investing in general. You can observe a great example of this in 2008, a terrible year for the stock market, and the ensuing market recovery in 2009.

In 2008, the S&P 500 fell a whopping 37%. But, interestingly, the Barclays U.S. Aggregate Bond Index actually rose 5.24% that year. So, if you had a 50% stock and 50% bond portfolio, you would have lost 15.88%. Not good, but far from devastating.

Then in 2009, the S&P 500 rose 26.46% and the Barclays U.S. Aggregate Bond Index rose 5.93%. The same 50 / 50 portfolio would have gained 16.20%. If the portfolio was rebalanced annually, then less than a year removed from the financial crisis and Great Recession, an investor in a plain vanilla balanced portfolio would have almost fully recouped all losses.

Lastly, in 2010, the same 50 / 50 portfolio would have generated 10.8% returns, putting the portfolio back in the black and well-positioned for robust returns in the years since. (Even without annual rebalancing, a 50 / 50 portfolio would have produced positive three-year returns from 2008 through 2010.)

As evidenced above, risk mitigation techniques do not need to be fancy, overly complex or expensive. Frankly, in our experience, the more esoteric these schemes, the less effective they are. Make no mistake, finding the proper allocation to high-quality bonds to complement your stock exposure is the best risk management strategy—it is straightforward, transparent and low-cost.

The chart below shows that even during a protracted bear market for bonds (1941-1981)—a time when interest rates rose and bonds prices fell—they still proved an excellent risk manager. The standard deviation (a statistical measure of variation around the mean) for a 50% stock / 50% bond portfolio was half that of an all-stock portfolio, or half the risk.

Ignoring the advice of Leonardo de Vinci that "Simplicity is the ultimate sophistication," many risk-averse investors will buy anything,

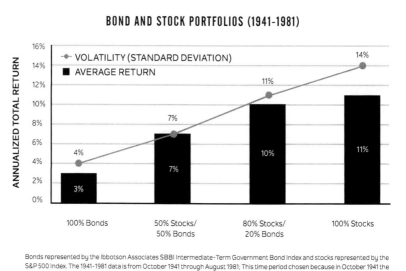

Bonds represented by the Ibbotson Associates SBBI Intermediate-Term Government Bond Index and stocks represented by the S&P 500 Index. The 1941-1981 data is from October 1941 through August 1981; This time period chosen because in October 1941 the yield on the IA SBBI Intermediate-Term Government Bond Index hit a low of 0.51% and in August 1981 the yield hit a peak of 16.4%. Source: Ibbotson Associates, FMRCo (MARE) as of 5/25/10. Past performance is no guarantee of future results.

as long as it sounds sophisticated, regardless of whether they understand it. Or maybe the fact that they don't understand it gives a certain level of comfort—if it's that complicated, it must be good!

The old economic axiom, "There's no such thing as a free lunch," provides a cautionary message to people looking to manage risk via magic trick. Investors are naïve to believe strategies actually exist that can consistently shuffle money from one asset class to another with precision, or predict which stocks will spike over the short-term even when the market declines, or that can use options to truly protect against the downside without considerable cost, etc.

The martial artist and movie star Bruce Lee believed that, "It is not a daily increase, but a daily decrease. Hack away at the inessentials." From an investment standpoint, be honest with yourself about what you are trying to accomplish. Don't subscribe to the myth that a black box exists that will protect you from high stock prices and low bond yields. Instead, avoid the temptation to purchase investments that are supposedly sophisticated enough to outperform the tried and true.

A final thought from Peter Lynch: "All the math you need in the stock market you get in the fourth grade." This may sound unreasonable, but it's surely true. A real investment discipline will outperform all of the gimmicks.

50

THE STOCK MARKET
IS RIGGED

"STOCK MARKET'S RIGGED. THE UNITED STATES
STOCK MARKET, THE MOST ICONIC MARKET IN
GLOBAL CAPITALISM, IS RIGGED."

AUTHOR MICHAEL LEWIS,
ON *60 MINUTES*, MARCH 30, 2014

L ast Sunday, *60 Minutes* Correspondent Steve Kroft profiled author
Michael Lewis and his new book, Flash Boys, which tells the story
of high-frequency traders and their millisecond "front-running"
of stock trades on American exchanges. This story was brimming with
hyperbole and was designed to generate buzz and sell books. In our
opinion, true long-term investors have nothing to fear.

Simply put, high-speed traders intercept information about
imminent stock trades and use advanced computers, algorithms and
telecommunications to execute orders in their house accounts and
make incremental profits.

As a basic example, the computer might see a buy order transmitted by a mutual fund for 500,000 shares of Microsoft stock. More quickly than you can blink, the computer would buy the stock before the mutual fund's order hits the exchange and then sell it back to the mutual fund at a slightly higher price, booking a small profit.

Presently, high-speed trading accounts for 50% of market volume, but this figure is down from 66% in 2008. It is our view that this percentage will continue to fall in the coming years. As the strategies become more sophisticated, competition and innovation will squeeze inefficiencies from the market, making it more difficult to turn a profit from high-frequency trading.

A vital detail that the *60 Minutes* story mentioned only once is that high-speed traders generally add just one or two cents to the price of a share of stock. While this may seem inherently unfair to viewers of the segment, *60 Minutes* exaggerated the severity of the problem with words and phrases like "rigged," "ripped off," "bait and switched," "illegal," and "shocking."

In the segment, the protagonist of *Flash Boys* went so far as to offer this embellished analogy: "You go onto StubHub, there's four tickets all next to each other for 20 bucks each. You put in an order to buy four tickets, 20 bucks each, and it says, 'You've bought two tickets at 20 bucks each.' And you go back and those same two tickets that are sitting there have now gone up to $25."

In reality, if a mutual fund puts in an order for shares of Microsoft, the first half might get filled at $41.35 and the next half might get filled at $41.36. In other words, there is a substantial difference between the 25% price increase in the ticket analogy and the 0.024% increase in an actual equity trade. And if you own Microsoft for ten years, collect the dividend and then sell the stock for, say, $90, does that extra penny you paid really matter?

The most galling aspect of the story is the utter dismissal of the liquidity benefits that high-frequency traders may bring to the marketplace. In theory, if high-speed traders currently represent half of market volume, it would seem logical that they help ensure that orders get filled quickly. In reality, nobody knows the ultimate impact of high-speed trading. What we do know, however, is that with high-speed traders in the market, it has never been less expensive to purchase shares of stock. Since we started in the investment business, transaction costs have done nothing but fall.

And looking back several decades, according to Charles Schwab, buying 1,000 shares of AT&T in 1975 would have cost $800 in commissions. Today it costs $7.95 through our firm's custodian—one hundredth of the price.

> "THE *60 MINUTES* PIECE MENTIONS NOTHING ABOUT THE CONTINUOUSLY FALLING COST OF TRANSACTING IN THE MARKET. BUT, IT DOES CITE A DUBIOUS EXAMPLE OF THE COSTS TO 'INVESTORS' FROM HIGH-SPEED TRADING."

Before high-speed traders, "specialists" and "market makers" provided the daily liquidity that makes the market function. When specialists and market makers dominated, stocks didn't trade in decimals or cents, but rather in 1/8ths and 1/16ths. The spread between the "bid" and "ask" on a stock trade was usually 1/16th, which is equal to six and a quarter cents. In other words, the "decimalization" of trades helped tighten spreads and, along with cheaper commissions, contributed to lower trading costs.

The *60 Minutes* piece mentions nothing about the continuously falling cost of transacting in the market. But, it does cite a dubious example of the costs to "investors" from high-speed trading.

According to Michael Lewis, a hedge fund managing $9 billion estimated that high-speed traders cost it $300 million in a year. But without any context, this example is meaningless. Is this hedge fund trading in equities? Using the penny a share figure and assuming the average stock trades at $40 per share, then this fund would have needed to generate $1.2 trillion in trades, a sum 133 times the size of the hedge fund itself. Or is this hedge fund day-trading in options and derivatives? If this is the case, perhaps the $300 million cost is accurate, but the *60 Minutes* piece was purported to be about the stock market.

Rather than proving that the market is rigged and high-speed traders are thieves, this example only illustrates the tremendous costs associated with hedge funds and why they ultimately underperform over full market cycles. The $300 million figure is 3% of the fund's value and most hedge funds charge fees of 2% of assets under management and 20% of profits. So you are more than 5% in the hole before the fund even starts implementing its investment strategy. And if the fund happens to have net gains, they are probably of a short-term nature, so high income earners could lose 20% of the profits to the fund managers and almost 50% to taxes.

High-speed trading is certainly not without risk. Our heavy reliance on information technology in all fields—from aviation to medicine to markets—makes us vulnerable to the occasional catastrophe. Moreover, some of the specific tactics that high-frequency traders employ probably violate ethical standards or even the law.

But if the stock market is rigged, it is rigged in favor of fundamental, disciplined and patient investors because it discourages excessive and wasteful trading. High-speed trading does no meaningful damage to long-term investors.

51

FEE-USUALLY

The Certified Financial Planner Board of Standards, a certification body, dictates that CFP® practitioners may use the term "fee-only" if they solely collect fees for advice and they do not own or work for a financial services business that charges commissions—even if the advisors themselves do not receive commissions.

The CFP Board recently investigated its own board chairman, Alan Goldfarb, over his compensation. Goldfarb disclosed his compensation as "fee-only" and "salary" and claimed that his salary stemmed exclusively from fee-only activities. However, he was drawing his salary from a wealth management concern, whose parent company owns a broker-dealer (a commission-generating enterprise) of which Goldfarb owned 1%.

The Board sanctioned Goldfarb, asked for his board resignation and he ultimately departed his firm—all fallout from his inaccurate compensation disclosure. Although this may seem draconian, the purity of the fee-only concept is crucial to its success.

Independent fee-only advice is resonating with consumers and brokers are taking notice. Unfortunately, too many advisors now claim to be fee-only just because they have access to a few fee-based products when they are still affiliated with a broker-dealer. But unless the advisor collects commissions in one capacity or another, there isn't much reason to have a broker-dealer affiliation. Even if an advisor within a broker-dealer-associated firm uses fee-based products, the firm still collects commissions and major conflicts of interest exist.

Commissions are a difficult temptation from which to turn. For example, a retiree with a $500,000 401(k) rollover might find a commission-driven advisor seeking to sell a variable annuity to provide "guaranteed" returns with limited downside ("Variable Annuities: A False Panacea," see page 181). The advisor may or may not mention the potential $50,000 gross upfront payout from the sale.

In our opinion, for the vast majority of people, the variable annuity is the most inappropriate and abused product our industry has ever devised. The risk of falling for a good sales story and buying a variable annuity is one reason to stay away from a commission-based planner.

In the world of financial planning, commissions are inherently dangerous, almost by definition. When an advisor can choose from a wide variety of products to present to you, they will undoubtedly consider how much the product pays them before making a recommendation. The degree to which the commission factors into this recommendation may vary based on the integrity of the advisor, but it clearly shrouds the advice in a cloud of doubt. Is the advisor having a rough month and needing a boost from a fat commission? Or is this really the best investment for your personal goals and risk tolerance?

Commissions are also front-loaded, so it might take a fee-only planner anywhere from three to ten years to earn commensurate compensation. Clearly then, the fee-only advisor has a much better incentive for a strong long-term relationship. Furthermore, fee-only planners who charge a percentage of assets under management have an incentive to grow your account over time as their compensation is directly tied to your continued success and not an upfront commission check. The fee-only structure is much more transparent, allowing you to truly understand what you are paying.

The actual legal standards for true fee-only planners are different from those of commissioned planners, or brokers. Brokers are required to follow a suitability standard. Under suitability, the recommended product doesn't have to be in the best interests of the client. The product just has to be suitable—in other words, satisfactory. For example, given two available annuities with different underlying annual fees, the advisor may sell the more expensive product without fear of repercussion.

On the other hand, regulators hold fee-only advisors to a fiduciary

> "COMMISSIONS ARE ALSO FRONT-LOADED, SO IT MIGHT TAKE A FEE-ONLY PLANNER ANYWHERE FROM THREE TO TEN YEARS TO EARN COMMENSURATE COMPENSATION."

standard, meaning they have a legal requirement to act in the client's best interest. As such, they must only offer advice that they believe is of the highest quality. In our view, this creates an environment of much greater consistency where instant gratification takes a backseat to enduring performance.

Because the opportunity for rip-offs is so rampant in the broker-dealer world, the compliance requirement for these operations is onerous. Unfortunately, like much government regulation, the compliance misses the forest for the trees. You can sell someone a terribly expensive and totally incomprehensible variable annuity as long as you fill out enough forms.

Just as counterproductive, this compliance handcuffs even the best commission planners from offering straightforward advice because their internal overseers are frequently unwilling to document simple, understandable recommendations. Rather, institutions prefer noncommittal and impenetrable ideas, regarding these as less hazardous from a liability standpoint.

As a matter of course, commissioned planners need to devote time to earning their next commission rather than managing their client's portfolio. Therefore, the advisor outsources the portfolio's management and moves onto the next commission.

Many clients have a true need for certain commission-based products, such as life, disability and long-term care insurance. For many high net worth individuals, these products are vital to protecting business and family interests. When considering insurance, we strongly advise collaboration with a fee-only financial planner, attorney and / or accountant to ensure the purity of the advice.

52

STILL A THING?

On HBO's weekly "faux news" program *Last Week Tonight*, John Oliver occasionally delivers a segment in which he poses the question, "How is this still a thing?" In one episode, the show pokes fun at the Commonwealth Games, an athletic event open only to members of the British Commonwealth. "Well, imagine the Olympics without the United States, China and Russia, then imagine a track meet dominated by sprinters from Wales...," the show's announcer quips.

After reading recent statistics about variable annuity sales, we began wondering, "How are variable annuities still a thing?"

Despite unflattering press and mind-numbing complexity, many financial advisors continue to peddle variable annuities. In 2013, consumers purchased $145 billion of these contracts, a slight decrease from the prior year but still impressive.

A common saying in the investment industry is that "annuities aren't bought—they're sold." And with commissions of up to 10% (paid directly to the advisor from the insurance company), it's easy to see why advisors continue to promote them. And consumers often succumb to their "sleep-at-night" appeal that promises gains if the stock market rises or a minimum guaranteed return should the market falter.

In reality, however, these products are almost invariably low-returning, highly complex and extraordinarily expensive.

According to Bloomberg, Prudential's Jackson National Life unit extended its lead in U.S. variable annuity sales through the first six months of the year, selling $12.7 billion in VA contracts.

Jackson National's flagship product is the "Elite Access" variable annuity. If you are an experienced contracts lawyer with a PhD in finance and plenty of time on your hands, a perusal of its 692-page prospectus reveals a yearly contract fee of 1% and average annual underlying sub-account expenses of 1.18%. But because this product touts its access to "alternative investments"—an asset class that is dramatically more expensive than traditional investment vehicles—sub-account expenses can run as high as 2.45% annually. And to avoid the surrender charges that range from 6.5% to 3% if you have buyer's remorse and pull your funds over the first five contract years, the "liquidity option" tacks on another 0.25% annual expense. Therefore, based on the average sub-account fees, total annual expenses would be 2.43% (but can easily run as high as 3.7%).

But the most vexing characteristic of variable annuities is the so-called "guaranteed" minimum return, often set at 5%. It is important to understand the financial impossibility of guaranteeing this level of return. To earn 5% net of the 2.43% fee calculated above, the annuity's underlying investments would need to average at least 7.43% gross returns—not an easy task in and of itself. Remember that insurance companies, by statute, are investing their "float" (i.e. policy premiums) primarily in bonds in an environment where the 30-year Treasury only yields 3.04%. Not only don't insurance companies have access to magic investments that guarantee lofty returns, but the law requires them to invest a majority of their assets in high quality bonds.

In reality, the guaranteed return applies to a fairy tale value that can only be annuitized at a future date—not simply withdrawn in a lump sum. And the insurance company gets to determine the future annuitization rate. In the end, the insurance company and the financial advisor are the real winners.

We strongly urge our clients to avoid variable annuities in nearly every scenario. If you already own one, we encourage you to engage us to review your statement and the prospectus. In some cases, it makes sense to terminate the variable annuity. In other situations where termination would trigger tax ramifications or surrender charges, another plan of action may be appropriate. For example, most contracts allow a 10% annual withdrawal that is free from surrender charges. In addition, our custodian, Fidelity Investments, offers a variable annuity "wrapper" that maintains the investment's tax-deferral but only carries a 0.25% annual fee.

53

INDEXING IS ALL
THE RAGE

Since 2006 investors have pulled more than $700 billion from actively managed U.S. stock funds and added an equivalent amount to index mutual and exchange-traded funds. As of year-end 2014, Empirical Research Partners found that index funds account for 35% of total stock "fund" assets (combined mutual and exchange traded funds), up from 25% in 2010.

To be sure, so-called "passively" managed funds have a cost advantage to "actively" managed mutual funds. Morningstar reports that the average actively managed U.S. stock fund has an expense ratio of 1.24% versus 0.73% for an index fund. Furthermore, since passively managed index funds were originally designed to mirror the holdings in a static index, they offer lower turnover and should be more tax-efficient. And most active fund managers have a long history of failing to outperform their respective benchmark indexes—a point that has been widely discussed in the financial media.

But indexing has been around for many years and has always had its advantages, so why are people so aggressively flocking to indexes right now?

215

The answer, we believe, is a familiar one—performance chasing. Over the last five years, a Standard and Poor's 500 Index Fund has dramatically outperformed the "endowment model" of investing and, as such, more and more investors are looking to index funds to accomplish their goals.

The endowment model of investing, which most financial advisors and wealth managers adopted over the last decade, is based on broad diversification across numerous asset classes and a variety of managers. For example, a relatively conventional portfolio of this type might include 30% in U.S. large cap stocks, 5% in U.S. small cap

> "OVER THE LAST FIVE YEARS, A STANDARD AND POOR'S 500 INDEX FUND HAS DRAMATICALLY OUTPERFORMED THE 'ENDOWMENT MODEL' OF INVESTING AND, AS SUCH, MORE AND MORE INVESTORS ARE LOOKING TO INDEX FUNDS TO ACCOMPLISH THEIR GOALS."

stocks, 20% in international (including emerging markets), 15% in U.S. core bonds, 5% in real estate, 5% in commodities and 20% in hedge funds. Over the last five years, this portfolio would have returned around 9.57% per year versus a return of 14.47% per year for the S&P 500, as of March 31, 2015.

Today when people say indexing is better, they are often referring to an S&P index fund. But it's not that simple. The S&P is not always the superior index. For example, from 1995 through 1999, the large capitalization S&P 500 more than doubled the performance of the small cap Russell 2000 index. But, from 2000 through 2004, in the wake of the tech stock bubble, the Russell did almost five times better than the S&P 500. The same performance rotation occurs among other asset classes as well. Sometimes emerging markets, real estate or commodities shine and sometimes they slump; hence, the concept behind the presently waning endowment model.

If you accept the idea that broad-based diversification is best because the S&P 500 will not always be the leading index, and you believe in using index funds to fill various asset classes, then you still need to decide how to weight the portfolio. Should emerging market stocks be 5%, 10% or 15% of the portfolio? Should you include any commodity exposure? What about real estate and, if so, what kind of real estate, etc.? This is a potentially never-ending deliberation, especially because fund companies are inventing new index funds on a regular basis. The point here is that "indexing" is not nearly as simple as buying an index fund.

To further compound the problem, it is becoming increasingly difficult to even define an index fund. For example, consider the iShares MSCI USA Minimum Volatility ETF. This fund "seeks to track the investment results of an index composed of U.S. equities that, in the aggregate, have lower volatility characteristics relative to the broader U.S. equity market."

Sounds good, but just because a stock has displayed less volatility in the past, will it continue to do so? Isn't an investor more likely to be attracted to this fund when markets are experiencing fear and are thereby poised to offer above-average returns? And is this fund a replacement for another broad U.S. market index like the Wilshire 5000 or the S&P 1500 or the Russell 3000 or merely a compliment?

"Indexing" can offer as many questions as answers. In addition to low-volatility index funds like the example above, fund companies have devised categories including leverage, equal-weighted, dividend-weighted, earnings-weighted and more. Certainly all of these new iterations of the index fund have blurred the line between active and passive management.

A leveraged ETF, for example, promises to return a multiple of a certain index, such as three times the returns of the Russell 1000 Financial Services Index. This particular fund is called the Direxion

Shares ETF Trust—Direxion Daily Financial Bull 3x. Notice the word "daily" in the fund's name. The reason is that the fund only tracks the index (by a multiple of three) if you buy it and sell it every day. Although it seems absurd, if you don't buy and sell this fund daily, it will not even come close to tracking the index (even directionally). Although this fund should only appeal to a day-trading speculator, it is important to recognize that many advisor-built ETF portfolios include gimmicky funds as a way to differentiate the portfolio and make clients feel like they have a complex strategy.

Traditional indexing's greatest triumph is that it has opened investors' eyes to the importance of fees, turnover, tax-efficiency and diversification. Although paradoxical, we continue to believe a portfolio of individual securities offers all the benefits of indexing. Our individual stock and bond portfolios avoid the second layer of product-level fees inherent in portfolios of actively managed funds. And our buy-and-hold approach limits turnover and improves tax efficiency. Additionally, our basket of stocks is diversified across a wide variety of industries and geographies. Finally, owning individual stocks offers investors the transparency they deserve. When it comes to buying individual securities at fair prices to hold for the long-term versus choosing which indexes to own and in what weights, we subscribe to the idea that it is "better the devil you know than the devil you don't."

54

REALIZING VALUE

> "OUT OF CLUTTER, FIND SIMPLICITY. FROM DISCORD, FIND HARMONY. IN THE MIDDLE OF DIFFICULTY LIES OPPORTUNITY."
>
> ALBERT EINSTEIN

From 1970 through 2014, large cap value stocks outperformed large cap growth stocks by 2.4% per year with an average annual return for value of 10.7% versus 8.3% for growth, according to Morningstar. Furthermore, since 1926, value beats growth in roughly three out of every five years, according to Bank of America Merrill Lynch.

More recently, however, value stocks have fallen on hard times. Since the beginning of 2009, growth has outperformed value by about 3.5% per year, based on Standard & Poor's 500 Growth versus Value indices.

Experts categorize growth stocks as having a high rate of earnings and sales growth, elevated price-to-book and price-to-earnings ratios and these stocks usually pay low or no dividends. Value stocks, on the other hand, have the opposite characteristics—slow growth of sales and earnings, low price-to-book values and price-to-earnings ratios, higher dividend yields and are often turnaround opportunities.

An interesting aspect of the outperformance of growth in this bull market is that these robust returns are in direct contrast to the advice many market pros offered coming out of the bear market, which was to tread carefully and buy dividend-paying stocks as a hedge against market turmoil.

Historically, over long time periods, value has consistently outperformed growth. As most know, though, investing is a cyclical proposition. Due to the overwhelming outperformance of growth over value of late, we know that eventually the tide will turn, the historical relationship will revert to its mean and more reasonably priced stocks will offer superior returns.

New leadership often comes from market turmoil. The current skittishness in stocks may well foretell a shift in performance from growth to value.

Over the last six years, growth has led because the overall advance of the economy has lagged in comparison with past economic expansions. This lag in aggregate economic growth led investors to prefer individual companies that have been increasing their sales and profits despite the tepid economy.

With worldwide economic expansion a seemingly enduring problem near-term, especially with the slowdown in China and other emerging economies, why wouldn't investors continue to prefer growth over value? Quite simply, growth has become too expensive and value stocks have become too cheap.

The S&P 500 Growth index has a price-to-earnings ratio of 21.41 compared to its value counterpart at 15.48, its price-to-book is 4.12 versus 1.86 for value and its dividend yield is 1.46% versus 2.42%. So, by these measures, growth stocks are anywhere between 38% and 121% more expensive than value stocks. This is a hefty premium.

Looking at the components of growth and value indices is also telling. Technology (including social media and Internet) and bio-technology companies have heavy weightings in the growth index, whereas energy, financial and traditional telecom have large weights in the value index.

Clearly the darlings of the market over the last six years have been stocks like Apple, Google, Amazon, Netflix, Gilead, and Allergen—growth stocks.

The laggards have been value names like Exxon Mobil, Chevron, J.P. Morgan Chase, Bank of America and AT&T.

An interesting factor in the growth versus value interplay is the effect that interest rates may have. In a recent Barron's article, Dartmouth economist Jonathan Lewellen compared growth and value indices during the five periods since 1983 when interest rates were rising and found that value returned 14.4% on an annualized basis compared to just 8.3% for growth stocks. In the six months leading up to the rate increases, however, growth had slightly outperformed value stocks.

Although the U.S. Federal Reserve decided last Thursday to continue their Zero Interest Rate Policy (ZIRP), citing recent market turmoil, an interest rate hike in the next several months is likely. If history is any indication, perhaps rising rates will coincide with an overdue transition in leadership from growth to value stocks?

Market shifts are often plodding, but historical relationships endure. We don't know for sure when the value segment of the market will again outperform, but we believe current valuation relationships are stretched.

55

WE THOUGHT SO

W e've been writing to you for many years about the flaws that we see in the "manager-of-managers" model of investing. In this model, wealth management and financial advisory firms build portfolios by choosing the "best" managers for various asset classes. In our minds, this practice is nothing more than performance-chasing.

An important new academic study, "The Harm in Selecting Funds That Have Recently Outperformed," offers empirical evidence that, indeed, the modern heuristic of building "best-of-breed" investment portfolios leads to poor performance.

Without a doubt, although other factors are involved, practitioners of the manager-of-managers approach replace funds that have underperformed with those that have outperformed. We'd venture to say that never has an advisor told a client that they were getting rid of a manager who has outperformed in favor of a manager who has underperformed because such a strategy would be unacceptable to most clients.

Such is the classic example of an agency conflict. It is easier for an advisor to "sell" a client on a fund that has done well versus trying

222

to persuade a client to purchase a fund that has done poorly. The conflict arises because the better advice is to purchase the fund that has performed poorly.

Analyzing the performance of mutual funds from January 1994 to December 2015, the study's authors identified the funds that performed in the top ten percent for a three year period versus the funds that performed in the bottom decile over the same three year period. They then compared subsequent three year performance and found that the bottom ten percent funds outperformed the top decile funds by 2.36% per year. In other words, the "worst" managers were found to have substantially outperformed the "best" managers.

Looking at this another way, the study "fired" or replaced managers that had underperformed their benchmark by 3% (cumulative) over a three year period and kept all the other managers (those that did not underperform by 3%). In this situation, the "fired" managers outperformed the "kept" managers by 1.06% per year. The damage in this context is less because, although the advisor's firing of the "bad" manager clearly hurt performance, the advisor doesn't compound the mistake by hiring an outperforming manager who subsequently underperforms.

To us, this study is fascinating. The manager-of-managers approach to portfolio management is horribly flawed. The study finds that, "If past performance is used at all in selecting funds, it is the best-performing funds that should be replaced. Realistically, however, a policy of replacing successful funds with poor performers is unlikely to gain widespread acceptance." The authors further state that, "While a contrarian approach to manager selection might seem ridiculous at first blush, leading thinkers have long advocated a contrarian approach to buying stocks."

And this is one of the reasons why we have long advocated for an individual stock portfolio over a mutual fund portfolio. As investors in individual companies, we are quite comfortable purchasing quality stocks that have underperformed. Investing in out-of-favor areas of the market at a discount leads to better returns as performance tends to revert to a mean.

So if past performance isn't a credible indicator of future performance, then what is? The study's authors point to various recent research papers that have been successful in predicting future performance. Here are a few of the criterion, along with our thoughts about how they relate to our investment approach:

- "performance-linked bonuses in fund manager compensation packages"—Our compensation is overwhelmingly dependent on the performance of client accounts. We charge a fee based on a percentage of assets under management, so we need to grow client accounts to grow our compensation.

- "a high level of fund manager ownership"—We personally invest in the same companies as our clients and manage our own accounts just as we manage client accounts—as the saying goes, we eat our own cooking.

- "a high active share"—This means that the positions we own in portfolios have a substantially higher weight (or concentration) in our portfolio than they do in a relevant index and that is certainly the case with all of our holdings.

- "lack of affiliation with an investment bank"—We are completely independent, which makes our investment process pure and assures no one is unduly influencing us.

Investing isn't about the next big winner; rather it is all about process. Although one could consider our process boring, stubborn or even obstinate, we think that is exactly what one should want in an investment process.

56

ROBO ADVISORS

The investment website Investopedia defines robo advisors as "an online wealth management service that provides automated, algorithm-based portfolio management advice without the use of human financial planners." Robo advisor sites tout themselves as tax-efficient, low-cost and hassle free. Interestingly, these are the same attributes we have been promoting since we began working with clients independently in September 2008.

Given this seeming incongruity, when thinking about robo advisors it is most important to look at what they aren't versus what they are.

Clients with proactive advisors are 20 times more confident about the future than clients without advisors. This study didn't include robo advisors (very few high net worth people use robo advisors). The reason for this is that most investors experience trouble during difficult times because without an advisor, investors generally don't have a disciplined process. And even more vital, they don't have anybody to offer reassurance using facts and experience during tough times in the market. Robo advisors won't be much help to people during the next major bear market, we can assure you of that.

225

Also, programmers have yet to develop a "magic" investment formula. Long before robo advisors existed, there were quantitative-based investment strategies. These strategies have never proven more effective than traditional investment approaches. Furthermore, there is absolutely nothing new, advanced or even truly quantitative about robo advisor investment models. Frankly, they are a combination of index funds weighted similarly to how most advisors approach asset allocation.

Betterment, one of the leading robo advisor sites, for example, claims that their performance model beats 88% of advisor models

> "CLIENTS WITH PROACTIVE ADVISORS ARE 20 TIMES MORE CONFIDENT ABOUT THE FUTURE THAN CLIENTS WITHOUT ADVISORS."

since January of 2004. The article they posted on their website about this supposed outperformance is somewhat amusing to us. Essentially, long after the fact, they created an investment model based on back testing (how it would have performed if it had existed). Then they say this model—that they created with the benefit of hindsight—beat 88% of everyone else. One would sure hope it did.

In reality, how has their performance been since these websites actually began managing investments? We found a reliable article stating that the major robo advisors don't publish performance. However, the author, Meb Faber, who is generally a fan of robo advisors, created models and estimated the performance of Betterment and Wealthfront for 2015. In each of the five allocations for each company that he estimated, their 2015 performance was negative, with 3% and 4%-plus losses in the all-equity allocations.

For now, robo advisors have severe limitations as holistic advisors when considering clients with any complexity. Even for simplistic scenarios, these sites don't offer much in the way of financial planning. The algorithms just don't exist, nor does an ability to truly understand a client's goals and motivations.

Robo advisors can be ideal for beginning investors looking for a low-cost, diversified approach to investing and who don't need financial planning. More sophisticated investors will find the investment approach pedestrian. And clients with planning needs will be frustrated. But, most importantly, to quote Meb Faber in his article about robo advisor performance—"I've always said the biggest benefit of a traditional advisor is being a coach, and they are worth their weight in gold if they can keep you from doing something really dumb." In our minds, our most serious responsibility is to avoid big mistakes, for us and for you.

57

ADVISOR ALPHA

In 2001, Vanguard introduced the concept of Advisor Alpha, a method by which advisors can attempt to quantify their value or, at the very least, be aware of the areas where we can maximize value for clients.

Recently, in a September 2016 paper, "Putting a value on your value: Quantifying Vanguard Advisor's Alpha," Vanguard expounded upon their latest thinking in this area.

We find this subject vital because it helps us better understand where to focus. Our priority needs to be at the intersection of what's important and what we can control. Because we can't predict the future, we instead need to know what to emphasize and how to adhere to a plan.

Vanguard breaks Advisor Alpha into seven modules—asset allocation, cost-effective implementation, rebalancing, behavioral coaching, asset location, withdrawal order for client portfolio spending, and total return investing.

It's been well known in academic circles for some time that the most important determinant of variability (risk) and performance (return) is asset allocation. We take a traditional approach to allocation.

We see stocks as a risk asset and high-quality bonds as the most consistent diversifier of equity volatility. When allocating clients between stocks and bonds, we test various asset allocations against projected income scenarios and work to determine—as a starting point—what is the lowest level of risk a client can assume and still meet their goals. In other words, how much equity does someone need to meet their long-term goals and how much can we invest in relatively less volatile bonds?

Vanguard puts it as well as anyone: "Complexity is not necessarily sophisticated, it's just complex. Simplicity is thus a strength, not a weakness, and can be used to promote better client understanding of the asset allocation and of how returns are derived. These features can be used to anchor expectations and to help keep clients invested when headlines and emotions tempt them to abandon the investment plan."

Therefore, regarding asset allocation, we need to 1) create a plan; 2) periodically test that plan against client goals; and 3) stick to that plan regardless of market volatility. If we can achieve these three things, then our clients have a higher likelihood of achieving their goals.

Next, let's look at the three components of cost-effective implementation: 1) fees and expense ratios; 2) trading costs; and 3) taxes. From the beginning, we designed our investment philosophy to be effective in these three areas.

We are fee-only advisors, so we don't collect any sales commissions, and our custodian's trading costs are among the lowest in the industry. Furthermore, since we manage individual stock and bond portfolios, we avoid product-level fees (e.g. mutual fund or exchange-traded fund expense ratios), which means our clients only pay an account-level management fee. Very few advisors manage their own portfolios, resulting in a second layer of product fees for clients. In most cases, purely from a fee perspective, we offer substantial savings over other advisors.

We seek to minimize trading costs and taxes as well. Since we are long-term investors, we do not trade frequently, reducing trading costs and capital gains taxes. Funds distribute capital gains annually as a matter of course, whereas we have complete control over whether to realize capital gains in any given year. And additionally, we have the ability to harvest tax losses when it is appropriate. Our use of individual securities (including tax-free municipal bonds) in taxable accounts offers us a unique ability to control tax consequences.

With our single fee, low turnover and control over when and where to realize capital gains, our approach is cost-effective, meaning our clients can realize higher net-of-fee and after-tax returns.

The third module is rebalancing. Vanguard points out that "the true benefit of rebalancing is realized in the form of controlling risk." In other words, in an ideal world, we hope to be adding to bond exposure after periods of stock outperformance, so that the next correction or bear market isn't as brutal.

For example, if a client's target allocation is 60% in stocks and 40% in bonds, then after a good stock market run, the client may now be invested 65% in stocks and 35% in bonds, potentially requiring a rebalancing of the client's accounts.

We monitor allocations as interest and dividends post, when clients add to accounts, when maturities occur or any other cash flow event. It is better to incrementally rebalance versus a wholesale and deliberate rebalance (especially in taxable accounts because of capital gains considerations).

Again, Vanguard sums-up well how we incrementally rebalance for clients: "Advisors who can systematically direct investor cash flows into the most underweighted asset class and / or rebalance to the 'most appropriate' boundary are likely to reduce their clients' rebalancing costs and thereby increase the returns their clients keep."

Our accounts are not synched to computers that "rebalance" for us and generate unnecessary trades and realized capital gains, which is harmful to long-term returns. Rather, we rebalance along the way and we make the uncomfortable decisions about buying stock when the market is correcting or trimming stock positions when equities have outperformed. Rebalancing sounds easy in theory, but it's much tougher in practice.

Vanguard points out that "the task of rebalancing is often an emotional challenge. Historically, rebalancing opportunities have occurred when there has been a wide dispersion between the returns of different asset classes (such as stocks and bonds). Whether in bull or bear markets, reallocating assets from the better-performing asset classes to the worse-performing ones feels counterintuitive to the 'average' investor. An advisor can provide the discipline to rebalance when rebalancing is needed most, which is often when the thought of rebalancing is a very uncomfortable leap of faith."

Our willingness to rebalance at unpopular times and our ongoing efforts to rebalance accounts as cash flows occur add value for our clients in the same way that asset allocation and cost efficiency do. Accomplishing one of these is not enough. We need to do the afore-mentioned three well to offer you a compelling value. So far, we've been largely successful in these areas and we will continue to work on "perfecting" our approach.

Behavioral coaching, the fourth way advisors add value for their clients, is perhaps the most impactful, adding 1%-2% to returns according to Vanguard's analysis. Advisors must establish trusting relationships with clients before times of market euphoria or stress, so they can properly influence client decisions.

It's a fact that investing has a counterintuitive component. When the market is gripped by fear, it is often a great time to buy, yet also an emotionally difficult decision. The opposite is also true, that when markets are firing on all cylinders, it can be hard to reduce equity exposure because of the fear of missing out.

Vanguard calculates that its average large cap blend fund returned 6.44% annually in the ten years ending December 31, 2015, but that the average investor in these funds only earned 5.06%. The 1.38% shortfall results from poor timing as investors moved in and out of the funds at inopportune moments. These results are similar to other studies, like

Dalbar's, which shows a far larger deficit of actual investor returns versus the returns of underlying funds.

The fifth factor is asset location, the allocation of assets between taxable and tax-advantaged accounts. First, we always analyze client tax brackets to judge whether to use tax-free municipal bonds in taxable client accounts. This can be an important factor in boosting after-tax returns. Next, when rebalancing a client relationship, we can look to take a larger amount of capital gains from tax-deferred accounts, so investors can avoid these taxes.

Furthermore, as individual stock and bond investors, we can strategically take gains and losses in taxable accounts when it suits each client's specific tax circumstances. Vanguard estimates that proper use of asset location can add up to 0.75% to client returns.

Withdrawal order for spending, which can add another 1.10% to investor returns, is the sixth component of Advisor's Alpha. When completing Retirement Income Evaluations for clients, we analyze the buckets from which a client funds his or her retirement in order to minimize taxes and get the most "bang for the buck."

A generic example involves funding retirement initially from taxable accounts, maximizing Social Security payments and waiting until age 70 and 1/2 (or the year after) to take one's first IRA withdrawal (the legally mandated required minimum distribution, or RMD).

A few other considerations that vary depending on the client's situation are reducing income by donating an RMD directly to a charity; carefully considering which assets will receive a step-up in cost basis at death (and therefore not liquidating them to fund retirement); preserving Roth IRAs for heirs; and determining the best assets from which to make gifts.

Finally, Vanguard highlights the importance of total return investing, i.e. taking a long-term approach to generating returns from a combination of interest, dividends and appreciation. Although Vanguard doesn't quantify a percentage value-add for this component, they argue that overweighting purely income-producing assets like long-term bonds, high yield debt, preferred stocks and dividend-paying equities to generate enough pure dividends and income to cover distributions can result in underperformance—particularly if these securities are out of favor for an extended period.

A diversified, balanced approach to investing will lead to less volatility and therefore less temptation to bail when things get difficult because a disciplined process controls volatility and helps calm emotions. Furthermore, a total return portfolio, particularly an approach like ours that is built around individual securities, can be more tax-efficient as we take advantage of favorable long-term capital gains tax rates.

We see these seven modules as critical to serving you. It's a complicated world...and now more than ever, a knowledgeable advisor is worth the investment.

THE INVESTMENT ENVIRONMENT

58

THE FUTURE IS NOT
WHAT IT USED TO BE

"THE TROUBLE WITH OUR TIMES IS THAT THE FUTURE
IS NOT WHAT IT USED TO BE."

PAUL VALERY, POET

After massive investment losses in many 401(k) and 529 plans, IRA accounts, and various other portfolios, people are wondering what they can expect from their investments over the coming years. Such prognostications are important when planning retirement dates, college savings and other important life events.

The foundation of most investment accounts are diversified stock and bond portfolios. In order to estimate future ten-year returns, we will start by building projections for stocks and bonds. While such projections can be helpful, we will also consider the advice of baseball manager Casey Stengel who said, "Never make predictions, especially about the future."

As a proxy for stocks, we will use the Standard and Poor's 500 Stock Index. This index contains most of the five-hundred largest companies in the United States and S&P weights the index based on market capitalization (stock price multiplied by number of shares outstanding).

Based on the last twelve months of operating earnings, this index has a price-to-earnings ratio (price of the overall stock index divided by the weighted average earnings of the index) of approximately fifteen as compared to a historical twenty-five year average of roughly seventeen. Even a measure of "normalized" earnings like the one that Yale Professor Robert Shiller calculates, which adjusts S&P 500 earnings for inflation and then averages these earnings over ten years, indicates that stock price-to-earnings measures are close to the historical average.

While valuations often trend higher or lower over multi-year periods, we will accept these average valuations and anticipate that they remain normal. There are then two more components that fundamentally drive returns.

The first is dividend yield, which for the S&P 500 is currently roughly 3%. The second is earnings growth. Historically, gross domestic product (GDP) has served as a reasonable predictor of earnings growth. A likely scenario for post-recession U.S. GDP growth is 3.0%.

Therefore, with average valuations, a 3% dividend yield and 3% earnings growth, stocks will most likely return about 6% per year—on average—over the next ten years. But, it is unlikely that stocks will return a smooth 6% annual return. Some years will be much better, others substantially worse.

Such an indicated return for stocks is much lower than the long-term historical average of over 10% per year. The index generated these often-cited returns from a lower-than-average price-to-earnings ratio and a higher-than-present dividend yield. The Irish-born philosopher Edmund Burke famously wrote, "You can never plan the future by the past." In investing, many continue to make this mistake.

As for bonds, we will use the Barclays Aggregate Bond Index as a proxy for the U.S. bond market. For reference, the weighted average maturity of this index is nearly six years. It is comprised of about 75%

U.S. government and agency debt, with the remainder primarily in corporate issues.

The current yield of this index is nearly 4.5%. Often, current yield is quite indicative of long-term returns for bonds. Principal values will fluctuate and if interest rates increase over this period, bond prices will fall. But investors will replace maturing bonds with higher yielding bonds. Therefore, although it could be a bumpy road, investors that hold high quality bonds to maturity will generally realize the current yield.

As always, significant risks exist to these ten year stock and bond return forecasts.

> "AS YOU PLAN YOUR RETIREMENT AND OTHER LIFE EVENTS, BE SURE TO USE REASONABLE ASSUMPTIONS. ALBERT EINSTEIN SAID THAT, 'REALITY IS MERELY AN ILLUSION, ALTHOUGH A VERY PERSISTENT ONE.'"

On the stock side, a further deteriorating economy could lead to deflation. Investor sentiment could cause contracting price-to-earnings multiples. Below-trend long-term economic growth and further cuts to corporate dividends could also drive returns below even 6%. Conversely, the opposite could occur in each factor, leading to better returns.

Higher inflation, leading to higher interest rates in the near future, could impair bond prices and generate lower fixed income returns. Whereas, a deflationary spiral would lower rates and increase bond returns over the period. Corporate credit risk, resulting in the default of some bonds, would also diminish returns.

Overall, indications are that over the next ten years stocks will return an average annual return of around 6% per year and bonds an annual average of about 4.5% per year. These somewhat meager returns demand either a low-cost index approach or true, strategic and fairly concentrated active management to prevent fees, taxes and transactions costs from destroying your savings even further.

As you plan your retirement and other life events, be sure to use reasonable assumptions. Albert Einstein said that, "Reality is merely an illusion, although a very persistent one." The possible reality of lower future investment returns should guide some investors to proceed very differently than they have in recent years.

59

MONEY MAKER

"Don't fight the Fed" is an important adage in the investment world. But, when times are tough, bears can find a million good reasons why the Fed's efforts will be ineffective.

The Federal Reserve's most potent tool is its control of the money supply. Simply put, the Fed buys bonds on the open market and the cash it pays for those bonds is often "new" money that the has Fed created.

Therefore, when you hear people throwing around the term "quantitative easing," they are referring to cash that the Fed is injecting into the system through its purchase of United States Treasury bills, notes and bonds—and, most recently, the Fed's purchase of mortgage-backed bonds.

One of the leading contributors to the turnaround in equity markets from their early 2009 lows was the Fed's efforts to purchase bonds.

This analysis is particularly interesting given the current debate over the fiscal cliff, which is garnering endless amounts of news coverage. Frankly, fiscal policy makers (Congress and the President) have done precious little to jump start our economy or financial markets. To date, monetary policy (the Fed) has been the driving force in helping to rejuvenate economic activity.

To further evidence the Fed's power, take a look at the 30-year fixed mortgage rate. Through its purchases of mortgage-backed securities, the Fed has driven this rate to 3.4%. The economic impact of this singular effort is proving to be hard to resist. With millions and millions refinancing and many more deciding the opportunity for home ownership is too compelling to ignore, this Fed stimulus is working.

As an investor, there are too many distractions. But if you pay attention to something, then pay attention to the Fed. The fiscal cliff "debate" is a made-for-TV reality show. Watching the Fed is more boring, but a lot more important over a multi-year period.

60

A LITTLE WOBBLY OF LATE

With the Standard and Poor's 500 struggling over the last several weeks, we wanted to update you with our current thoughts.

Just two weeks ago, we indicated in a similar update that the stock market was trading uncomfortably above its 50-day moving average (a common technical measure). In other words, the market was "overbought."

As it happened, through Monday equities suffered losses in nine of the prior eleven trading days, pushing the S&P 500 just below its 50-day moving average of 1,657.

We believe there are two primary reasons for the decline.

For one, from a seasonal perspective, the first two weeks of August are poor for the market. Historically this rectifies itself in the last two weeks of August, during which the S&P 500 has been positive in seven of the last ten years with an average gain of 1.26%. We could use a little rally now because September is seasonally the worst month for the market.

Secondly, investors are terrified that the Federal Reserve will decide to taper some of its bond purchases at its September meeting.

242

With initial jobless claims falling to their lowest level since October 5, 2007, registering only 320,000 claims last week, many commentators see stabilization in employment, which helps fulfill one of the Fed's two legal mandates (full employment and stable prices).

This fear of subdued Fed asset purchases has caused long-term rates to jump substantially over the last four months—from 1.7% on the 10-year Treasury in mid-April to 2.9% now, a sizeable percentage increase.

In the near term, we would be encouraged if the market makes it through August and September right around its current levels. This would alleviate some of the seasonal problems as October, November and December constitute a strong quarter more often than not.

As for monetary policy, we think it would be irresponsible for the Fed to decrease asset purchases at this time. The economy has come a long way over the last four years, but it is still weak. Furthermore, inflation is low, which eliminates the need to reign in monetary stimulus. We think the Fed recognizes this reality. Therefore, if interest rates can retreat slightly or remain steady for the balance of the year, it would be bullish for equities.

61

A SUPER 2013 AND
THE YEAR AHEAD

The Santa Claus rally finally arrived and the Standard and Poor's 500 stock index is now up 2% in December after a lackluster start to the month. Since the Federal Reserve announced its tapering on December 18th, the market has rallied 3.39%. As we head into the final two trading days of the year, the market is severely overbought, trading more than two standard deviations above its 50-day moving average.

2013 was quite a year. If it were over now, it would be the 10th best year since the S&P 500's inception in 1928. For the Dow, which constituted in 1901, it would be the 24th best year. And for the Nasdaq, with its origins in 1972, it would be the 7th best year.

Looking ahead to 2014, January frequently foreshadows the rest of the year. Since 1950, this "January Effect," also known as the "January Barometer," has indicated the rest of the year with remarkable accuracy. As a matter of fact, 76.2% of the time, the market has followed the fate of January. This includes just seven major errors to the indicator and eight "flat" years (+/- 5%). Further, ten of the last sixteen (62.5%) midterm election years followed January's lead. So, clearly, we will be carefully observing the year's beginnings.

244

However gradually, interest rates are finally (and, perhaps, irreversibly) heading higher. The ten-year U.S. Treasury Bond hit 3% last week. This is a milestone. The long-term compounded rate of inflation is 3% per year over the last one hundred years. Therefore, you can now, theoretically, purchase a "risk-free" Treasury Bond and at least protect the purchasing power of your money.

Over the next few years, we continue to see equities providing competitive average annual returns, but there does come a day in a rising interest rate environment when bond coupons will offer an enticing enough return. For now, though, there is still significant principal risk in bonds, especially co-mingled bond mutual funds and exchange traded funds.

After a robust 2013, it is prudent to continue to rebalance portfolios to target asset allocations. And with value more difficult to discern in the stock allocation of portfolios, we will continue our focus on underappreciated areas of the market.

62

HAPPY BIRTHDAY
BULL MARKET

Earlier this week, the equity bull market celebrated its sixth birthday. Since World War II, only three other bull markets lasted this long. After 72 months without a drop of 20% or more, the stock market isn't as cheap as it used to be. And while far from exuberant, investors have grown more comfortable with stocks, particularly in the U.S.

On March 14, 2009, we penned a client update entitled "Could It Be?" (see page 56), in which we noted that the S&P 500 had reached a trailing price-to-earnings ratio of 13.4, just below the average bear market low of 13.9. While we weren't trying to time the market, the low P/E ratio was one of the reasons we were so bullish about stocks.

As of the end of February, the trailing price-to-earnings ratio for the S&P 500 stood at 18.6, according to Standard & Poor's. However, this figure is weighted toward the larger market capitalizations in the index that carry lower valuations, such as Apple, Exxon Mobil and Microsoft. Looking at a simple average of S&P 500 companies without weighting by market cap, the average trailing P/E ratio looks even loftier at 27.9 times earnings, according to Stock Investor Pro.

Bespoke Investment Group reports that the average P/E since 1929 for the S&P 500 is 15.35. In other words, U.S. large cap equities have gone from a 12.7% historical discount to a 21.2% premium since 2009.

Sentiment has also shifted since the crisis days of 2009. On March 12, 2009, the American Association of Individual Investors (AAII) sentiment survey measured bearish sentiment at a majority 54.47% of investors. Over the last six years, bearish sentiment has fallen by more than half to just 25.41%. Bullish sentiment, on the other hand, has been less resilient. Six years ago, AAII reported that just 27.64% of investors were bullish on stocks. Despite the historic stock market run, bullish sentiment today stands at just 31.6%—not far from the bear market bottom.

While the AAII sentiment survey would indicate a greater level of comfort in owning equities, we believe investors are still more pessimistic than one would expect given a six-year bull market run. For example, investors don't appear to have adopted a disregard for bad news (something that might signal a stock market top), and, if anything, events like plummeting oil prices or Greek debt negotiations still send financial commentators into a tizzy. When we do finally witness the 10% correction that everyone has been waiting for, our guess is that investors will be in full-fledged panic mode.

From a portfolio management standpoint, we don't believe the market has reached valuation and sentiment levels that warrant a dramatic shift to fixed income or cash (particularly given today's rock bottom interest rates). However, we do believe that whereas valuation was a major tailwind over the past six years, it is more likely to serve as a headwind over the next five years.

As contrarian investors, we believe our equity portfolio is well positioned for the decade ahead. Our holdings have a substantially lower valuation (P/E ratio) than the broad market, a higher dividend yield and are more exposed to international markets (our companies derive over two-thirds of their revenues outside of the United States). Although adopting unpopular ideas can be difficult in the short-term, like owning stocks at all in early 2009, we continue to see a powerful long-term benefit to a contrarian approach.

63

THE VOLATILITY

Augustwas awful for the stock market. The iShares Core S&P 500 exchange-traded fund lost 6.14% for the month and the iShares MSCI All-Country World Index declined 6.81%. Adding insult to injury, with today's action, September is off to a pitiful start.

When experts point to the reasons for the recent market slump, they cite a slowdown in China and the potential for a September Federal Reserve rate hike. In our updates we will continue to examine these two important issues, but today we want to point out that market declines are normal regardless of the reasons commentators happen to identify.

Even in relatively recent history, going back to 1980, Fidelity reports that, on average, 5% pullbacks occur three times per year, 10% falls happen once a year and 20% drops occur every three years. We haven't had a 20% pullback since early 2009. Before the present correction, we hadn't seen a 10% retracement in 47 months. Whatever the harbinger, the correction was overdue.

As we have suggested in recent notes, we think last week's move higher was a relief rally, rather than the end of the declines. First, selling begets continued selling until investors find a panic bottom. Second, the seasonality for September is extraordinarily week.

The S&P 500 recently experienced a technical (chart) pattern called a "Death Cross." Basically, when a formerly up-trending market sells off violently, a death cross can occur. According to Bespoke Investment Group:

> "...it occurs when an index...sees its 50-day moving average cross below its 200-day moving average and both moving averages (50 and 200) are declining themselves...it has only happened 10 times in the index's history...the S&P has run into trouble in the month following the "Death Cross." The index's average one-month return has been -1.38% with positive returns just 20% of the time...Over the next six months following these crosses, the S&P has been up nine of ten times for an average change of +8.23%."

In other words, a very quick market fall usually leads to more selling over the short-term, but then a relatively robust rebound a few months later. In addition to the selling itself suggesting deeper declines, September is unfavorable to begin with. Again, from Bespoke Investment Group:

> "September is the only month of the year where the Dow has averaged declines over the last 100, 50 and 20 years... [we just experienced] the worst August for the S&P 500 since 2001, and just the 15th August in the index's history to see a decline of more than 4%...Septembers following down Augusts have been even worse than the average September, but the market has tended to bounce back when looking at the final four months of the year, which includes the down Septembers."

So perhaps it will be a long September, but hope is not lost as history has shown the market to recover in similar circumstances. Furthermore, there have only been three occasions since World War II where there was a bear market without a recession. As such, the government's release last week of revised 2nd quarter GDP showing growth of 3.7%, is not only encouraging for the economy, but for the market as well. In the tepid growth environment that the U.S. has experienced—average GDP growth of 2.45% since 1996—a 3.7% number is very strong and is probably not predictive of an imminent recession.

And finally, selling stocks and waiting for a better time to reinvest is a fool's errand. From 1980 through 2012, if you hypothetically invested $10,000 in the S&P 500 (reinvesting all dividends and ignoring taxes) your money would have grown to $332,502 over these 32 years. However, if you just missed the 10 best days during that 32-year period, your investment would have only grown to $160,340—substantially less than half. As we saw in the wake of the 2008 market crash, when the market turns around, it does so quickly—leaving investors who bailed in the dust.

54

INDIGESTION

After exactly seven years of zero interest rate policy, the Federal Reserve raised its short-term interest rate on Wednesday by 25 basis points, or one quarter of one percent. Despite months of investor angst leading up to the rate increase, all seemed well. The stock market rallied, bond yields rose slightly and the dollar fell. But the relief was short-lived...

On Thursday and Friday, the stock market sunk, bond yields fell and the dollar rallied aggressively. In a note last month, "The Future of Interest Rates" (see page 126), we suggested that when the Fed raised short-term rates, longer rates might fall, resulting in a flattening of the yield curve. This came to fruition with the 20+ Year Treasury Exchange Traded Fund rallying 1.74% post-Fed.

Market participants, even though many hoped for a Fed rate hike, are worried that higher short-term rates will slow the economy, further curtail benign inflation and perhaps even cause a recession. Long rates fell as short rates rose because traders see muted prospects for long-term inflation and growth.

Another manifestation of predictions for stalled future growth is the continuing bear market in oil. We write about this often because the tumble in oil prices is having a devastating effect on investor psychology and doing real damage to pockets of the global economy, particularly in emerging markets.

The price of a barrel of oil bottomed during the financial crisis at $33.87 in early 2009 from its high of $150 in early 2008. Presently, the price of oil stands at $34.85—less than a dollar above its level at the depths of The Great Recession. Meanwhile, the average energy stock in the Standard and Poor's 500 is down 41.36% from its 52-week high. Also of note, the average energy stock is trading 26.37% below Wall Street analysts' price target and these same analysts rate 58% of the energy stocks they cover as "buys."

It's hard not to see value in energy right now, but many of the major integrated oil companies have held-up surprisingly well. Exxon Mobil and Chevron, for example, have seen year-to-date losses of just 13.57% and 16.35%, respectively, versus West Texas Crude's 42.70% nosedive. If these names experience another leg lower, they might pique our interest.

Although the Fed has made a very poor argument for why it raised rates, we continue to believe that they were seeking to create a more normal interest rate environment and stave off intense political pressure from inflation hawks (who, we should note, have been dead wrong about the market since 2009 and who have cost investors dearly with their prognostications).

The economy is arguably slowing with key survey measures like the Philly Fed General Business Conditions Index and the Institute for Supply Chain Management's Manufacturing Index both recently falling into contraction territory. On the other hand, housing starts and auto sales continue their trend higher, offering mixed signals.

The markets and the economy are a mixed bag and there is no clear indication where things are heading. But then again, when investors reach a consensus about the market's direction, that's usually the time to head for the hills.

This bull market has persistently climbed a wall of worry, with very few vocal optimists. We think that a rational Fed will be limited as to how quickly and how high it raises rates, particularly because deflation risks remain and long-term rates are low. We also believe, over time, businesses will adjust and thrive in an environment of lower energy costs and a strong dollar. For now, though, we need a strong stomach to digest the dramatic changes afoot.

65

VOTING MACHINE

J ust four trading days into the New Year, stocks are off to a bad start. As China's stock market crashes, oil prices continue to plummet and investors question the effects of the Federal Reserve beginning to raise interest rates, fear and volatility are taking hold.

Since peaking on May 21st of last year, the Standard & Poor's 500 is down 6.60% through yesterday's close, ignoring dividends. A more global basis, the Morgan Stanley Capital International All-Country World Index is down 14.08% since its May 10, 2015 high, also ignoring dividends. Today's market rout is extending these losses both in the U.S. and abroad.

An often-quoted nugget of investment wisdom from the famed value investor, Benjamin Graham, reads as follows: "In the short run, the market is a voting machine but in the long run, it is a weighing machine." In other words, on a day-to-day basis, stock prices are dominated by fear and greed and speculative traders will follow the market's momentum, often overpaying for equities or, conversely, selling perfectly good companies.

As a long-term investment, however, stock prices will follow the trajectory of the underlying companies' fortunes. As publicly-traded firms grow their revenues, profits and cash flows, they will reinvest in the business and return money to shareholders. More importantly, strong companies will largely endure recessions and adapt to a changing business landscape, including a strong dollar, low energy prices, higher interest rates, etc.

A second implication of Benjamin Graham's quote is that because fear instead of fundamentals can drive short-term returns, equity investments require a long time horizon. This fact is paramount to our investment process. In designing each client's personal investment policy, we avoid allocating funds to stocks if we cannot wait for market losses to recover. For clients drawing "income" from their investments, we maintain a heavy allocation to high-quality fixed income to stabilize the portfolio. Furthermore, in an environment like the last few days, wherever possible, we raise funds for client distributions from more stable fixed income investments.

The final implication of Graham's quote is that short-term volatility can offer a long-term buying opportunity. Therefore, we will continue to use maturing bonds and cash flows from dividends and interest to add to stock positions on weakness, while paying close attention to each client's target asset allocation.

66

OIL

Low energy prices were once considered good for the U.S. economy. Cheap gas used to be a boon for consumers whose savings at the pump were compared to a tax cut that boosted consumer spending.

So, why are lower oil prices so bad for the stock market this time around? Why do stocks tumble on days when oil falls? What is different this time?

- The panic-like plunge in the price of oil is causing extensive fear in financial markets which, by their nature, don't want to see anything crash. The uncertainty of the price collapse is leading to falling asset prices. These price drops are inhibiting economic confidence around the world.

- Investors are questioning banks' exposure to energy and the potential default ramifications of outstanding loans to the oil and gas industry.

- In 2012 and 2013 the oil and gas industry in the U.S. was responsible for more than 10% of all capital expenditures, a number that has dropped to around 5% recently. Business spending in the U.S. has been generally weak since the Great Recession ended, so seeing a boost from the energy sector was helping to drive economic growth, particularly in Texas and other fracking states.

- In 2014 only 27% of petroleum used in the U.S. came from imported oil, the lowest level since the last domestic oil boom in 1985. This means that more of our petrol dollars stayed domestic.

- Capital Economics reports that, since mid-2014, Americans increased personal savings by $120 billion, which has largely offset consumers' boost from the fall in gas. Meanwhile, the J.P. Morgan Chase Institute reports that lower gas prices result in more gas purchases because people tend to take longer trips and buy larger vehicles. Higher savings and increased gas consumption have minimized any immediate benefit to the broader economy.

- Markets are fearful that the Federal Reserve—which calls the decline in energy prices "transitory"—is substantially underestimating the deflationary impact of the oil crash. As the most hawkish developed market central bank in the world right now, the Fed continues to anticipate inflationary pressures while the U.S. (with a strong dollar and falling commodity prices) faces a real and immediate deflation threat. Investors are becoming concerned that as the Fed plays the fiddle, oil could cause a deflationary burnout.

Legendary investor John Templeton once said, "The four most expensive words in the English language are, 'This time is different.'" In our view, over the longer-term, lower energy prices are still good.

257

Consumers and businesses will eventually filter their savings through to the broader economy, particularly if prices stay low for an extended period. This has been the pattern in the past and should ultimately prevail in the future.

For now, though, the market remains vigilant about a prolonged deflation threat. Until oil stabilizes or consumer spending picks up, equity markets will likely suffer. We continue to think the best position for now is patience. Increasingly, there are bargains to be had among individual stocks. Much to our pleasant surprise, recent earnings announcements from our portfolio companies have been largely better than expected. Hang in there...and treat yourself to some cheap gas!

57

DISCONNECT

As the selloff in global stocks continues, we have been noticing the kind of nonsensical phenomenon that might indicate the selling is closer to its end than its beginning.

Clearly, nobody, including us, is ready to declare the current correction over. The market has a mind of its own and is far too unpredictable for mere mortals.

Experts almost universally agree that the primary trigger for the present market drop is the collapse in oil prices. Indeed, over the last three months, as the selloff has intensified, energy has led the market down. A drop in financial stocks has been following closely on the heels of energy.

The fear is that weakness in energy could create broader contagion throughout the economy and financial markets. And as energy companies slow production because of collapsing commodity prices, they will in turn fire workers, stop spending for capital expenditures and default on their bank loans.

Interestingly, though, over just the last month, U.S. financial stocks have greatly underperformed relative to energy, and even

259

the broader market has performed worse than energy.

In our view, this short-term trend indicates that panic may be setting in. Investors are selling financials first and foremost, and the broader market overall, but energy stocks—the supposed original culprit for all of the misery—are holding-up. Such silly behavior tells us that sellers are overwrought with anxiety and might be reaching a point of capitulation.

Furthermore, investors haven't forgotten the credit crisis that stemmed from the housing bubble's collapse from 2007 through 2009. While some may fear that energy's crash will cause a similar crisis, the reality is that with stringent bank regulation and ample reserves another financial crisis seems like a very low probability.

Lastly, energy stocks could be sending a signal that oil is near its bottom. If so, stabilization, or even a rally in energy, could be the impetus for a short covering rally in financial markets.

58

NEGATIVE INTEREST RATES

The European Central Bank adopted negative interest rates in late 2014 and the Bank of Japan followed in March of this year. These actions led many politicians and commentators in the U.S. to condemn the idea with gusto. While negative interest rates are probably not likely in the United States, the deflationary pressure oversees has prompted central bankers to take dramatic action.

Several clients have recently asked how interest rates can be negative. Negative interest rates arise in two specific situations.

One is primarily market-based. For example, during the Great Recession in the United States, our U.S. T-Bills (short-term government debt) traded at negative yields for a brief period. By and large, this was the result of too many investors demanding "safe" short-term government paper during a major financial crisis. In a hunt for safety, investors actually paid more than face value for zero-coupon bonds, leading to a negative yield.

The other form of negative interest rates stems from central bank action and this is the type that upsets many commentators.

Commercial banks hold their deposits with government central banks, like the U.S. Federal Reserve. These deposits take two forms—required and excess. The government legally mandates a certain amount of required reserves as a safety net for commercial banks. Excess reserves represent funds that the commercial banks keep at the central bank because they're not lending it and they have no other place to deposit it.

Central banks create this second type of negative rate by charging commercial banks to hold its excess reserves (instead of paying a small interest rate on that money). The goal of this policy is to incentivize banks to lend money to businesses and consumers, which stimulates the economy. Basically, under this regime, if the commercial banks don't lend, it costs them.

The first kind of negative interest rate, where demand for government bonds outpaces supply, is a market-based occurrence and is currently playing out in German, Swiss and Japanese government bonds. In the case of Switzerland and Japan, negative yields extend all the way to a 10-year maturity. In these cases, one could argue that the European Central Bank, the Swiss National Bank and the Bank of Japan were simply following the market's lead in instituting negative interest rates on excess reserves.

This is not the case in the United States. No U.S. government obligation has a negative yield. Meanwhile, the Federal Reserve has not proactively discussed negative rates; they have addressed the issue only in response to inquiries. As such, we believe that the likelihood of negative rates in the United States is currently quite low.

Perhaps the most important takeaway from negative interest rates is how sluggish global growth and inflation presently are. Furthermore, negative yields may also indicate just how far the world is from a "normal" interest rate environment.

59

EXPENSIVE[2]

Happy New Year!

2016 was a very successful year for our clients and we are rooting for a strong 2017 as well. Markets are crazy things. Last year at this time investors were pessimistic and stocks were struggling. But, by mid-February, after the worst start for the Standard and Poor's 500 since 1930, stocks began a major turn. Except for a brief panic following Brexit in late June, the year ended-up being a boon.

This year seems to be beginning in an altogether different fashion with optimism for equites surging and pessimism about bonds growing. In our view, it's not quite that simple. We believe that both stocks and bonds are overvalued as we embark on 2017.

The historical average price-to-earnings (P/E) ratio on the Standard and Poor's 500 is 15 and we are presently at 24.95 times earnings according to The Wall Street Journal. Effectively, this means that investors pay almost $25 for each dollar of earnings for the average S&P 500 company.

Meanwhile the ten year U.S. Treasury Bond, the global benchmark for bonds, yields 2.477%. The long-term average yield on the 10-year is 4.59%. Bond prices move inversely to yields, therefore, a low yield means a high price.

So, as you can see in this very simple framework, both stocks and bonds are expensive—you have to pay more for a dollar of earnings than average and you get a lower interest rate on bonds than average.

This presents a dilemma. However, we believe it is a surmountable one.

Recently, stock prices have increased robustly, while bonds prices have dropped substantially.

Both stock and bond markets are impossible to time. You should be highly skeptical of the nearly unanimous current predictions for continued stock market gains and a prolonged bond market funk. Of course, these forecasts may prove accurate for a time, but the stock bull market (which began in March 2009) will not last forever.

More likely, we will see increased stock and bond volatility as the bull market matures. With the recent jump in stocks and the recent dip in bonds, we are generally recommending that clients marginally increase their bond exposure.

We are not buying bonds for return. The expected return on bonds is still very low. Instead we are recommending small additions to bonds as a placeholder for cash so that funds are available when stocks fall. In other words, we want the ability to act in the event the market corrects over the next few years. Bond maturities should ultimately offer us a disciplined source of cash to buy more stocks at lower prices.

MAY 17, 2017

DEAR MR. BRENNAN

M r. John J. Brennan
Lead Independent Director
General Electric Company
41 Farnsworth Street
Boston, MA 02210

Re: Jeffrey Immelt[1] and General Electric stock performance

DEAR MR. BRENNAN,

As a registered investment advisory firm based in Lancaster, PA, we help individuals and families manage their savings and prepare for retirement. In this capacity, we have long held shares of General Electric common stock. We are small shareholders in GE, but we share a fiduciary dilemma with you and the rest of the GE Board. This dilemma, of course, is the exceptionally poor performance of Chairman and CEO Jeffrey Immelt. His dismal track record is persistently destroying tens of billions of dollars of value.

The public markets are far from a perfect arbiter; however, they are a good guide. In the case of Mr. Immelt, they indicate that he has resoundingly failed us. Over the last ten years, the Standard and Poor's 500 has returned 97% while GE has returned 9.58%, both with dividends reinvested. Furthermore, Morningstar identifies 3M, Siemens AG and Honeywell as GE's closest industry peers. Over the last ten years these companies have returned 198.2%, 64.19% and 192%, respectively.

Rather than focusing exclusively on operational excellence (running businesses), Mr. Immelt has repeatedly chased "capital allocation" strategies by acquiring and divesting businesses, almost universally at inopportune times.

On December 3, 2009, GE announced the sale of NBC Universal to Comcast Corporation. Since then, Comcast has returned 390% and Disney (a network, studio and theme park business analogous to NBC Universal) has returned 302.2% versus GE's return of 125%, all with dividends reinvested.

On July 20, 2012, at the midpoint of a slew of oil and gas acquisitions (John Wood Group, Wellstream, Dresser, Lufkin, Salof, etc.), GE decided to increase its strategic focus on oil and gas and dedicated a separate business unit under GE Energy to emphasize the expansion and investments. Since then the price of a barrel of West Texas Intermediate Crude has fallen 49.3% while the spot price of Henry Hub Natural Gas is now roughly flat, up 0.99%.

On April 10, 2015, GE announced the sale of its finance arm. Since then, the Financial Select Sector SPDR ETF (XLF), a fair proxy for GE capital, has returned 24.47% verses GE's 5.67%, both with dividends reinvested.

On January 15, 2016, GE announced the sale of its home appliance business. Since then, Whirlpool, a home appliance business, has returned 46.59% while GE has returned 3.15%, both with dividends reinvested.

A post on GE's website entitled *Waking Up as a Software and Analytics Company* boasts that the company has "spent five years and a billion dollars learning how to become a software and analytics company." Meanwhile, actual software companies and the tech-heavy

NASDAQ are setting new all-time highs. Maybe Mr. Immelt will finally get one of his capital allocation decisions right, but we suspect he is already late to the game.

The bottom-line results surely speak for themselves. Over the last ten years, GE's normalized diluted earnings per share have fallen 32.5%, while free cash flow per share has dropped a startling 144%. Perhaps most disturbing, quarterly free cash flow has been negative since the fourth quarter of 2015. Deutsche Bank's recent downgrade of GE stock reinforces our concern about free cash flow and the impact on future dividends and share repurchases.

All of these appalling results occurred on Jeffrey Immelt's watch. If these were the stats of an athlete, the general manager would cut him; if these were the scores of a student, the professor would fail him. As a board of directors, you have a fiduciary duty to respond to Mr. Immelt's inferior performance and terminate him immediately.

There are no extraneous factors that can explain GE's underperformance. The buck stops with Mr. Immelt. You have a responsibility to General Electric's millions of employees and investors to elect a new independent Chairman and recruit a competent CEO.

1: On June 12th, 2017, GE announced the "retirement" of CEO Jeff Immelt.

THE FUNDAMENTALS
OF INVESTING

71

INVESTING SERVED SIMPLY: BUYING BUSINESSES

American cartoonist Rube Goldberg (1883 to 1970) was famous for his illustrations of overly engineered machines designed to perform relatively simple tasks. More often than not, today's investment products are akin to his "self-operating napkin." But when it comes to investing, we do not believe that complexity yields better results than simplicity.

At the most fundamental level, we invest in businesses for our clients. The shares of each stock that we purchase represent small ownership stakes in large companies. Folks will often dispute this fundamental truth and instead "play the market" like the roulette wheel at a Las Vegas casino. But at a casino the house profits while the naïve fall flat.

To the contrary, this gambling concept only applies to stock investing if investors take the wrong approach. Let us consider the right approach to buying companies.

Although it is seemingly a cliché, a long-term mindset is paramount. Think about a successful small business owner that you know and ask yourself whether the owner started or bought the business with the intent

270

to sell the company in a day, a month, or even a year. The very idea is ridiculous. Instead, the entrepreneur is committed to the business for many years, even decades. True stock investing should be no different because, over the long-term, history shows that a company's stock price will almost always track its earnings growth.

The inherent problem with stocks is that the market prices them on a second-by-second basis. To ignore this manic pricing is one of the disciplines of investing.

If the busiest and most profitable restaurant in town was valued minute-to-minute, what do you think would happen to its price when a blizzard blows into town? What would the talking heads on CNBC declare if a talented sous chef quits? But in reality, neither of these events fundamentally changes the value of the town's best restaurant.

A long time frame can compensate for unpredictable events that bear on day-to-day pricing, but even the long-term is not foolproof.

The purchase price of a business also matters. If you pay too much for the neighborhood Laundromat, it is likely that no amount of management savvy or entrepreneurial ingenuity will save you. After all, there is a limited quantity of washers and dryers in the building and a finite number of hours in the day.

The good news, we do not need to buy stocks when we cannot find a company selling at an appealing price, just as an experienced landlord can delay acquiring a new apartment complex if the appropriate return on investment is not available.

For diversification reasons, we do not limit our portfolio to just one or two companies. Rather, we build a collection of businesses. The term diversification is another example of over-used investment jargon. The purpose of diversification is simply to spread risk among a variety of enterprises.

Only the wealthiest investors could own the aforementioned restaurant, Laundromat, apartment complex plus twenty other varying businesses in their community. It would require an enormous amount of capital. But, with stock investments you can diversify among businesses of all different stripes and also obtain global geographic exposure.

This is not to say that one cannot make fundamentally bad decisions. For example, five years ago an entrepreneur would have wanted to avoid buying a DVD rental store because of the imminent impact of on-demand, Netflix, and Redbox. Diversification, though, does mitigate the damage of an individual miscalculation.

Even with adequate diversification, it is necessary to understand that being a business owner is inherently risky. There is no such thing as a riskless business. For many years, General Motors franchisees

> "THINK ABOUT A SUCCESSFUL SMALL BUSINESS OWNER THAT YOU KNOW AND ASK YOURSELF WHETHER THE OWNER STARTED OR BOUGHT THE BUSINESS WITH THE INTENT TO SELL THE COMPANY IN A DAY, A MONTH, OR EVEN A YEAR."

in communities all across America may have thought they had a virtually bulletproof proposition. But, Honda, Toyota and the Great Recession changed all of that.

So, in addition to being diversified, remaining price-conscious and thinking long-term, investors need to make personal decisions about how much they should allocate to risky assets. Do not be fooled like many were in 2008 and believe that combinations of risky assets magically produce a riskless portfolio. Now, more than ever, as the result of globalization, risk-based assets will continue to move with extreme correlation in the event of a crisis.

Therefore, investors should determine how much of their assets they will commit to low risk fixed income. Matching relatively safe bonds according to anticipated cash flow needs and holding each bond to maturity is an optimal strategy. In our present extreme environment of low interest rates, we view bond mutual funds as inherently risky and unlikely to provide the stability that many are anticipating.

15th Century Renaissance man Leonardo da Vinci once said, "Simplicity is the ultimate sophistication." When building portfolios, we adhere to da Vinci's words of wisdom by creating a mix of strong businesses and safe assets that meet the individual goals of our clients.

72

BLOCKING AND TACKLING

Renowned Green Bay Packers coach Vince Lombardi once stated, "Some people try to find things in this game that don't exist, but football is only two things—blocking and tackling."

Success in investing, much like football, is not about completing the Hail Mary pass. Executing the seemingly minor tasks, like blocking and tackling, lead to victory.

Many investors seek strategies that can very quickly turn a pittance into a fortune. Others look for complicated schemes that they may not fully comprehend, hoping that someone else's genius will result in outsize profits. Over the long-term, these people nearly always lose.

Nevertheless, money management firms have catered their products to meet these investors' desires, ignoring efficacy in favor of market-ability. These firms generally over-engineer the process of investing, orchestrating trick plays that obscure the underlying weaknesses of their skill players.

Perhaps the most fitting example is the manager-of-managers approach that most modern day investment advisors follow, in which they claim to monitor the performance of a platform of third-party

274

funds, hiring the best performing managers and firing the poor ones.

But according to Standard and Poor's, "very few" funds consistently rank among the top half of their peer group. In fact, "over the five years ending March 2011, only 0.96% of large-cap funds, 1.14% of mid-cap funds and 2.59% of small-caps funds maintained a top-half ranking over five consecutive 12-month periods." Amazingly, S&P calculates that statistically at least 6.25% should meet this criterion purely on the basis of random probabilities.

Recent numbers from Dalbar, the Boston-based mutual fund research firm, continue to show that individual investors commit the same sin as many financial advisors—switching funds at exactly the wrong time. Over the 20 years through December 2011, the average stock fund investor realized annualized returns of 3.8% compared with a 9.1% return for the Standard and Poor's 500.

Trading in and out of managers is just as harmful as churning individual stocks or bonds. Both indicate an inability to stick to a long-term game plan. To keep with our sports theme, think of the New York Yankees during the 15-plus years before Joe Torre took the helm.

Recently, the financial services firm Barclays commissioned a wealth study: "Risk and Rules: The Role of Control in Financial Decision Making." The survey included 2,000 affluent people from around the world with a net worth in investable securities of approximately U.S. $1.5 million (or its foreign-currency equivalent).

Forty percent of the survey participants said they practiced market timing and these folks were "over three times more likely to believe they trade too much." Trading can be a compulsion. Of the respondents who said that "you have to buy and sell often" to be a successful investor, fifty percent believed they "buy and sell investments more than they should."

One of the study's primary conclusions is that "investors feel they need to engage in active trading, but they cannot then control how much they do it." Lack of restraint is not a fundamental strength in sports (see Woods, Tiger) or investing.

When one considers both (1) the underlying fund managers trading on a day-to-day basis and (2) the financial advisor swapping managers to justify his or her fee, many investors have no idea how much turnover exists in their portfolios. With investing, as in sports, turnovers will lose you the game.

In many sports, it is not considered gentlemanly to run-up the score. With investing, on the other hand, it is human instinct to reach for as much as possible. This phenomenon helps explain why stocks became so popular during the tech bubble of the late 1990s, and perhaps why gold has attracted so many speculators of late.

> "REMEMBER THAT INVESTORS WHO WIN ARE THE ONES WHO BLOCK AND TACKLE."

In 1999, with a big lead in the game—a tremendous decade of stock market returns in the rearview mirror—the California Public Employees' Retirement System (Calpers) decided it wise to recommend to the California legislature that public employees retire earlier and that the state raise the pensions of existing retirees. Lawmakers agreed to lower the retirement age of some workers to fifty and raised certain pensions to ninety percent of retirees' former salaries.

Now, with the decade of the 2000s encompassing two major bear markets for stocks, Calpers is asking the State of California to contribute $3.6 billion to its funds this year and $3.5 billion next year. Clearly, these are numbers that California can ill afford.

The lessons of market timing show that it pays to focus on fundamentals. We are not advocating inaction, but investing should be viewed as a slow and steady race to the top. It takes enormous time and patience and will only ultimately work if the right game plan is in place.

Instead of shooting for the moon or outsmarting oneself, focus on the little things: choose an appropriate asset allocation, pay modest fees, minimize turnover and resist the urge to time the market. Remember that investors who win are the ones who block and tackle.

If you do this, you will pick-up a little luck along the way as well. Former Oriole Manager Earl Weaver captures this sentiment well: "The key to winning baseball games is pitching, fundamentals and three homeruns."

277

73

BONDS AWAY

> "A BULL MARKET IN BONDS IS A LITTLE LIKE YOUTH;
> YOU TAKE IT FOR GRANTED AND DON'T APPRECIATE IT
> UNTIL IT'S GONE. ONE DAY, YOU LOOK IN THE MIRROR
> AND SEE SAGGING FLESH AND RISING YIELDS."
>
> NICK PAUMGARTEN, THE NEW YORKER,
> JULY 8 & 15, 2013

In the first six months of 2013, the Barclays Capital Aggregate Bond Total Return Index fell 2.4%, posting its worst first half since 1994. Meanwhile, the main gauge of U.S. equities, the Standard and Poor's 500, rose 12.6%, its best start since 1998.

Over one year, the Barclays Capital Long-Term Treasury Bond Index (price only) is down 19%. This feat has only occurred six times since 1980.

In the week ended June 26, bond funds had $28.1 billion in net redemptions, the largest weekly withdrawals since the Investment Company Institute began tracking these figures in January of 2007.

The world's largest mutual fund, Bill Gross's Pimco Total Return Bond Fund, fell 4.7% in May and June. This led investors to redeem $9.9 billion from the fund in June alone—the most on record.

Individual investors should find these numbers alarming. The vast majority of mass affluent investors own bond funds, rather than individual bonds. (It is worth noting that bond exchange traded and index funds basically have the same characteristics as managed mutual funds.)

Although bond funds can be advantageous in a falling rate environment, they are potentially disastrous when rates rise. Bond funds suffer from three major problems in a rising rate environment: 1) as rates increase, bond prices fall, along with the net asset value of the fund; 2) a plummeting fund value motivates investors to sell, forcing bond managers to liquidate bonds at low prices; and 3) fund managers are then left with no capital to purchase new, higher yielding bonds.

Investors in bond funds usually believe they are participating in a low-risk investment. But as the numbers above attest, bond funds are more risky than many acknowledge.

We invest in individual bonds with the intention of holding them to maturity. Therefore, the price swings in the bonds are less relevant and the actions of others do not force our clients to realize losses. Furthermore, we ladder our bond portfolios, engineering annual maturities so that with each passing year we reinvest in a new interest rate environment. This process introduces a discipline to fixed income investing that removes emotion from the equation.

74

INVESTING IS BORING

> "TO ESCAPE BOREDOM, MAN WORKS EITHER BEYOND
> WHAT HIS USUAL NEEDS REQUIRE, OR ELSE HE INVENTS
> PLAY, THAT IS, WORK THAT IS DESIGNED TO QUIET NO
> NEED OTHER THAN THAT FOR WORKING IN GENERAL."
>
> FRIEDRICH NIETZSCHE, HUMAN,
> ALL TOO HUMAN JULY 8 & 15, 2013

More often than not, "paralysis by analysis" sets in when making investment decisions. The global investment landscape seems rife with political and economic concerns. And to further confuse consumers, the financial services industry has created a vast array of absurdly complicated investment products.

Many investors turn to financial news outlets like CNBC and Bloomberg for guidance. But these businesses exist to attract viewers and traffic and so, by way of recent example, they promote political turmoil in Ukraine and economic crisis in Turkey. And although these

280

stories are important and interesting, they are not historically unique or meaningful to long-term investors.

The commonly-held belief today is that scrutiny of every imaginable detail is more important than ever. This mindset stems from the enormous complexity of the world and the instantaneous dissemination of new information. The theory goes that today's investor needs heightened speed and sophistication in order to "beat the system."

In our view, the truth is the exact opposite. As people scurry from one scenario analysis to another, they overlook the basic fundamentals of investing. They "miss the forest for the trees."

Modern psychology has identified a similar concept called mindfulness, which advocates a focus and appreciation of the present versus regret of the past or fear of the future. Consistent with this concept, people may avoid investing now because they are disappointed about missing the big run-up in stocks from the March 2009 bear market bottom. Or they may hesitate today because they worry about the political, social, and economic future of the country.

Many overcome their investment anxiety with layers of complexity, buying into convoluted portfolio strategies that they do not understand. Such an approach offers distance.

However, we recommend a straightforward, understandable strategy that is easy to implement and we offer the following five tips:

1) Keep your portfolio simple. Seek transparency that permits you to easily view your actual, underlying investments. Do not trust a "black box" that is too complicated to understand, but promises to produce enhanced returns. Be able to look at each one of your holdings and estimate the return that you can expect from it over a decade. In other words, view a stock or a bond the same way you would a piece of real estate, but without the carrying costs.

2) Remember the seeming cliché that investing is a long-term proposition. This is true. Most people's timeframe is at least

five years and often in excess of thirty years. With investing, it is self-defeating and counter-productive to evaluate results in short intervals. Any long-term proposition takes time—you will not know if you have a good marriage, a gifted child or a challenging career after a week or a month's experience.

3) Do not invest today because you think the price of a security is about to spike. This is speculation. Betting that a security's price will continue to increase or that some catalyst will occur in short order is gambling. Rather, look for long-term value (for example, a low valuation or an indelible franchise).

4) Do not feel like you are missing something. This envy just gets people into trouble. Rather, understand your goals, your actions and your strategy. Do not believe in "game changing" paradigms. They exist, but you will go broke trying to identify and invest in them.

5) Economists, strategists and political commentators have nothing to offer other than confusion and distraction. These people make their money based on quantity of words—be skeptical. You are making an investment in the long-term future of a stock or a bond. Don't get bogged down in nonsense that is unlikely to truly impact your investment over a decade.

One advantage of investing experience is the anecdotal lessons that you cannot replicate in quantitative analysis. Managing money has proven to us that one's results are directly linked to our above five principles. Over the years, we have seen three kinds of investing play out in a variety of clients' accounts.

1) The meddling investor always has the worst results. These folks generally believe they know what the next big trend is and how

to capitalize on it. Or, just as dangerously, they believe they have a really good idea of where the market and the economy are heading.

2) Asset allocators who build a portfolio of funds are often over-diversified and almost always chasing performance. Rather than making transparent investments in a portfolio of stocks and bonds, they choose investments based on the popularity of an asset class or the short-term track record of a third-party fund manager. These investors realize sub-par returns mainly as the result of multiple layers of fees and tax inefficiencies.

3) The authentic investor gets the best results. They own their investments directly and for the long-term. They avoid excessive turnover and maintain tax efficiency. And they significantly reduce costs and market timing mistakes by owning actual assets that they can see, understand and control.

When it comes to investing, boring is better. Complexity adds nothing. We cannot overemphasize that our basic principles of investing—transparent, low-cost, independent and contrarian—should be the authentic investor's fundamental tenets.

75

IF THE WORLD
WERE PERFECT

"IF THE WORLD WERE PERFECT, IT WOULDN'T BE."

YOGI BERRA (1925-2015)

With financial markets in turmoil, we want to reflect on a positive scenario, recap some of the hardest hit areas of the market and talk specifically about what we are doing for clients.

Thinking back to 2011, the market was relatively flat but stable coming into August and then experienced a big drop. After a short-lived rally, the market fell substantially again in September, but on October 3rd changed course and rallied to end the year where it started. This year has been remarkably similar to 2011 thus far.

Obviously, there is no guarantee that history will repeat itself. On the positive side, unlike 2011, the world is not on the verge of a European debt crisis and the U.S. economy is much stronger. However, we do face serious challenges including the slowdown in China, a confused

Federal Reserve and the potential for harmful political gridlock spurring yet another debt-ceiling fiasco. Furthermore, entering 2015 stocks were quite a bit more expensive, as measured by price-to-earnings ratios, than they were in 2011.

The internals of the market are nothing short of awful. Ignoring dividends, 25 stocks in the S&P 500 have fallen 50% or more from their 52-week highs and 169 have dropped 25% or more, all the while the average S&P 500 stock is down 22.55%, and the median is down 19.61%. The index as a whole, though, because of its market capitalization weighting, is down just over 11%. In other words, on the surface—believe it or not—the market looks better than it is.

One area hit particularly hard of late is biotech stocks. The iShares Nasdaq Biotechnology ETF has fallen about 25% from its high. Even after this fall, the ETF still sports a price-to-earnings ratio of over 26. The sector has been clearly overvalued, but investors chased the biotech story and have learned another hard lesson about buying expensive stocks.

We continue to believe that there are no shortcuts to long-term investment success; instead, we must endure the psychologically difficult work of owning a diversified basket of fairly-priced stocks and making incremental moves, rather than swinging for the fences. Biotech is yet another cautionary tale of exuberance.

In hindsight, another area of extreme market speculation was the energy and commodity complex. Many commodity bulls, not least of which the doomsday crowd, whose belief in the decline of America, worries over profligate federal spending and Fed money-printing encouraged investors to load the boat with hard assets, resulting in gigantic losses. Additionally, many wealth management firms made commodities a core part of their model portfolios and have suffered. Since peaking on June 30, 2008, the iShares S&P Goldman Sachs Commodity Index (GSG) has experienced a truly remarkable 77% drop from its peak.

Right now, we are working to remind clients of their true time horizon. Investing is a long-term proposition, as current retirees may have a multi-decade life expectancy. Even for some elderly clients, we are often investing more for their children and grandchildren, lengthening the time horizon of these relationships by multiple decades. And clients who are still working, even if they are approaching retirement, should realize that they have a very long road and staying the course and adding to stocks on dips is absolutely vital.

One year from now, most investors probably won't remember the market events of October 2015. Frankly, we don't spend much time contemplating the 14% peak-to-trough decline in 2003 or the 19% mid-year decline in 1997. These swings happen all the time and smart investors embrace the volatility instead of fleeing from it.

In mid and late 2014, we did a great deal of rebalancing. Since stocks had done so well, many clients were over-allocated to equities as compared to their long-term allocations, so we trimmed stock positions and bought additional bonds. The market continued to do well and the additional bond exposure was a short-term drag, but presently those moves are working in our favor. And now as bonds mature and dividends and interest post to accounts, we are marginally adding to stock positions on market weakness. In other words, we are opportunistically rebalancing in the other direction. We believe these incremental and patient moves, which are integral to our overall investment philosophy, will benefit clients.

We understand times like these are stressful and we are not dismissing recent events. However, solid long-term stock market returns are the direct result of volatility.

76

FAST AND SLOW

> "I BELIEVE IN THE DISCIPLINE OF MASTERING THE BEST
> THAT OTHER PEOPLE HAVE EVER FIGURED OUT. I DON'T
> BELIEVE IN JUST SITTING DOWN AND TRYING TO DREAM
> IT ALL UP YOURSELF. NOBODY'S THAT SMART."
>
> CHARLIE MUNGER, VICE-CHAIR,
> BERKSHIRE HATHAWAY

The psychologist Daniel Kahneman's book, *Thinking, Fast and Slow*, outlines the theory that people have a fast system and a slow system that they use in decision making. The fast system is intuitive and comes in handy if the house is on fire. The slow system is more deliberate and can sometimes override the fast system, telling you why you shouldn't buy that dream house, which is outside your price range.

According to a just-published paper in *Psychological Review*, frequently the fast system is simply too overpowering and despite the irrationality of a decision, the slow system can't win the day. Even worse, the slow system can be resolute in rationalizing the intuition and convince us that, given the circumstances, our decision was correct.

In no environment is this truer than with investing. Many still believe that hedge funds, traders, algorithms, etc. can move quickly, consistently and successfully to generate outsize returns. This is despite overwhelming academic evidence to the contrary.

The temptation is to hop aboard the best performing ideas and to avoid the worst performing. The reality, though, is quite different; bubbles often pop and out-of-favor investments often do recover.

Successful investing requires a slow system. The manifestation of a slow system is an investment discipline. Our investment discipline is to first find the proper asset allocation—the balance between risky and safer assets—for our clients. When we rebalance to this allocation, we ideally add to stocks when the market is weak and subtract from them when the market is strong.

Although our fast system often tells us to sell a stock when bad news strikes, we overrule the temptation with our slow system when we believe the company is still viable, despite the poor news. In exhaustive scholarly work and in our own internal studies, we know that the temptation to trade is most often foolhardy.

Fast is far more exciting than slow. But, with investing, slow and steady wins the race.

7

CASINO

To some, the stock market resembles a casino. And on a day-to-day basis, frankly, it is.

Equity investing is a game of chance in the short-term with fear, greed, headlines and sound bites driving prices. Unpredictable swings in sentiment make stocks rise or fall by significant percentages. But in the long run, public companies, which shareholders own, actually have an intrinsic value. If this intrinsic value grows over time, we expect the share price to trend in the same direction.

One of the reasons we prefer to invest in individual companies, rather than throwing money at "the market" through opaque investment products, is that we view our equity investments much like business owners contemplate the value of their companies. Each business has an intrinsic value, which we can reliably estimate by looking at cash flows, dividends, earnings growth, book value, etc.

In this way, a publicly-traded stock is similar to a small business. As an example, an owner of a manufacturing firm sells its widgets and uses the resulting cash flow to pay employees and suppliers, maintain equipment and invest in the business. If there is money left

289

over, the business owner reaps her cash profits. As these cash flows and profits grow over the years, the value of the business also rises.

Similarly, a shareholder of Apple (AAPL) owns an infinitesimal stake in the company and receives a tiny share of the company's future profit distributions. In the case of Apple, these profit distributions took the form of a $2.03 dividend per share over the last 12 months. We expect Apple (along with the other companies in our portfolio) to continue growing its revenue, profit and cash flow. It will likely use its cash to increase the dividend, repurchase shares and expand its business, both organically and by acquiring other companies. Although AAPL stock will have good years and bad years, over an extended period, the share price will very likely follow the trajectory of Apple's underlying business.

One of the most important differences between the share of AAPL stock and the privately-owned manufacturing firm is that the market quotes the price of AAPL every second of the day as the ticker tape rolls across the screen, whereas traders aren't buying and selling small businesses throughout the day and the price at any given moment is unknown. But, just because investors can buy and sell a business interest at any time doesn't mean that they should. Rather, like a private business owner, a true investor in public companies should allow time and persistence to bear fruit.

Many small business owners will tell you that building a business is a marathon; not a sprint. We view investing in much the same way. Making short-term calls on the direction of a stock is nothing more than a guessing game. Investing success comes from an extended time horizon, patience and the magic of compound returns.

78

WHY WE INVEST

After a tough month like January, and, frankly, following a lack-luster couple of years for financial markets, some investors may be wondering why they even bother investing.

The answer is relatively simple: We invest to achieve goals. If you're not investing to meet a goal, like generating retirement income, building a nest egg for retirement, accumulating wealth for children and grandchildren or saving for college, then investing is guaranteed to be a murky and unfulfilling proposition.

Why are goals so important?

Because investing is a long-term proposition. The stock market is volatile. It provides competitive returns over long periods of time, but only if you remain invested in it. You cannot time the market.

Without clear long-term financial goals, it is too easy to convince yourself that you shouldn't be in the market when times get tough.

If an investor put $10,000 in the Standard and Poor's 500 index on January 1, 1980, reinvested all dividends, paid no taxes or fees and

291

held the investment through December 31, 2012, they would have grown the portfolio to $332,502.

If during this 32-year timeframe the investor missed the 10 best days in the market, fate would have cut their return to just $160,340. This is a compelling statistic because it illustrates the devastating damage from timing the market incorrectly.

The expression that it's not about timing the market, but rather time in the market, is true. From 1926 through 2015, the entire history of the S&P 500, there have been 88 rolling three-year periods, and only 15 of these periods have experienced negative returns while the other 73 have been positive. Similarly, the S&P has had 81 rolling ten-year periods over this time and only 4 have been negative. Historically, staying in the market yields positive returns.

Having a goal also means having a strategy. For many clients we test what asset allocation (the percentage in stocks versus bonds) is the least risky while still meeting their goals. This process offers a "sleep at night" advantage for clients (and us) during market upheavals. This is our preferred method for clients that have a highly specific and attainable retirement goal.

Other clients, especially those with a significant net worth, believe in the power of equities over bonds because, despite the higher volatility of stocks, they earn higher long-term historical returns (and bonds yields have been low for many years). This approach is also a strategy, an admirable one in many ways, but it comes with particular indigestion at times. The stark reality is that people investing 100% in equities have endured a great deal of risk for meager returns the past couple of years. This too shall pass, but in the meantime it's a reality that everyone needs to acknowledge.

It seems to us, and many surveys affirm this, that we are in a period of extreme negativity about the world, America, the stock market, etc. Such an environment makes goals (and faith in achieving them) all the more important.

Although it seems difficult to imagine, the pessimistic sentiment that abounds today is bullish for markets that do their best when "climbing a wall of worry." With everyone so skeptical, there is no "irrational exuberance" in markets. This skepticism has the potential to trigger a short-covering rally in the near-term.

Although the market has done well since 2009, it has fallen on hard times of late. We believe that the U.S.—spurred by low energy prices—has the potential to see accelerating economic growth over the spring and summer, which could drive stocks higher. Unlike many others, we haven't given up on 2016 yet.

79

TOOLBOX

I n a note last month, we wrote that sellers were "overwrought with anxiety and might be reaching a point of capitulation." Two days later, February 11th, we saw a short-term bottom for the market. Although we have no great sense of where things go from here, we have been happy for the reprieve. And regardless of how the market trades in the days and weeks ahead, we feel like we have the proper tools in place to continue to navigate a challenging market environment:

- **INDIVIDUAL STOCKS**—There is no better time to own individual companies than when the market seems lost. And with a built-in bias toward value-oriented and dividend-paying companies, our portfolio tends to perform relatively well in tough markets. We are long-term investors in the future prospects of our companies, rather than short-term market speculators. Over time, stock returns are inextricably linked to valuation, earnings growth and dividend payments, so we can remain confident that our investments will deliver strong results over decades regardless of their day-to-day swings.

- **INDIVIDUAL BONDS**—Being diversified in tumultuous times is of utmost importance. In periods of panic, owning high-quality individual bonds in balanced accounts reduces volatility. Furthermore, given the low interest rate environment, a laddered strategy offers protection against rising interest rates. If lower energy prices ultimately boost economic growth, interest rates will slowly rise. As rates gradually increase and our laddered bonds mature each year, we will have opportunities to reinvest in issues with higher yields.

- **REBALANCING**—Our laddered bond strategy further allows us to rebalance if a bond matures and stocks have fallen (using the maturity proceeds to purchase out-of-favor equities). Disciplined rebalancing entails selling high and buying low and often requires time to blossom. Having the courage of conviction to rebalance from bonds to stocks or vice versa results in incremental benefits over the long run.

Your investment portfolio should be low-cost, straightforward and transparent: paying a low fee in a low-return world is more important than ever; being straightforward about articulating investment goals takes on added importance in times of turbulence; and a transparent investment strategy makes difficult decisions easier.

80

EARNINGS
SHMEARNINGS

The most popular measure of a stock's valuation is undoubtedly the price-to-earnings ratio, otherwise known as P/E. Investors and analysts commonly reference a stock's P/E ratio when estimating whether a stock is cheap, expensive or fairly valued. Quite frankly, the P/E ratio is also the first number that we look at when beginning to analyze an equity investment. The second is price-to-free-cash-flow, more as to why later in this note.

In reality, however, the P/E is only as good as its inputs: a stock's price and its earnings per share. In other words, "garbage in" can lead to "garbage out."

All publicly-traded American companies are required to report their profits according to Generally Accepted Accounting Principles, or GAAP. However, many companies—some more creatively than others—also calculate "adjusted" earnings.

While companies must report official GAAP numbers, they often create myriad supplemental adjusted figures that may or may not be legitimate. And in our experience, the adjustments invariably paint a prettier picture—never the other way around.

These adjusted profit figures typically remove "one-time" or "extraordinary" items. For example, Kraft Heinz (KHC), one of our portfolio companies, recently presented adjusted earnings per share that excluded the one-time costs from merging Kraft and Heinz into a single company. As an additional example, in recent years, many multinational companies are releasing adjusted earnings that remove the harmful effect of a strong U.S. dollar as part of their supplemental disclosures.

According to a recent article from *The Economist*, "For firms in the S&P 500 index, the gap between these official profits and the more flattering 'adjusted' numbers that they shove in front of investors is now about 20%, well above the long-term trend." This is an unsettling development as it leaves investors in the dark when gauging a company's performance and valuation.

The Economist goes on to state that, "Microsoft's latest profits rose by 6%, dipped by 3% or sank by 25%, depending on the metric." This could lead to wildly different calculations of Microsoft's P/E ratio and earnings growth.

Fortunately for investors, public companies must also report their cash flows. Free cash flow (operating cash flow less capital spending) essentially removes noncash elements from a company's profit figures and is more difficult to fudge. Free cash flow's trend over time also offers a sense for whether the current dividend payout and future increases are sustainable, as dividends are funded with either cash or debt.

In theory, a stock is worth the discounted present value of its future cash flows to investors. This fact makes dividends, and therefore free cash flow, immensely important. We focus on long-term investments in a basket of high-quality companies that have historically grown their free cash flow and will likely continue to do so. Allocating capital based on anything else, such as instinct, hunches and short-term trends, is simply speculation and guesswork.

81

CONCENTRATED INVESTING

n a new book, *Concentrated Investing*, authors Michael van Biema, Allen Benello and Tobias Carlisle examine the characteristics of successful concentrated investors. They define "concentrated" as a portfolio containing 10 to 30 positions.

Before we get into the traits required for success in such a portfolio, we'll point out that in balanced client accounts—those that own stocks and bonds—we further diversify a concentrated equity portfolio with positions in high quality bonds that have a low risk profile. This fixed income allocation allows us to customize each client's risk and return parameters.

Looking at the risk side (the equity part) of the portfolio, we continue to believe that our method of investing in individual companies is superior. We are heartened to see that we share many of the prerequisites for success that the authors uncovered in their study.

Many people believe that markets are efficient and that you can put your money in a "market" portfolio and achieve success. This is largely true. However, as Charlie Munger, the legendary Vice Chairman of Berkshire Hathaway points out, "If markets are efficient, then they are only as efficient as the individual investing in them." This statement is all too accurate.

First, investors must define the "market" portfolio. This definition can range from U.S. large cap stocks to the whole U.S. stock market to the entire global equity market, with different long-term results depending which index you select. Second, investors tend to make poorly-timed decisions, jumping in and out of markets and asset classes at the wrong time. In our view, it is much easier to make rational decisions when you believe you are investing in a business for the very long-term, versus trying to pick an investment product.

Investing for the long-term requires a commitment of capital. You can't invest in a stock thinking that you'll be out of it in a year or two; rather, you have to have the wherewithal to think in terms of a five, ten or twenty year commitment. Lou Simpson, the head of investments at the insurance giant GEICO, says, "We do a lot of thinking and not a lot of acting. A lot of investors do a lot of acting, and not a lot of thinking."

Concentrated investors need to truly think of their holdings as ownership in individual businesses, not as a tradeable security. Norwegian investor Kristian Siem explains why this worldview is vital: "Industry, by nature, is long term, and the fund management business, by nature, is short term. Financial investors come in and out: They can push a button any day and get out. The principal industrial investors don't have that luxury. They have to think for the long term." We see ourselves as financial investors with the time horizon of industrial investors.

The authors found that successful concentrated investors have "a strong focus on the long term" and "an abhorrence of action for action's sake." We couldn't agree more.

82

TWO THINGS THAT MATTER

We have long stressed the importance of avoiding over-diversification while making patient, long-term investments. Recently we were pleased to see academic evidence that high active share and long fund duration lead to superior investment results—average outperformance of 2% per year over the long-term.

A forthcoming academic study in the *Journal of Financial Economics* by Drs. Martijn Cremers of the University of Notre Dame and Ankur Pareek of Rutgers Business School finds, "Among high Active Share portfolios—whose holdings differ substantially from their benchmark—only those with patient investment strategies (with holding durations of over two years) on average outperform, over 2% per year."

A high active share portfolio is one that overweights holdings relative to an applicable benchmark (index). For example, if Apple is 1.48% of the MSCI All-Country World Index, a high active share manager who favors Apple might hold a 4% or 5% position in the stock versus a low active share manager who might hold a 1% to 1.50% position, in effect shadowing the index. In other words, a high active share manager owns outsize positions relative to the benchmark, while avoiding

300

other index holdings altogether. A low active share manager, on the other hand, tends to mimic the index, hugging the shore, so to speak.

A long holding duration (patient investment strategy) is generally correlated with low turnover, but they are not entirely the same concept. If a manager turns over the same 5% of her portfolio twenty times a year, that manager would have 100% turnover. However, if the other 95% of her portfolio remained static, this manager would have a long holding duration. Said differently, duration is the amount of time a manager holds the vast majority of their stocks; this study indicates the longer the better.

The study, which is dense, accounts for fees (but, not mutual fund loads) and analyzes mutual fund performance as well as the performance of institutional portfolios like banks, insurance companies, independent investment advisors, pension funds, etc.

Overall, the study concluded that managers with long fund duration are associated with better performance than shorter fund duration managers; and that frequently traded portfolios systematically underperformed "regardless of how different their holdings are relative to their benchmarks."

Vitally, however, only the combination of the most active share and patiently managed funds were able to outperform in a meaningful way. The authors also concluded that patient active management is most fruitful during periods of market turmoil.

Why does owning meaningful positions in stocks and being a loyal, long-term investor pay off? The authors conclude that it is mainly a scarcity phenomenon—so few people actually do it and, therefore, opportunities exist:

- It's a contrarian approach because "relatively few fund managers combine patient strategies with a high Active Share approach. Most patient funds (i.e., with long Fund Duration) have low Active Share."

301

- Because managers don't widely use the approach, the market allows for "more long-term mispricing and thus greater profitability for the more limited set of arbitrage capital that is able to invest in patient strategies."

- "... investing in patient and active managers generally also requires that investors themselves be patient. Such investor patience may be relatively rare as well, as both fund managers and their investors may need to wait years before getting rewarded for their patience."

Since launching our firm eight years ago, we have maintained a consistent investment philosophy built around individual securities with a high active share. Furthermore, we have made each investment with a long-term mindset, largely ignoring the day-to-day noise generated by financial markets.

FINANCIAL AND
RETIREMENT PLANNING

83

FRUSTRATED BY 529s?

Since its creation in 1996, the 529 plan has become the most popular college savings vehicle for American families. However, many parents have become frustrated by their 529 plans' lackluster performance while college tuition costs continue to skyrocket.

A 529 plan is an education savings account offered by a state or an educational institution as a vehicle for families to build assets to fund future college costs.

Two distinct types of 529 plans exist: prepaid plans, which permit participants to pre-pay for future college expenses, and savings plans, which allow participants to invest in mutual funds. Because savings plans are subject to the whims of the market, they have also been subject to the ire of frustrated participants.

These investment vehicles offer several benefits, but the primary appeal is tax-deferred growth. Participants can also ultimately withdraw "qualified" distributions tax-free. While your contributions are not deductible on your federal tax return, Pennsylvania residents are allowed a current deduction in calculating Pennsylvania taxable income.

Additionally, anyone can fund a 529 plan, regardless of age, income and relationship to the account beneficiary. Plan contributions are classified as gifts, so a person can make contributions of up to $14,000 a year without filing a federal gift tax return. Moreover, an exception exists that allows for the prefunding of five years of gifts ($14,000 x 5) in one lump sum. (The annual exclusion amount is now $14,000.)

It is important to note that there is a 10% penalty for withdrawing earnings from a 529 plan when not used for higher education expenses, in addition to paying income tax on those earnings. However, most 529 plans allow a change in beneficiaries. So, if the beneficiary decides not to attend college, one can transfer the account to a new individual who is directly related to the original beneficiary.

Despite the theoretical advantages of a 529 plan, it is tough to find a participant who has been thrilled with their results. Consider what has happened to college tuition costs versus equity market returns since the advent of 529 plans roughly 15 years ago.

The U.S. Bureau of Labor Statistics reports that college tuition and fees have increased at a rate of 5.94% from 1996 through 2009, roughly double the long-term average rate of inflation. In other words, a $10,000 college tuition bill in 1996 would cost over $22,000 today.

And according to a recent New York Times editorial by Mark C. Taylor, chairman of the religion department at Columbia University, "if recent trends continue, four years at a top-tier school will cost $330,000 in 2020, $525,000 in 2028 and $785,000 in 2035."

Since the advent of 529 Plans, the S&P 500 index produced total returns of 6.19% through 2009, lower than the market's long-term average return and just barely keeping pace with tuition inflation. And along the way, it was anything but a smooth ride. We experienced a tech stock bubble, two recessions, a housing bubble, and a major financial crisis.

But, as the investment disclosure statement says, "Past performance is not indicative of future returns." The past ten years have been a "lost decade," but the United States stock market has never endured two consecutive decades of flat or negative returns in its modern history. As contrarian investors, we see value in a stock market that most investors have largely been shunning for the past two years.

For 529 plan participants who are gun-shy about investing in equities, the most likely alternative would be fixed income. Interest rates are at all-time lows, and rising interest rates would lead to losses for bond fund investors, making it unlikely that bond returns will keep up with the rise in college expenses.

We advise 529 plan investors to focus on creating an appropriate asset allocation given the beneficiary's time horizon and minimizing fees.

> "SO, IF THE BENEFICIARY DECIDES NOT TO ATTEND COLLEGE, ONE CAN TRANSFER THE ACCOUNT TO A NEW INDIVIDUAL WHO IS DIRECTLY RELATED TO THE ORIGINAL BENEFICIARY."

For a young child with more than ten years until college, consider a stock-heavy portfolio to allow for growth. For a young teenager with five years or less, bonds, cash and a small allocation to equities may be more appropriate in order to protect principal. Time frames in between probably call for a more balanced asset allocation. Seek the help of a fee-only investment advisor for guidance in developing an asset allocation strategy.

Next, choose a low-cost plan. According to Savingforcollege.com, a website that offers extensive information on 529 plans, you can find the lowest-cost 529 investment options in Ohio (CollegeAdvantage), Virginia (VEST) and Utah (UESP). In addition, Vanguard Group recently cut its fees for participants in New York's College Savings Program Direct Plan to 0.25% from 0.49%, according to *The Wall Street Journal*. A Pennsylvania resident is free to participate in any state's plan and still receive a Pennsylvania income tax deduction.

Although 529 Plans have discouraged many, saving for college is a wise investment regardless of the returns available in the savings vehicle. A recent report from the U.S. Census Bureau reveals that over an adult's working life, high school graduates can expect, on average, to earn $1.2 million; those with a bachelor's degree, $2.1 million; and people with a master's degree, $2.5 million.

84

THE FUTURE STARTED YESTERDAY AND WE'RE ALREADY LATE

> "IF YOU HEAR THIS MESSAGE, WHEREVER YOU STAND / I'M CALLING EVERY WOMAN, CALLING EVERY MAN / WE'RE THE GENERATION / WE CAN'T AFFORD TO WAIT / THE FUTURE STARTED YESTERDAY AND WE'RE ALREADY LATE."
>
> JOHN LEGEND, "IF YOU'RE OUT THERE"

There is no better time than today to start planning for retirement, whether you are looking ahead twenty days or twenty years. When retiring, or simply planning for retirement, clients often ask us if they have sufficient funds, or how much money they will ultimately need.

Each investor's situation is unique and requires a detailed analysis. But as a general rule, a target retirement age is the best starting point (When do you hope to retire?). Once a retirement date is established, we consult actuarial projections to determine life expectancy (How long do I need my retirement savings to last?). The estimated duration of retirement is, quite clearly, essential.

Many retirees commonly make the error of implementing an asset allocation that is too conservative given the long lives that Americans lead today. According to the IRS, an individual who turned 62 in 2011 is expected to live another 23.5 years. A retiree who makes the mistake of investing his entire nest egg in "safe" low-yielding bonds will diminish the odds that his savings last, particularly given the erosive effects of inflation.

When assessing the level of income needed post-retirement, we suggest a three-part strategy.

First, track all of your expenses over twelve months. Using a credit card for as many daily expenses as possible, and paying each monthly balance in full, is an easy way to consolidate and monitor miscellaneous spending. We also advise clients to avoid subtracting "extraordinary" or "one-time" expenses. Unfortunately, unanticipated expenditures do not end just because paychecks stop coming.

Second, confirm this figure's accuracy by subtracting your annual savings from your annual income. This process is especially simple for wage earners because an end-of-year pay stub includes both income taxes and employer-sponsored retirement plan contributions, so you need only subtract other savings (e.g. IRAs). This final calculation should very closely match your expense total. If not, you probably missed some expenses.

Third, in conjunction with your expense tally and your income-minus-savings arithmetic, it is helpful to consider a replacement ratio, i.e. the percentage of your income earned in working years that you will need in retirement. For middle- to high-income earners, the replacement ratio is normally less than 100%; often around 80%.

There are several reasons to expect a replacement ratio below 100%. Taxes are often markedly less for retirees because they no longer receive W-2 wages, which are the most heavily taxed category of income. W-2 wages are subject to higher marginal rates, Social

Security and Medicare taxes, and state and local taxes. Furthermore, a retiree typically begins "distribution mode" and therefore is no longer setting aside income for savings.

Retirees who plan extensive travel or other costly leisure activities, such as daily golf outings or African safaris, will likely need more, not less, retirement income. In other words, the replacement ratio may indeed be north of 100%.

> "MANY RETIREES COMMONLY MAKE THE ERROR OF IMPLEMENTING AN ASSET ALLOCATION THAT IS TOO CONSERVATIVE GIVEN THE LONG LIVES THAT AMERICANS LEAD TODAY. "

The ultimate expense wild card in retirement is healthcare (including long-term care). Retirees who plan to retire before they are eligible for Medicare will face a major expense for health insurance premiums, unless a former employer offers subsidized insurance until they are Medicare-eligible. For investors without healthcare at retirement, we strongly recommend seeking insurance quotes before making a final retirement decision.

Our next step is to take inventory of retirement income sources— Social Security, pensions, annuities, real estate rental income, part-time work, etc. Then evaluate your retirement savings—IRAs, 401(k)s, 403(b)s, Thrift Savings Plans, brokerage accounts, cash value life insurance, savings bonds, etc. Finally, consider other potential sources of cash— buyout agreements, proceeds from downsizing homes, anticipated inheritance, sale of assets, etc.

The final step requires retirement evaluation software to project investment growth while accounting for inflation related to expenses, cost of living adjustments to pensions and Social Security and income and capital gains taxes.

A chief benefit of software analysis is a projection of long-term investment performance while withdrawing funds on a regular basis. For investors who are regularly adding to savings, volatility can actually be advantageous. For retirees making recurring withdrawals, volatility can be terribly detrimental. Software analysis is also crucial because it models a multiplicity of scenarios, based on random historical market returns and life expectancies, in order to forecast the probability that an investment portfolio will last a lifetime.

Lastly, we advise caution regarding "guaranteed" investment products such as variable annuities that are commonly peddled to retirees. These products come with a variety of claims, when in reality they are frequently low returning, highly complex and extraordinarily expensive. Remember the famous admonition "if it sounds too good to be true, it probably is."

Overall, modeling retirement investment "income" is not overly complicated, but does require experience and coaching.

85

INVESTING IN RETIREMENT

> "THERE ARE TWO MISTAKES ONE CAN MAKE ALONG THE ROAD TO TRUTH...NOT GOING ALL THE WAY, AND NOT STARTING."
>
> BUDDHA

Two months ago, we wrote an essay about the process for determining how much money you need to retire. However, saving for retirement is only half the battle. This article will take the next step in the retirement planning progression and address how to invest during retirement to provide "income" throughout your golden years. While far from an exciting read, this subject is extremely important, especially for the "baby boomer" generation.

To be fair, there is more than one way to skin a cat. For example, at retirement a risk-adverse individual can invest in an immediate fixed annuity from a top-tier insurance company. This would be a sensible strategy for a retiree who wants maximum certainty. But, there is no silver bullet, as even an appropriate product like a fixed annuity will face the detrimental certainty of a long-term inflation headwind. For a "safety first" investor with frugal spending habits and a limited interest in bequests, though, a fixed immediate annuity might be just right.

A clever salesman seeking a high commission might entice you into a "guaranteed" annuity that offers a minimum rate of return and also the opportunity for appreciation that keeps pace with inflation—caveat emptor! Such tricky products are low returning, highly complex and extraordinarily expensive. As always, remember the admonition, "if it sounds too good to be true it probably is."

But, with interest rates historically low, how do you invest in a traditional stock and bond portfolio to fund retirement? Over the past couple of decades, endowments—pools of dollars that charities invest for perpetuity—have adopted the concept of "total return" investing.

This style of investing takes into account two categories of returns: income and appreciation. Income is the coupon payments from bonds and the dividend payments from stocks, while appreciation is the long-term increase in the value of the stocks and bonds. Over the past ten years, appreciation has mainly come from bonds, but historically appreciation comes from stocks (and we think this will be the case over the next ten years).

Now, let's address the mix of stocks and bonds that create an ideal retirement portfolio.

It is vital to note that equities are inherently risky. History, including recent history, has shown that equities can tumble in the event of a financial bubble, international crisis, etc. Analysts and other experts cannot anticipate such losses. On the fixed income side, bonds still have various risks, including credit and interest rate risk. This means that bonds can and do default; and that as interest rates increase the market values of bonds decrease.

A greater allocation to higher-risk investments, such as equities, is typically more appropriate for investors with a long-term time horizon (ten years or more). Despite intuition to the contrary, retirement is a long-term endeavor, as you can retire at sixty-five and still be retired thirty years later. An outsized allocation to "lower-risk" investments, such as fixed income and cash equivalents, could be problematic over this thirty year period because inflation will do significant damage to the purchasing power of the portfolio.

The most significant risk-reward decision you will make in investing is the allocation to stocks (high risk investments) versus bonds (low risk investments) and this determination will dictate your portfolio volatility and performance.

For those who need safety, stability, and a steady stream of income, you should adopt the time-tested strategy of "laddering" a portfolio of high-quality individual bonds. Building a bond "ladder" involves purchasing a series of individual bonds and staggering the maturity dates.

This strategy protects against the risk of rising interest rates in two ways. First, each bond is held until maturity, at which point the issuer returns the original principal (face value), rendering any temporary slump in the market value of the bond irrelevant. Second, the manager can reinvest the proceeds at maturity in a new interest rate environment. This strategy relies, though, on clients being comfortable holding bonds to maturity. Credit risk remains a primary consideration.

A successful retirement investment strategy will combine diversified and / or government guaranteed bonds with a diversified portfolio of individual stocks. A bias toward larger, dividend paying and high cash flow generating companies is likely in a retiree's best interests. However, the portfolio should include international exposure as well as a few speculative stocks. Diversification is the key to success because trends change on a dime; what appears reasonable today will look foolhardy tomorrow.

So, with a stock and bond portfolio, how much "total return" can you expect? Although no one likes to admit the probability that future long-term stock and bond returns will be similar to historic returns, it is sensible to give history the benefit of the doubt.

Using Ibbotson data from 1926 through 2011, large U.S. stocks have returned 9.8% per year and U.S. government bonds have returned 5.7% per year. (Over the last ten years, stock returns have been far lower and bond returns higher.) If you assume a portfolio of 60% stocks and 40% bonds, based on these historical returns, your portfolio would

> "AFTER BACKING OUT PORTFOLIO COSTS AND AN INFLATION FACTOR, HISTORY SUGGESTS THAT A SUSTAINABLE BALANCED PORTFOLIO WITHDRAWAL RATE IS 3% TO 5%."

generate an average annual return of a little more than 8%. After backing out portfolio costs and an inflation factor, history suggests that a sustainable balanced portfolio withdrawal rate is 3% to 5%.

Because markets achieve their average annual returns manically (up 20% one year, down 10% the next), it is best to use computer software that randomly analyzes historical market performance to evaluate your spending rate based on your portfolio and your goals.

More than likely, there is little room for error regarding your retirement investments. For this reason, avoid headwinds; insist on a low-cost, transparent retirement investment plan. Be wary of cure-all, pre-packaged products that claim to meet your needs—the complexity and fees will derail your best intentions.

86

DON'T WASTE YOUR 401(K)

Fifty-one million American workers have an active 401(k) account and *Smart Money Magazine* estimates that the balances in these plans accumulate to $4.3 trillion. Without a doubt, 401(k)—or their brethren 403(b)—plans are the primary retirement vehicles for the majority of American employees.

Not so long ago, retirees relied on pensions for their retirement, but the traditional defined benefit pension program is nearing extinction. Of the pension plans that still exist, some are so financially strained that their futures are uncertain.

The 401(k) industry has come under heavy criticism since its advent, much of it well-deserved. Increasingly, however, such cynicism is also an excuse for inaction among plan sponsors (employers) and plan participants (employees). Although many plans are extremely flawed, they are almost always workable and worthy of employee participation.

Instead of getting hung-up on the investments within the plan, employees should focus first on how much they are able to save. After all, this is the part that the employee can control. In our view, obsessing over the investment choices before maximizing your

318

savings harkens back to the old expression about putting the cart before the horse.

Many employers offer a match to encourage 401(k) savings. For example, if you save 6% of your pay, your employer might match your contribution $0.50 on the dollar and therefore put an additional 3% of "free money" into your 401(k). For legions of people, this is a strong incentive to contribute up to the match.

Ironically, though, clients we talk to often cite the employer match as a disincentive as well. In other words, people think, "Why should I save more than my employer will match?"

The answer is simple—taxes. Employees defer federal income taxes on traditional 401(k) contributions (Roth 401(k) plans have different rules) until the money is withdrawn during retirement, so middle income earners can save 25% in current taxes on the money they contribute (high income earners can save 35%). Not a bad return, especially in a world with near zero interest rates.

Even if the plan's investment options are less than ideal, the employer match and the tax benefits of contributing to traditional 401(k) plans are in and of themselves a sound investment. Remember too that all of the dividends, income and appreciation that occur within the 401(k) plan are also tax-deferred until the time you withdraw the funds.

Make no mistake, the first line of retirement savings should be maximizing 401(k) contributions. This is the "no brainer" route to retirement success. While some plans may restrict annual contributions below government limits for certain reasons, the maximum legal contributions for 2017 and 2018 for traditional 401(k) plans is $18,000 and $18,500, respectively, and those over 50 years of age can make additional "catch-up" contributions totaling $6,000. Sophisticated plans allow for even greater tax-deferred savings through safe harbor and profit sharing add-ons.

After maximizing 401(k) contributions, your savings options are less compelling and more complex. Of course, you can only save what you can afford, but "paying yourself first"—the withholding of your pay to automatically invest in your 401(k)—is an ideal route to disciplined savings.

After maxing-out savings, it is time to turn to the investment side of the 401(k) equation. Our first rule of investing your 401(k) is "don't be too clever." A disciplined and consistent fund allocation over a long period of time—especially in a situation where you are adding money with every pay period—has a high probability of success.

Determine your stock and bond mix based on your age, retirement year and risk tolerance, not based on your personal forecast for the global economy or your political outlook. Invest in a diversified basket of funds, don't attempt to be tactical. Find lower cost funds with limited portfolio turnover; these two traits are amazingly prescient indicators of long-term performance.

Although seemingly self-serving, we cannot overemphasize the importance of getting professional help with your 401(k) investment strategy. You don't fill your own cavities or pull your own teeth, so don't be coy about getting assistance with your retirement.

> "EVEN IF THE PLAN'S INVESTMENT OPTIONS ARE LESS THAN IDEAL, THE EMPLOYER MATCH AND THE TAX BENEFITS OF CONTRIBUTING TO TRADITIONAL 401(K) PLANS ARE IN AND OF THEMSELVES A SOUND INVESTMENT."

Seek advice from your investment manager or your financial planner. Coordinating your 401(k) investments with your other assets is crucial. If you don't have a full-time financial professional working with you, then consider a fee-only planner that you can compensate on an hourly basis to examine your 401(k) and recommend an allocation.

Many employers, about 60% according to consultancy Aon Hewitt, offer investment recommendations to employees through a 401(k) provider. One word of caution, however—it is critical to definitively determine if the 401(k) provider's compensation is linked to the funds that you pick. Be sure to walk into the consultation with your eyes open.

For a variety of reasons, perfection within a plan is an impossible utopia. The best plans have reasonable and fully disclosed fees and dedicated service providers who have a fiduciary duty to act in the best interests of the plan sponsors and participants. Plans should offer a variety of investment choices, but not every investment strategy under the sun. Regardless of a plan's specific limitations, the benefits of tax deferral, company match and systematic savings almost always make 401(k) plans a vital endeavor.

87

WHAT DOES
A 529 BUY?

5 29 Plans have become the go-to vehicle for funding future college expenses. But like most savings programs designed by lawmakers, they can be confusing.

Two distinct types of plans exist: Prepaid Plans, where participants pre-pay future tuition expenses; and Savings Plans, where participants invest in the market and use the proceeds to pay for various college costs.

With only a few exceptions, most Prepaid Plans simply cover tuition, not other expenses, like housing or supplies. Savings Plans, on the other hand, allow greater discretion, but IRS rules for their use are murky.

The growth within 529s is tax-free as long as withdrawals are used for qualified higher education expenses. When withdrawals are used for non-qualified expenses, on the other hand, the investment earnings are subject to income taxes and a 10% penalty, so it is important to follow IRS guidelines.

Our general rules of thumb for 529 Savings Plan withdrawals are (1) if the school requires it, it's probably qualified and (2) keep documentation of everything. However, please contact us with questions about specific costs.

529 PLAN QUALIFIED HIGHER EDUCATION EXPENSES (QHEE)

- Tuition
- Fees (not all colleges consider application fees as qualified educational expenses; additionally, you can only apply 529 funds to the school your child actually attends, so it's not recommended to use 529 funds for application fees)
- Textbooks that a class requires
- Supplies
- Equipment (calculators, software, Internet access, etc. as long as a class requires it)
- Expenses for "special needs" beneficiaries

STUDENTS PURSUING A DEGREE AT LEAST HALF-TIME ALSO QUALIFY FOR:

- Room (generally limited to on-campus housing costs or equivalent) and board

NON-QUALIFIED EXPENSES (SUBJECT TO INCOME TAX AND A 10% PENALTY)*

- Insurance, sports or club fees, other fees not required as a condition of enrollment
- Medical expenses
- Electronics, smartphones, computers, and tablets
- Transportation costs (gas, airfare, etc.)
- Repayment of student loans
- Non-credit courses
- Room and board costs in excess of what the school housing/meal plan cost (room furnishings do not qualify; they are considered "lifestyle expenses")

Expenses do qualify if they are directly required as part of enrollment or attendance

IMPORTANT NOTES

- You must subtract the costs already covered by tax-free educational assistance (Pell grants, tax-free scholarships, fellowships, tuition discounts, Veteran's Educational Assistance Program, and tax-free employer educational assistance programs).
- If you receive educational tax credits (ex. American Opportunity tax credit or Lifetime Learning credit), you cannot use 529 funds to pay for the amount the credit was used to support. However, if some excesses occur as a result of tax credit adjustments, the IRS will waive the 10% penalty.
- Keep all receipts for purchases made with 529 funds as well as documentation from the school supporting what a student is required to own (textbook lists, lab fee notices, etc.). 529 statements will show earnings, contributions, and withdrawals, but you will be responsible for matching your QHEE against the withdrawals on your income tax return.
- It's a good idea to make qualified and non-qualified purchases separately to clearly show that you used the funds appropriately and to simplify record-keeping.
- Setting up tuition payments directly to the school is convenient and reduces the reporting an account owner is responsible for, but some schools treat 529 payments as evidence of reduced "financial need," and may consequently reduce a student's financial aid package. Check with the school's financial aid department about their treatment of 529 payments before authorizing direct payments.
- It's important to take out withdrawals in the same calendar and tax year when the expense occurs. For example, don't take out money in December to pay for a January tuition payment (different calendar years). In general, it is best to withdraw money close to the time a payment is due.

38

HEALTH SAVINGS ACCOUNTS

In the spirit of tax season, below is an explanation of Health Savings Accounts (HSAs). These vehicles are another way to defer dollars and lower your annual tax bill if you have access to an HSA-qualified plan. If you are self-employed with a higher income, such a plan is probably worth exploring. If your employer currently offers an HSA plan, contributing to the plan throughout the calendar year is likely prudent.

OVERVIEW

- A tax-favored savings account used in conjunction with a high-deductible health insurance plan
- Contributions to the HSA are tax-deductible up to the legal limit (see below)
- Withdrawals to pay for qualified expenses are never taxed
- Earnings accumulate on a tax-deferred basis; if they are used to pay for qualified expenses, they are never taxed
- Unused money at the end of the year is not forfeited but allowed to continue growing tax-deferred

• Money used on non-qualified expenses is taxed at your income tax rate with an additional 20% penalty if you are under age 65

> "HOWEVER, SINCE ANY INVESTMENT GAINS USED FOR QUALIFIED EXPENSES ARE TAX-EXEMPT, MORE AGGRESSIVELY ALLOCATING IN HSAs MAY PRESENT AN EXCELLENT INVESTMENT OPPORTUNITY."

CRITERIA FOR HSA-QUALIFIED INSURANCE PLANS

You must verify that your healthcare plan is HSA-qualified before opening an HSA account. Your insurance carrier can provide you with more information about whether your plan is qualified. A 2017 (and 2018 in parenthesis) qualified plan would have the following criteria and contribution limits:

* INDIVIDUAL COVERAGE
+ Minimum Deductible: $1,300 ($1,350 in 2018)
+ Maximum Out-of-Pocket: $6,550 ($6,650)
+ Contribution Limit: $3,400 ($3,450)
+ 55+ Contribution Limit: $4,400 ($4,450)

* FAMILY COVERAGE
+ Minimum Deductible: $2,600 ($2,700)
+ Maximum Out-of-Pocket: $13,100 ($13,300)
+ Contribution Limit: $6,750 ($6,900)
+ 55+ Contribution Limit: $7,750 ($7,900)

* Out of pocket expenses include deductibles, copayments, and other qualified expenses, but not premiums
* After the out-of-pocket limit is reached, health insurance pays

for the remaining qualified expenses (unless exceptions for certain expenses are detailed in the plan)

INVESTMENT OPTIONS

Some HSA accounts only function as savings accounts while others offer investment opportunities. Investment options differ widely depending on the account custodian. Some institutions may just offer a handful of mutual funds that they themselves manage. Other health savings account administrators have a much wider selection, such as the HSA Bank which offers upward of 10,000 mutual funds along with the ability to purchase stocks.

The majority of HSA owners (around 87%) hold their accounts in cash or money market funds because their balances are relatively small. However, since any investment gains used for qualified expenses are tax-exempt, more aggressively allocating in HSAs may present an excellent investment opportunity.

HSA PLANS AND MEDICARE

Individuals are no longer able to contribute to HSAs once they enroll in Medicare (starting the first month of enrollment, enacting a pro-rated contribution limit for the year). However, the funds already within the account may still be used as before, remaining tax-exempt if used for qualified medical expenses. Premiums for Medicare Parts B, D, C (Medicare Advantage Plans), and some Medicare supplement programs are eligible for tax-exempt reimbursement (premiums are often taken directly from Social Security payments).

QUALIFIED MEDICAL EXPENSES

While the complete list of qualified medical expenses is exhaustive, here is a sampling of the more commonly occurring items:
• Hospital bills and lab tests

- Surgery
- Ambulance services
- Eyeglasses
- Prescription drugs
- Alternative therapies (e.g., Acupuncture)
- Dental care and braces
- Premiums for continuation of coverage plans (e.g., COBRA), health insurance while you are receiving unemployment compensation, qualified long-term care insurance, and Medicare (see above)

For a full list, refer to IRS Publication 502:
http://www.irs.gov/publications/p502/

Items not included on the list may still qualify if they fall under the IRS description of a medical expense: "Medical expenses are the costs of diagnosis, cure, mitigation, treatment, or prevention of disease, and the costs for treatments affecting any part or function of the body. These expenses include payments for legal medical services rendered by physicians, surgeons, dentists, and other medical practitioners. They include the costs of equipment, supplies, and diagnostic devices needed for these purposes."

NON-QUALIFIED EXPENSES
As with the qualified medical expenses, a more detailed list of non-qualified expenses can be found in the link above, but here is a sampling:
- Surgery for purely cosmetic reasons
- Health club dues
- Maternity clothes
- Toiletries
- Vitamins and dietary supplements
- HSA insurance premiums

POTENTIAL HSA FEES
Fees vary based on the particular plan you enroll in and may include some of the following:
- One-time set up fee
- Monthly service fee
- Debit card transaction fee
- Check order fee
- Overdraft fee
- Trade fee

Be aware of which fees your plan may be subject to before making a decision. Some plans may also waive maintenance fees as long as you maintain a minimum balance within the account.

CONTRIBUTING TO AN HSA
Many HSA accounts allow users to go online to make contributions electronically. If your custodian has a physical location, you may go in and use a deposit slip as with a normal bank account (or use their ATM). A coupon may accompany your monthly statement to let you mail in contributions. Finally, many employers facilitate automated payroll deductions.

HOW TO PAY QUALIFIED EXPENSES
The bank holding your HSA will typically issue you a debit card and/ or checks, allowing you to use HSA funds at the point of sale. Some banks also allow you to reimburse yourself for qualified expenses through electronic deposit into the account used to pay the expense.

OTHER INFORMATION
- If you switch to an insurance plan not HSA-qualified, you will not be able to contribute further to your HSA account, but you still have access to and control over the funds within it. Using remaining funds for qualified expenses will remain tax-free.

• The HSA custodian will issue tax form 1099-SA every year to account holders, reporting all distributions taken from your account. You must file Form 8889 with your tax return to report your distributions. It is also recommended that you keep all receipts for qualified medical expenses in case the IRS audits you.

39

AUGUST 17, 2015

LONG-TERM
CARE INSURANCE

As Americans live longer and the population ages, more and more people worry about outliving their assets, especially given the risk of an extended stay in a nursing home or a long-term period of in-home assistance. To address this concern, the insurance industry devised long-term care insurance. According to the National Care Planning Council, insurance companies created the first long-term care policies about 30 years ago and since 1987, the number of policies has increased at an average annual rate of 21%.

More than a third of our clients are retirees and many more are approaching retirement. As such, we often field inquiries about long-term care insurance. While the product protects against an important risk, it does not come cheap. Clients should carefully weigh the cost and benefits within the framework of their personal circumstances before purchasing a policy.

The following is a general overview of the product category:

Most traditional insurance policies cover predetermined periods of time, excluding benefits for long-term services such as an extended nursing home stay. Companies design long-term care insurance to address longer benefit periods.

TYPICAL COVERAGE ITEMS
• Skilled nursing care
• Occupational, speech, physical and rehabilitation therapy
• Personal care (bathing, dressing, meal preparation, etc.)
• Nursing homes
• Assisted living facilities
• Hospice care
• Special care facilities (e.g. Alzheimer's)

INSURANCE ELIGIBILITY
A social worker or nurse hired by the insurance company will assess a person's eligibility for long-term care insurance. They will look for impairments to the individual's activities of daily living (ADL) or cognitive abilities. Benefits are triggered when a cognitive impairment or a certain number of ADLs is recognized.

Clients are advised to purchase long-term care insurance before they need it because some insurance companies may deny coverage for pre-existing conditions. However, each company's criteria are different, so even clients denied from one company may still be accepted by others. Pre-existing conditions sometimes used to deny coverage include:
• Already using long-term care services
• Already needing help with ADLs
• Presence of certain diseases: metastatic cancer, dementia, Parkinson's, multiple sclerosis, AIDS, etc.
• Experiencing a stroke

ELIMINATION PERIOD
After benefits are triggered, clients must wait a certain period of

time before coverage actually starts. This is called the elimination period. It is often compared to a deductible, but it is measured in time rather than a dollar amount. The elimination period often lasts 30, 60, or 90 days depending on the particular insurance plan. During this time, clients must pay for services themselves.

POLICY PAYOUTS

- Most policies pay up to a daily limit until the lifetime maximum is reached.
- Some policies pay a pre-determined amount every day clients qualify for benefits whether they actually receive services that day or not. These plans are usually more expensive.

PURCHASING CONSIDERATIONS

- Don't over-purchase: After assessing the costs they face, clients may just need a small policy, particularly if existing income or family assistance can help offset some of the costs.
- Don't under-purchase: Long-term care services can potentially create a financial hardship on a client's expenses if they do not purchase enough insurance to assist them. Generally though, it is better to buy too much insurance rather than too little. Insurance coverage can be decreased much more easily than it can be increased.
- Examine each policy carefully, particularly the benefit triggers and elimination periods as these are subject to change from plan to plan and can greatly affect premium pricing.
- The younger a client is, the cheaper insurance policies generally are.
- Keep in mind how your monthly income may change approaching or during retirement to ensure that insurance premiums are financially feasible over the long-term.

ESTIMATED INSURANCE COSTS

Buyers pay a pre-determined premium for insurance, averaging

$2,000-$3,000 per year according to the American Association for Long-Term Care Insurance. Prices vary widely (ranging from less than $2,000 to upwards of $5,000 per year), but they are based mainly on:
- Age at the time of purchasing the policy (industry recommended age is mid-50's)
- Policy type (e.g., set period vs. lifelong)
- Coverage options (e.g., elimination period, daily benefit, specific services covered, etc.)

ESTIMATED COSTS OF CARE IN THE U.S

Understanding the expected costs of care is important to decide an appropriate level of care. Costs vary by state, and, of course, provider, but below are the most recent national average costs (2017) for the most frequently used long-term care services.
- Personal services aide: $129/day
- Home health aide: $131/day
- Adult day health care: $70/day
- Assisted living facility: $123/day
- Nursing home (private room): $261/day

90

POST-DIVORCE BUDGETING

Budgeting is one of the most important financial aspects of divorce. Unfortunately, given its significance, individuals facing a divorce too often overlook this topic. Even for the affluent, dividing assets and then supporting multiple households, children and other relationships, while trying to maintain previous living standards, can prove difficult.

Divorcing couples justifiably focus on their children, their home, vacation properties, personal possessions and retirement accounts. They may also fiercely negotiate alimony and child support payments. Too often, however, they insufficiently consider the impact that the divorce settlement will have on their lifestyle. In other words, once the dust settles and the divorce is behind them, will they be able to meet expenses while continuing to prepare for their financial future?

The higher-earning spouse typically needs to balance his or her own household expenses with alimony and child support payments and an ongoing plan to save and invest for the future. Even in cases where this "breadwinner" earns a substantial income, meeting post-divorce obligations can be a challenge and, as a result, people too often neglect

335

saving. At the same time, his or her nest egg, in the form of 401(k)'s, IRA's, and brokerage accounts, may be less than half of what it was before the settlement.

It is vital that higher-earning spouses prepare a detailed post-divorce budget that includes a plan to rebuild savings. This often involves maximizing contributions to 401(k) plans and IRA accounts, including catch-up contributions for those 50 years and older. In addition to understanding everyday expenses, a budget will help determine how much to spend for housing, vehicles and vacations (skiing in the Alps might take a backseat to Vermont). Importantly, if budgeting is done early enough in the divorce process, it may even drive decisions

> "EVEN FOR THE AFFLUENT, DIVIDING ASSETS AND THEN SUPPORTING MULTIPLE HOUSEHOLDS, CHILDREN AND OTHER RELATIONSHIPS, WHILE TRYING TO MAINTAIN PREVIOUS LIVING STANDARDS, CAN PROVE DIFFICULT."

about which accounts and assets to pursue more aggressively during divorce negotiations.

For financially dependent spouses who have been out of the workforce and possibly caring for their children, post-divorce income planning is even more critical. In many scenarios we have encountered, these clients, who are often responsible for primary custody of children, may receive a settlement that includes alimony, child support, the family residence and an investment portfolio. They and their children are frequently accustomed to a standard of living that may or may not be feasible in the future, particularly over a period of many years. A detailed budget will go a long way in making this determination.

A spouse who receives an investment portfolio as part of a marital settlement, particularly when their absence from the labor market for years impairs their ability to rebuild their savings, must develop a plan to meet spending needs without making excessive withdrawals from their portfolio. Large withdrawals in the early years after a divorce can decimate an investment portfolio and squander an opportunity to ensure a financially sound retirement.

Early budgeting can clearly illustrate whether a client needs to look for full-time or part-time work. In some cases, full-time work may not be realistic, especially when children are young. But a regular withdrawal strategy to supplement part-time income, alimony and child support is far better than simply tapping an investment portfolio until it runs out.

Financial independence, providing for children and a healthy retirement should serve as the primary financial goals for clients facing divorce. Budgeting and income planning can help your clients set realistic expectations and develop a sound financial plan to achieve these goals.

337

91

401(K) TIPS

1) START EARLY

Albert Einstein said, "Compound interest is the eighth wonder of the world. He who understands it, earns it...he who doesn't, pays it." The long-term impact of saving early can be powerful, even in small amounts. A saver who begins socking away $500 a month at age 40 and earns a 7% return would end up with $405,000 at age 65. But if the same person also set aside just $100 per month from age 25 to 40, she would have over $586,000 at age 65. An extra $100 a month and an earlier start date would lead to $181,000 more retirement assets thanks to the long-term effects of compound returns.

2) TAKE ADVANTAGE OF THE COMPANY MATCH

Say a company matches your 401(k) contributions, dollar-for-dollar, up to 4% of your W-2 wages. If you don't contribute at least 4% to your 401(k), you're essentially leaving money on the table...money that could grow to substantial sums over your working years.

3) DON'T GET EMOTIONAL

Emotional investment decisions are almost always mistakes. When stock prices are falling, which they inevitably do sometimes, it feels like the pain will never end. And when markets are hitting new highs, investors often worry about missing out. The best approach is slow-and-steady dollar-cost-averaging through all the peaks and troughs, while rarely switching your investments unless your financial circumstances or long-term goals dramatically change.

4) THINK LONG-TERM

Many investors underestimate their true time horizon. Younger savers should largely ignore short-term market fluctuations because today's bull and bear markets are inconsequential when you're not retiring for several decades. Even an investor retiring in 2018 could make the same mistake, forgetting that he will likely remain invested for 20 or 30 years while withdrawing only a small portion from retirement savings each year.

5) CONSIDER TARGET DATE FUNDS

Target date retirement funds can be an ideal solution to the issues outlined in #3 and #4. These all-in-one investment vehicles offer a diversified portfolio that becomes more conservative as you age. For example, a 30 year old saver might opt for the Vanguard Target Retirement 2050 Fund, which currently holds about 90% in equities. As time passes, the fund will gradually reduce stock exposure and add bonds for safety and stability. Conversely, the Vanguard Target Retirement 2015 Fund holds just 45% stocks.

Investing from a young age, maximizing contributions, avoiding common mistakes along the way and taking advantage of the discipline offered by target date funds, most 401(k) plan participants will be well on their way to a healthy retirement.

92

THREE TIPS FOR CLAIMING SOCIAL SECURITY

1) CLAIM AS LATE AS POSSIBLE

Delayed retirement credits begin to accrue when you wait to claim Social Security after your Full Retirement Age (FRA). This will increase your benefit at a rate of 8% per year, plus cost of living adjustments. A retiree can claim as late as age 70, when payments will automatically begin. This translates to a 26%-36% increase in benefits depending on your exact FRA. This is an especially important strategy for married couples. It is often wise for the higher earner to delay Social Security to maximize the survivor benefit.

2) AVOID TAKING SOCIAL SECURITY WHILE WORKING

It may be tempting to claim Social Security benefits when they become available at 62, but if you still work, you may end up reducing your benefits. Taking Social Security before FRA while working will result in an earnings test. For those who stay below FRA the entire year, $1 is temporarily withheld for every $2 earned over the annual limit ($16,920 for 2017). For those who will reach FRA in the current year, $1 is temporarily withheld for every $3 earned over the limit ($44,880 for 2017). It is possible to completely wipe out your benefit this way. Social Security repays withheld benefits after you reach FRA, when earnings no longer result in reduced benefits, but a permanent reduction in benefits will still apply due to the early withdrawal penalty, which can be as much as 30% less than the benefit at FRA.

3) CONSIDER SPOUSAL AND EX-SPOUSAL BENEFITS

Your Social Security statement shows your benefit based on your earnings record, but it does not show your spousal or ex-spousal benefit. The maximum spousal benefit is half of your spouse's benefit at FRA (delayed retirement credits will not increase the spousal benefit). To claim an ex-spousal benefit, you must have been married for at least 10 years and be currently unmarried. When you file for benefits, you will automatically receive the higher of your personal or spousal benefit. However, knowing ahead of time what the approximate values are will help you determine when to claim. For example, if you are planning to wait until 70 to claim benefits on your record when they will be highest, but your spousal benefit is about the same as your age 70 benefit, it may be better to claim the spousal benefit at your FRA (when the spousal benefit has already reached its maximum value) instead of delaying another 3-4 years.

To retrieve your Social Security benefit statement and find answers to common Social Security questions, visit the Social Security Administration online at **www.ssa.gov**.

93

MEDICARE

M edicare is vital for Americans after age 65. Knowing the basics of Medicare is important not only for beneficiaries, but also for their children—and even their grandchildren— as relatives often need assistance navigating the system. Whether you're approaching Medicare age, currently enrolled in Medicare or simply looking for more information to help friends and family, we encourage you to read over the information we are providing and contact us with questions.

Americans qualify for Medicare at age 65. You must enroll in Medicare beginning in the three months before your 65th birthday, the month of your birthday or the three months following your birthday. If you don't sign-up for Medicare during this period you will face a *lifetime penalty* on your premium. Do not sign-up late for Medicare.

MEDICARE PART A:
- You are automatically enrolled in Medicare Part A *if* you are receiving Social Security.
- For those that have worked for ten years, most will have

accumulated enough credits to receive their Part A premium at no cost.

• Part A covers inpatient hospital care, skilled nursing facility and home health care (for up to 100 days per benefit period and only for temporary conditions), and hospice care.

MEDICARE PART B:
• Medicare bases Part B premiums on income levels.

• Part B covers portions of doctor's services, outpatient hospital care, lab tests, outpatient physical and speech therapy, home health care, ambulance services, and medical equipment and supplies.

MEDIGAP/SUPPLEMENTAL PLAN:
• Recipients should pair a Medigap or Supplemental Plan with Part B.

• There are ten types of these plans (Plan A through Plan N) that each have slightly different coverage schemes.

• Private insurance companies offer these policies according to a diligent set of government mandated standards, but pricing and service can vary widely.

MEDICARE PART C:
• Part C is better known as Medicare Advantage Plans.

• This is used as an alternative to Medicare Part A and Part B (and Medigap).

• Private insurance companies offer these plans.

• If you are in good health, need limited medical services and generally stay within one geographic area, these plans are worth a look as you can potentially save money on premiums.

• Medicare regulates these plans, but the plans are not standardized and require careful shopping.

• Part C plans include a drug coverage component, effectively bundling Part D with Parts A and B (and Medigap).

MEDICARE PART D:
- Part D plans are independent of Part A and Part B plans.
- This is the prescription drug benefit.
- You can choose your plan from private insurance companies.
- There are a variety of Part D plans available, the more comprehensive the prescription coverage, the higher the premium. There is also a premium adjustment for higher income earners.
- You cannot enroll late without facing a *lifetime penalty* on your premiums.

Even for the wealthy, healthcare is an important aspect of retirement planning. Under current law, clients over 65 years of age can rely on Medicare to cover a majority of their doctor and hospital expenses. Over one's lifetime, the premiums, deductibles and co-pays for Medicare (Parts A, B (paired with Supplemental) and D *or* Part C) will add-up, but Medicare offers relatively comprehensive coverage at affordable prices.

MAGNIFICENT SEVEN

A s food for thought, here are seven anecdotes about retirement investing that we recently encountered:

1) In 1889, Germany created the first national pension scheme and set the default retirement age at 70. In 1919, Germany reduced this age to 65, which has persisted as the most common retirement age with Medicare eligibility and Social Security full retirement age (for those born before 1954) at 65. However, German life expectancy in the late 19th century was only 47. It's no wonder entitlement programs are financially stressed.

2) The Society of Actuaries assigns a 45% likelihood that at least one spouse of a 65-year-old couple will live to age 95 or longer. They place the odds of one spouse living to age 100 at almost 18%. Outliving your savings is a real risk for Americans today.

3) What is the true risk for a portfolio that will be used to fund a liability such as retirement? It's not the day-to-day or even

345

year-to-year volatility. Rather, it's the risk that the portfolio won't be available to pay for that future liability. This is important to remember when volatility once again picks up and investors become fearful. An irrational, emotional decision can permanently impair an investor's returns.

4) The stock market has delivered robust long-term returns and will probably continue to do so. But these returns do not come in a straight line, with brutal bear markets along the way. "Sequence of returns risk" describes the risk that a major market decline occurs immediately before or after retirement, when a

> " 'SEQUENCE OF RETURNS RISK' DESCRIBES THE RISK THAT A MAJOR MARKET DECLINE OCCURS IMMEDIATELY BEFORE OR AFTER RETIREMENT, WHEN A SAVER'S ASSETS ARE THEORETICALLY AT THEIR PEAK. IN OTHER WORDS, A BEAR MARKET HURTS THE MOST RIGHT WHEN YOU RETIRE."

saver's assets are theoretically at their peak. In other words, a bear market hurts the most right when you retire. This specific risk confirms a strategy of focusing on asset allocation above all other investment considerations, having detailed retirement income projections to determine the minimum risk you must take to achieve retirement goals and strategically rebalancing your accounts after major market moves.

5) A rule of thumb for retirement spending is that investors can afford to spend 4% per year from a balanced investment portfolio. This approach has worked well for American investors, as a portfolio of 60% stocks and 40% bonds would have generated

real returns of 5.01% per year since 1900. The experience in other countries, however, paints a gloomier picture. Over the same time period, real returns were 4.06% in the U.K., 2.72% in Japan, 2.34% in France, 1.84% in Germany and 1.28% in Italy. On the one hand, we are lucky to live in a country with a dynamic economy, healthy markets and a record of winning World Wars. On the other hand, past performance is no guarantee of future results.

6) The low interest rate environment continues to harm retirees due to paltry bond yields. However, one retirement income strategy actually benefits from low interest rates. Reverse mortgages allow homeowners to turn their home equity into a series of regular "income" payments in retirement. Low rates translate to higher payments because of discounted cash flows. Reverse mortgages do come with major drawbacks but may warrant consideration in certain situations.

7) In a 2013 *Journal of Retirement* article entitled "Alpha, Beta, and now...Gamma," Morningstar estimated that financial advisors can add value of about 2% per year from tax planning, asset location, behavioral coaching, withdrawal strategies, etc. This echoes results from Vanguard's recent Advisor's Alpha study, which estimated a 3% benefit from working with an advisor. Regardless of the actual number, retirement investing is complex and often requires expert assistance. Whether you are grappling with when to retire, longevity or sequence of return risk, rebalancing and market timing temptations, total return investing and / or a non-traditional retirement strategy, it is beneficial to have help from an advisor who has a fiduciary duty to you.

EPILOGUE:
INVESTING VALUES

INVESTING VALUES

As we compiled and selected our essays for this book, we had a chance to reflect on our investing values and our financial planning methods. At its core, we believe our approach forges a judicious and disciplined path to meeting financial goals.

We wrote our first essays nine years ago when the world was in the throes of a severe financial crisis and recession. Now, as we pen this epilogue, we are experiencing one of the longest bull markets in American history. During this period, the world has gone from bust to boom, particularly for global equity markets. But, all along the way, we've done our best to maintain our investing values.

In the dark days of the crisis, and during the corrections since, we maintained a certain optimism among the gloom. And now, with the market booming, we find ourselves harboring a heightened skepticism. We are, without a doubt, contrarian investors.

In our opinion, a contrarian mindset prevents us from getting carried away in either good times or bad times. It is at these extremes when many investors make the most harmful investment decisions that jeopardize a lifetime of savings.

The investment values we laid out in this book—and that we summarize below—serve as sound fundamentals for a responsible investor. These five core values are diversification, tax-efficiency, low turnover, transparency and consistency. We have not perfectly executed on these values. Perfection in investing does not exist. Rather, we have done some things right and others wrong. However, the goal is for the positive to outweigh the negative, which we believe we have accomplished thus far.

DIVERSIFICATION

Diversification has become a cliché in investment lingo today, but it's

350

nevertheless a vital concept. At its core, diversification is risk management. Owning different kinds of assets serves to lower the volatility of an investment portfolio.

We love simplicity. In our world, there are two kinds of investments: 1) securities with a high-risk premium that are inherently volatile and 2) securities with a low risk premium but with greater stability. In our clients' portfolios, individual equities and individual high-quality bonds fill these two buckets, respectively. Over the years, many advisors have created complex portfolios with byzantine asset classes like hedge funds, smart beta, managed futures, leveraged ETFs, and so on. The theory is that greater complexity will lead to higher returns with less risk. But the financial crisis proved the only true hedge against severe bear markets is high-quality bonds. Therefore, the simple determination of the proper mix between stocks and bonds is the most important risk management decision an investor will make. We overwhelmingly base this mix on long-term objectives, not on our market, economic or political forecasts.

On the stock side, our primary method of diversification is ensuring the companies we own are in different businesses. We aim for companies that work in different areas of the economy but have strong brands, excellent multi-decade track records and an enduring ability to generate free cash flow and return it to shareholders. We believe 20 to 25 equities offer more than enough diversification, which has been reinforced when comparing our clients' year-to-year volatility to major market indexes.

On the bond side, we often own government guaranteed instruments, mixed with some high-quality corporate bonds and municipal bonds where appropriate. We ladder bond exposure, which means we own bonds maturing each year (2018, 2019, 2020, etc.). This helps us manage interest rate risk without making predictions about the direction of rates. It also offers regular cash flows within a portfolio that we can then redirect into equities during market downturns. The discipline inherent in a bond ladder is a perfect fit for our investment strategy.

LOW TURNOVER AND TAX-EFFICIENCY

Turnover and tax-efficiency go hand-in-hand. Low turnover is the cornerstone of an effective investment strategy and tax-efficiency is one of the direct, but wholly underappreciated, benefits of low turnover.

As equity investors, we believe our strong suit is finding good businesses that are out-of-favor and waiting for the market to fully appreciate them. Our most common mistake has been impatience. Almost all of our unforced errors have resulted from selling too soon, e.g. lack of fortitude.

We think about buying businesses, not buying stocks. Few successful entrepreneurs start a business in an overheated industry and expect to sell the company in two months. Great entrepreneurs build a business in an area with sustained growth or turn a business around over a multi-year (if not multi-decade) period. We shouldn't treat stock investing any differently, no matter the temptation to think otherwise.

We have a similar mindset with bonds. We purchase a bond to hold until maturity, not to trade. This allows us to ultimately minimize interest rate risk. By holding a bond to maturity, the interest rate-inspired price fluctuations that occur (when rates rise, bond prices fall and vice versa) become only paper events because we ultimately see a return of the bond's face value.

Portfolio managers report investment returns net-of-fees, but you rarely hear anyone discussing after-tax returns because the calculation isn't straightforward and most managers would have poor after-tax returns. Although rarely discussed, owning individual stocks for long periods of time is a surprising source of tax-deferral. After all, you are not responsible for paying capital gains taxes until you sell the shares, so you can defer gains for decades, even a lifetime. Taken to an extreme, holding stocks until death results in a "step-up" in basis, meaning heirs receive your shares with the cost adjusted to the date-of-death value. In this case, not only did you defer your capital gains, but you eliminated them. Individual equity investing also facilitates tax loss harvesting, another great tax management opportunity.

On the bond side, we evaluate whether municipal bonds make sense based on a client's tax bracket and the nature of the account. Yields on most municipal bonds are lower than comparable taxable bonds, but the income is often tax-free at the federal, state and local levels.

TRANSPARENCY

Investments in individual stocks and bonds are, by definition, transparent. Part and parcel with this transparency is a lower cost because you avoid product fees for mutual funds, exchange traded funds and other opaque investment vehicles. Due to the compounding of returns, over a long period of time, this fee differential is meaningful.

In addition to the cost savings of owning individual stocks and bonds, this strategy, most importantly, helps to eliminate "market noise." Instead of listening to a parade of manic market punditry, you can evaluate the companies and credits you own and have faith their value will materialize despite market drama. Transparent and direct investments facilitate detailed analysis rather than broad speculation.

CONSISTENCY

This brings us nicely to the idea of consistency and its importance to the investment process. Following a disciplined strategy through market cycles maximizes long-term returns. Every market, sector, style and country will have its day in the sun and its day in the doghouse. Unfortunately, predicting these trends is impossible. Investing directly in securities rather than in "markets" promotes a thoughtful, thorough and long-term perspective.

A final point on consistency: investing is not about home runs; rather it's a game of singles and doubles. The runs come over time by avoiding strikeouts. So, whether you create bond ladders to take the guess work out of interest rate movements or you analyze stocks to better understand your risk, the consistency and repeatability of the underlying approach is vital.

Truly practicing these values—diversification, low turnover, tax-efficiency, transparency and consistency—is essentially a form of contrarian investing. Almost every investor pays lip service to these values, but they succumb to the pressure to follow the herd. If everyone stuck to these values, the herd wouldn't exist. Adhering to these values regardless of the market environment is a contrarian investment decision in itself.

For example, even today, as you hear the drumbeat of exuberance...It is easy to ignore diversification because outperformance is found in U.S. growth stocks; no need for low turnover and tax efficiency because algorithm-based trading will always generate outsized returns; it's not necessary to evaluate free cash flow and profitability for social media and ecommerce companies because the giant tech juggernauts will grow forever; and who cares about consistency when many are abandoning the endowment theory of global, multi-asset diversification in favor of an S&P 500 index fund.

Beware the shifting currents of markets or they will wash you away.

Ben Atwater and Matt Malick
Fall, 2017
Lancaster, PA

ACKNOWLEDGEMENTS

Since we founded Atwater Malick in September 2008 we have been writing essays about markets, investments and financial planning.

Beginning in the summer of 2014, our intern Morgan Bodell took the first steps in selecting and compiling the essays in this book. When Morgan returned to Fairfield University, our portfolio assistant, Briana Van Craeynest, picked-up the book and worked on it. By the winter of 2014, we put the book aside. Fast forward to the summer of 2017 and Aaron Zuo came to us as an intern from the University of Virginia with the task of taking this book to the finish line. We express our sincere gratitude to Morgan, Briana and Aaron for their diligent efforts.

A big thanks to Mike Feldser for his help in reviewing the manuscript.

We are grateful to our families and our friends for their unwavering support not only when we started our business with no clients and no revenue, but also for their continued patience as they've lived the ups and downs of entrepreneurship and markets. We cannot thank you enough.

We dedicate this book to our clients for without them there would be no essays. We feel particularly indebted to our earliest clients who took a chance on us and who also made many introductions for us. Without you, we would have been back in the job market.

Also, we'd be remiss not to thank each other. We were luckily paired as business partners and wouldn't have made it very far alone.

As with these kinds of things, support comes from many people and we thank everyone who has had a hand in helping us.

Ben Atwater and Matt Malick
Fall, 2017
Lancaster, PA

ABOUT THE AUTHORS

BEN ATWATER began his career in portfolio management in 2000 following his graduation from Miami University with a B.S. in Finance. He earned a Masters of Business Administration degree from Lebanon Valley College in 2003. In 2008, Ben co-founded Atwater Malick, an independent fee-only registered investment advisory firm.

Ben has been extensively involved in the Lancaster, PA community throughout his career. He is a former Board Chair of the Lancaster County Community Foundation and the American Red Cross of the Susquehanna Valley. Ben was a long-time Board Treasurer for Power Packs Project and the Occupational Development Center. He currently serves on the Planned Giving Committee of the LG Health Foundation and on the Asset Development Committee of the Lancaster YMCA. Ben is also the Co-Chair of the Lancaster County Community Foundation's Forever Lancaster initiative.

Ben and his family reside in Lancaster, PA.

MATT MALICK started his career in economics and finance in 2001 after graduating with a B.A. in Economics from Millersville University. In 2006, he earned his Certified Financial Planning™ (CFP®) designation. Matt co-founded Atwater Malick, an independent fee-only registered investment advisor firm, in 2008. Matt completed a three-year course of study and three levels of exams to earn his Chartered Financial Analyst® (CFA®) charter in 2014.

Matt splits his time between Mount Joy, PA and Pittsburgh, PA, where his wife is in medical fellowship.